THE
Prairie Schooner
ANTHOLOGY OF
CONTEMPORARY
JEWISH AMERICAN
WRITING

Edited by Hilda Raz

University of Nebraska Press, Lincoln and London

© 1997 University of Nebraska
Press Introduction © 1998 by the
University of Nebraska Press. All
rights reserved. Manufactured in
the United States of America.
⊗ The paper in this book meets the
minimum requirements of American
National Standard for Information
Sciences – Permanence of Paper for
Printed Library Materials, ANSI
z39.48-1984 First Bison Books
printing: 1998
Most recent printing indicated
by the last digit below:
10 9 8 7 6 5 4 3 2 1
Library of Congress Cataloging-in
Publication Data. The Prairie
Schooner anthology of contemporary
Jewish American writing / edited by
Hilda Raz.   p.   cm.
ISBN 0-8032-8971-5 (pbk. : alk. paper)
1. American literature – Jewish
authors. 2. Jews – United States –
Literary collections. 3. American
literature – 20th century.
I. Raz, Hilda. PS508.J4P73 1998
810.8'0924'09045 – dc21
97-41201 CIP
Originally published as *Prairie
Schooner* 71:1 (spring 1997), a special
issue of Jewish American writers
published with support from the
Lucius N. Littauer Foundation of
New York City and from the Milton
and Pauline Abrahams Judaic
Studies Fund, Harris Center for
Judaic Studies, University of
Nebraska–Lincoln.

Contents

Hilda Raz

Introduction

Why did the venerable literary quarterly *Prairie Schooner* in its seventy-first year of continuous publication decide to gather a special issue on Jewish writing in America? Well, as Irena Klepfisz says, *Ober, far vos nisht?* /Why not?

One reason why not may have been that Jewish writers were not welcome to submit their work to literary quarterlies like *Prairie Schooner* in the early days of this century. As Sanford Pinsker says, "literature – pronounced *liter-a-toor* by them in the know – had the look of a closed Anglo-Saxon shop." That has not been the case for a long time now. In fact, Jewish American writing has enjoyed such success in recent decades that renown, inevitably, has been followed by announcements of its death. Yet as Sanford Pinsker again reminds us – and the book in your hand amply demonstrates – "the demise of Jewish-American writing has been much exaggerated."

Since 1987 our series of special issues – *Writing from Australia; China; Japan; Czech and Slovak Writers in Translation; Canadian Women Writers;* and others – has published new work by contemporary writers outside the United States. This most recent special issue offers aspects of post-Holocaust identity expressed by some American Jewish writers at work as we approach the millennium. Thanks to the Littauer Foundation in New York City and the Norman and Bernice Harris Center for Judaic Studies at the University of Nebraska–Lincoln for help, and to the University of Nebraska Press, which now makes this book available to a wider audience.

What did we learn as we read manuscripts from fiction writers, essayists, and poets? First, that American Jews often cite non-American progenitors in their writing. A turn of phrase, a tone of voice and my Russian grandmother pops off the page. From them, Yiddish is our heritage as Hebrew is our language of learning, and English is now the tool with which we make our art. *Bobe*s prevail, even in America. From them and other cultures the language of American Jews takes words like *Mah-Jongg* as well as *metabolism, inoculation* and *goyische, lesbian* and *epilepsy.* As Marilyn Hacker wonders,

> . . . Did she speak
> Yiddish to me? With whom did she speak Czech?
> German was what my father spoke till his
> sixth year, first grade (did he? she? tell me this?)
> – his parents' common tongue. And did they make
> love in their second language? The air's thick
> with cognates, questions and parentheses. . . .

Second, we learned that American Jews are remaking our identity, just as our forebears have done for 5758 years. "So when the time comes, I will have no choice," writes Klepfisz. "Somehow I will take my place on the historical continuum and try to observe and take notes. I will go to Sally and Linda's seder and recline on the Moroccan, Israeli, and Native American rugs. Together we will retell the ancient story as it was passed from *bobe* to *bobe* and read out of our xeroxed *hagadah*s decorated with images of ancient goddesses and interspersed with texts of witches' incantations, peace songs between Hagar and Sarah, tributes to midwives, toasts to the liberation of Palestinians, and praisesongs and poems. . . . At appropriate moments, my women friends and I will raise our cups of grape juice and greet Miriam the Prophetess, drink the vegetarian chicken soup, dunk the parsley in the bitter waters, chew the symbolic mortar, and burn the sweet-scented incense."

Third, we learned that reconciliation is the necessary addendum to prayer; and prayer sometimes is couched in the language of outrage. Our cry to God, enunciated by Alicia Ostriker, may be "Can you understand, you, that this is not what I intended? / Not what any of us intended?" Savage divisions of our world – even after the Holocaust, even then – continue.

We learned that our American past is often embodied by catalogs of detail. Here's Norman Harris's "Ikey":

> I weighed ninety-five pounds when I started High School.
> I weighed a hundred twenty-five when I graduated.
> I got all A's except for typing and freshman gym.
> When I was a sophomore, my biology teacher
> was the gym teacher, so I got an A in gym, too.
> Some tough guys in gym used to call me Ikey.

They never knew any Jews and thought they could
Rile me. But "Ikey" wasn't so bad.
I'd been called "Christkiller" too many times
By Catholic kids in the neighborhood parochial
School. But I knew they didn't know what or why
they were doing it. It made me mad, but I never cried.

Sadly we learned that our encounter with the Holocaust comes always and only as a visitor to historical sites, "*To* [only] *touch the walls of the execution*," as Michael Blumenthal says, quoting Hungarian writer George Konrad. But to touch these walls is a "duty no nation can afford to ignore." We were aware this issue went to press on the fifty-first anniversary of the Nuremberg Trials.

And finally we learned that contemporary American Jewish identity is manifold. *Prairie Schooner's* original cover, Deborah Kass's gloss of Andy Warhol's *Double Elvis*, is called *Double Red Yentl (My Elvis)*. It shows Barbra Streisand as Yentl, a girl dressed in boy's clothing, the necessary disguise for devout Jewish girls who want to study Torah. As Warhol's iconic Elvis speaks to an apparently unified popular American culture and its values – Elvis dressed as a cowboy, his six-gun drawn – Kass's image incorporates complex cultural icons and expresses our need both to retain and to deconstruct them. Streisand as Yentl holds a book, not a gun. She wears glasses, not gun belts. Unlike Elvis, whose roles were put upon him, Streisand puts on her many roles – artist, director, producer, Jewish woman, hero in a Christian consumer culture, reviser and maker of fables, "herself fabulous."

Jewish writers are busy in the larger American cultures. We wear our *zaideh's* [grandfather's] robes even as we reweave them.

Irena Klepfisz

Di yerushe/The Legacy: A Parable about History and Bobe-mayses, Barszcz and Borsht and the Future of the Jewish Past

This is no *bobe-mayse*.* I never knew my grandmothers, both of whom died in the war, and it's only recently that I've gotten even a glimpse of what my *bobes* might have been like by watching my eighty-one-year-old mother, Mama Lo. Oddly enough I, too, though childless, am experiencing a state of *bobe*-hood. More and more, Mama Lo and I are sharing the aches and pains of getting old and older and bridging our lifelong generation gap. Who would have thought? But then these are peculiar times.

For example, lately Mama Lo has been instructing me about "when the time comes . . . " and showing me the desk drawer with her living will and the jewelry box with Elza's watch, not especially valuable, but the only physical link to my twenty-four-year-old almost-sister who committed suicide over thirty years ago. Occasionally she walks me through the apartment, pointing to this or that. Sometimes she stares at her well-stocked book-cases of Ringelblum, Levi, Charlotte, Herman Wouk, Howard Fast, and Jane Austen and George Eliot, at the framed reproductions of Chagall and Van Gogh, and at the *tshatshkes* of kittens, vases, miniature musicians (many of them presents from me). In a gesture of puzzlement (perhaps despair), she throws up her hands: "What are you going to do with . . . ?" she begins, then stops and changes the subject with a shrug.

Though she has experienced two world wars, poverty, and serious illnesses, I suspect Mama Lo is admitting to herself for the first time that she has no choice but to accept her lack of control over her own life and mine. Knowing my forgetfulness and essential anarchism, she cannot feel easy about passing on

* *Bobe-mayse:* fantasy, fabrication (pejorative); grandmother's story (literal)

the pots of sturdy jades and blossoming African violets. Actually, I'm not certain what she feels because I have no idea what it is like to be eighty-one, and also because, with iron-clad tenacity, Mama Lo has kept her inner life a locked vault. It is a vault to which she is not about to bequeath me the key – History be damned, she is saying – What is private is private.

So these days we are both silent about what we both know: that at some point, I will take possession of her possessions, dismantle her apartment, and, barring catastrophe, continue with my life for possibly two or three decades without her. In other words, my life as a daughter will come to an abrupt end and I will cease being Mama Lo and her generation's future and be transformed into a true *bobe*, the next generation's past.

Theoretically, legacies and inheritances are simple: some things we accept and keep, even if with great sadness; others we discard because they're inconvenient, useless, simply passé. A watch like Elza's – orphan child-survivor, dreaming poet, determined suicide – embodies so much public and private history that I've never been able to claim it for myself. So when the time comes, the watch will be transferred to my desk drawer. But I am determined eventually to bequeath it to someone, someone younger – not a relative, because I have none – but someone to whom its fierce and painful history will be important, and whose arm will display it like an honor, rather than a wound.

Mama Lo's other bequests will be more problematic. Should I, for example, keep a leaky pot – its white enamel worn, its rim dented – but Mama Lo's (and my own) sole physical link to Poland (post-war, of course, but Poland nevertheless)? What historical purpose will it serve standing on a shelf behind my teflon pans, my well-used wok and bamboo steamers? Does such a pot belong in a museum and should I try to donate it? ("It's the very pot in which Mama Lo cooked her *borscht* – on *both* sides of the Atlantic. Believe me it tells the quintessential twentieth-century Jewish story.")

And then there's the album with photographs of people I don't quite remember: a man and woman standing by the white brick oven in our Lodz apartment or a teenager kneeling by a sandbox in a park – ordinary people who, because of their imagination, stupidity and/or luck, just happened to survive. Should I ask Mama Lo to name them? I've no family, so what does it matter? Won't such an album inevitably end up in some collectibles barn in Columbia County in upstate New York to be browsed through by eager weekenders trying to furnish their newly built A-frame with an aura of history? On the other hand, the album is part of *my life, my past* – one which my aging brain has increasingly more trouble retaining, a past which, I confess, I've already distilled (or thinned – depending on your point of view) as I've tried to "get on" with my life.

The truth is that for most of my adulthood I've been braced against Mama Lo's disapproval, conscious I did not fulfill her wish and emulate her and her one-bedroom apartment in a three-bedroom one of my own, fully furnished with a husband and children. Instead, I went off and settled into a wall-less, closet-less loft which I share with another woman who has no legal relationship to me, but with whom I also share my life.

Yet, for all my rebelliousness and alternativity, a part of my identity – the *Jewish* part – has been inextricably intertwined with Mama Lo and the life of her generation. *My* vaulted secret is that I've been a dependent Jew – dependent on Mama Lo's generation to provide me with a sense of *hemshekh*/continuity. They've been the visible *goldene keyt*/the golden chain to which I've wanted to hook the link I've been forging through my life and my work. With them gone, where am I supposed to hang myself?

To put it another way: *Vos iz geshikhte?*/What is history and what is my place in it? And how is time defined with any accuracy by human events? The Middle Ages. The Renaissance. The Age of Reason. How do we know when one age ends and another begins? I wonder with increasing urgency as I ready myself to begin the Jewish generation relay race in which I've been entered.

Take *borscht,* for example. Consider that beets were unknown to us at the time of the destruction of the Temple and were not among the hastily packed foods our *bobes* took into Babylon or later into the northwestern *goles*/exile. Then consider the centrality of borscht in modern Eastern European Jewish culture. By what process did this essential component of Jewish life emerge?

Borscht entered Jewish life many centuries ago – through the kitchen. The first Jewish mention of beets, I believe, occurs in *A bobe, an eydes/A Grandmother, A Witness*, a recently discovered collection that is bound to rival Glickl's *Memoirs*. Among its many fragmentary stories, *A bobe, an eydes* contains a series of tributes to a certain Gitl *bas* Frume *di frume** who, according to one *bobe mayse,* lived in the later part of the thirteenth century in the town of Knin. Knin was far from her ancestors' beloved

* Gitl *bas* Frume *di frume:* Gitl daughter of Frume the pious

Ashkenaz, very far east in fact, in a region we nostalgically remember today as *poyln*/Poland – the cradle of *yidishkayt, der yidisher oytser*/the Jewish treasure – but where, in Gitl's time, the buds of *yidishe geshikhte un kultur*/history and culture were barely formed, much less beginning to bloom.

It was some time during that Yiddish dawn that Gitl *bas* Frume *di frume* forged a secret friendship with Grushenka, even though Janek, Grushenka's brother, beat up Yankl, Gitl's brother, on a regular basis. One Sunday morning after sneaking out of church, Grushenka led Gitl (without Frume's knowledge) into her mother's Christian kitchen, where, for the first time, Gitl smelled the sweet, dark aroma of *barszcz*. "*Treyf!*" *undzer yidishe tokhter*/ our young Jewish girl declared that night to her younger sister Chava, thereby conveying her understanding of the nature of the soup's bones and, indeed, its entire culinary context. But then, much to her sister's horror, Gitl added with *emesdike benkshaft*/heartfelt longing: *Ober es shmekt azoy gut!*/But it smells so good!"

Like other texts whose authors were neither official recorders nor note takers, but ordinary homemakers focused more on an event's ingredients than on its development and denouement, *A bobe, an eydes* gives scant information about the process of Judaization of the Polish *barszcz*. Perhaps once, perhaps more than once, the girl tasted the forbidden friend's forbidden food. In any case, at some point, after numerous visits and sniffs, much finger-pointing at the market place, two or three public tantrums, and repeated posings of the proverbial "*Ober, far vos nisht?*/Why not?" – the impetus behind all creative leaps – Gitl convinced Frume *di frume* to act: ("*Dos meydl makht mir in gantsn meshige. Tog un nakht redt zi bloyz fun* buraki *un* barszcz!/The girl's driving me completely mad. Day and night she talks only of *buraki* and *barszcz!*") And so the frazzled mother peeled the bleeding vegetables into a pot of boiling water, added some *beyner, tsiker, knobl, un tsibeles*/bones, sugar, garlic and onions and, through trial and error – *tsu gedikht, tsu shiter, tsu zis, tsu zoyer*/too thick, too thin, too sweet, too tart – the soup looked, tasted, and smelled exactly like the *barszcz* in Grushenka's mother's kitchen with the added advantage it could pass rabbinic inspection: *s'iz geven kusher*/it was kosher.

The rest *iz poshet*/is simple. By the first decade of the fifteenth century when Gitl's great-granddaughter, Frume *di freylekhe*,* was already a married *baleboste*/homemaker, the Slavic-rooted

* Frume *di freylekhe:* Frume the joyous/gay

barszcz had become *borsht*, the Yiddish word for the quintessential Jewish soup.

Given such history, it is not surprising that today, near the end of the twentieth century, I am preoccupied with leaky pots, with Elza's watch (which, despite being idle for almost thirty years, began ticking the second I wound it), with photo albums, and with the survival of *borscht* itself in Jewish kitchens dominated by woks and bamboo steamers. Nor is it surprising that I am preoccupied with Mama Lo's entire *yerushe,* including everything she lost almost sixty years ago so that when she debarked in *di goldene medine*/the golden land, Mama Lo had nothing but a goosedown *koldra* (which a year later caught fire from a faulty heating pad), some crumbling photographs, a pot purchased in Lodz shortly after liberation – and me. That year *poyln* was no longer a blooming garden, but a country-sized wall-less graveyard and Mama Lo's past a *vistenish*/a void, something that history and nature abhor and immediately engulf, thereby allowing the transformation of alien weeds into beloved indigenous flowers and a *treyf barszcz* into the embodiment of a *kushere heym.*

So when the time comes, I will have no choice. Somehow I will find my place on the historical continuum and try to observe and take notes. I will go to Sally and Linda's seder and recline on the Moroccan, Israeli, and Native American rugs. Together we will retell the ancient story as it was passed from *bobe* to *bobe* and read from our xeroxed *hagadahs* decorated with images of ancient goddesses and interspersed with the texts of witches' incantations, peace songs between Hagar and Sarah, tributes to midwives, toasts to the liberation of Palestinians, and praisesongs and poems to Hannah Senesh, Yokheved and Gitl *bas* Frume *di frume.* At appropriate moments, my women friends and I will raise our cups of grape juice and greet Miriam the Prophetess, drink the vegetarian chicken soup, dunk the parsley in the bitter waters, chew the symbolic mortar, and burn the sweet-scented incense. Each year we will substitute this for that and add that to this and sing and chant recalling the tears and losses and recite (in English, of course) *"hayntiks yor knekht, dos kumendike yor fraye froyen*/this year we are slaves, next year liberated women."* And a few years from now, sometime around the year 2000, we will feel familiar, comforted, and grounded in our tradition and look back upon the seders of our childhoods as the ancient ceremonies of another century and era – which is exactly what they will have become.

But until then, I am at Mama Lo's service. Whenever she wants to recall more vividly the *poyln fun ire kinderyorn*/Poland of her childhood and the sweetness of my *bobe* Rikla's *kikh*, a kitchen whose ashes and dust are now indistinguishable from those of the Second Temple – I will take Mama Lo to Second Avenue and Teresa's Polish Cafe and order *borscht*, the same *treyf barszcz* Gitl *bas* Frume *di frume* first smelled in Grushenka's mother's kitchen. As Mama Lo and I breathe in its dark, rich aroma, we will begin talking for the first time *bobe tsu bobe* about the miracles of our common past and the mystery of our separate futures.

Marilyn Hacker

Squares and Courtyards

Across the Place du Marché Ste-Catherine,
the light which frames a building that I see
daily, walking home from the bakery,
white voile in open windows, sudden green
and scarlet window-box geraniums
backlit in cloud-encouraged clarity
against the century-patinaed grey
is such a gift of the quotidian,
a benefice of sight and consciousness,
I sometimes stop, confused with gratitude,
not knowing what to thank or whom to bless,
break off an end of seven-grain baguette
as if my orchestrated senses could
confirm the day. It's fragrant. I eat it.

Confirm the day's fragrance: I eat, bit
by bit, the buttery pain aux raisins
shell-coiled beside my steaming afternoon
tea. It's the hour for a schoolchild's treat,
munched down, warm in waxed paper, on the street,
or picked at on chipped earthenware (like mine)
beside books marked with homework to be done
while the street's sunlit, dusk-lit, lamp-lit.
She sucks her pencil, window-framed. I sip
nostalgia for a childhood not my own
Bronx kitchen table, with a fire escape
in the alley shaded by sumac trees
which filtered out the other languages
I heard the airshaft's crosscurrents intone.

I heard the airshaft's crosscurrents intone
below the minyan davening morning offices.

A childish rasp that slurred and sputtered was
the Polish janitor's red-knuckled son
helping his father empty garbage cans.
His voice was why I thought him rough (as is
English when uttered by its novices)
– a voice I never heard speaking its own
language. His name was Joseph. He was six.
Other syllables connected news
from gutted Europe to the dusty motes
of Sabbath morning. Ash settled on bricks,
spun up the shaft with voices of old Jews,
was drawn down garrulous chain-smokers' throats.

Drawn up from garrulous chain-smokers' throats
at square tin tables on wet cobblestones
just hosed down by a green-clad African
street-cleaner: strikes, prices, who still votes
Left, sex, a sick child. Hands unbutton coats
halfway. The wind's mild, but it looks like rain
above the Place du Marché Ste-Catherine
where charcoal-bellied clouds converge like boats
in the mutable blue harbor sky.
Another coffee, another blanc sec –
as if events were ours to rearrange
with words, as if dailiness forestalled change,
as if we didn't grow old (or not) and die
as long as someone answered when we spoke.

As long as someone answered when I spoke
– especially someone walking a dog –
I'd launch into juvenile monologue:
Greek myths, canine behavior – and could I stroke
the Lab or spaniel? Speech and touch evoked
my grandmother, the bookkeeper from Prague
who died as I emerged out of the fog
of infancy, while lives dispersed in smoke
above the camps (and Dresden, and Japan)

and with them someone else I might have been
if memory braided with history.
I pressed my face into the dog's warm fur
whose heat and smell I learned by heart, while she
receded into words I found for her.

Receding into words I found for her
delight, someone was dispossessed of her own
story (she thought) by mine.
                          Receding in-
to words, the frail and early-rising neighbor
who died during my cancer-treatment year
is not summed up by "centenarian."
Her century requires a lexicon.
I wrote a girl on paper when I bore
a child, whose photocopied life became
letters tattooed across a watermark,
a woman's in the world, who shares her name.
And Gísela, who took me to the park,
for whom I pieced together sentences
– it's all the words she said to me I miss.

– It's all the words she said to me I miss,
down to unechoed accents. Did she speak
Yiddish to me? With whom did she speak Czech?
German was what my father spoke till his
sixth year, first grade (did he? she? tell me this?)
– his parents' common tongue. And did they make
love in their second language? The air's thick
with cognates, questions and parentheses
she'll scribble down once she's back in her room,
chewing her braid, tracing our labyrinthine
fragments. She zips her anorak
and shifts the heavy satchel on her back
watching low clouds gather as she walks home
across the Place du Marché Ste-Catherine.

Not knowing what to thank or whom to bless,
the schoolgirl at the window, whom I'm not,
hums cadences it soothes her to repeat
which open into other languages
in which she'll piece together sentences
while I imagine her across the street
as late light shifts, sunlit, dusk-lit, lamp-lit.
Is there a yellow star sewed to her dress
as she exults, confused with gratitude:
her century requires a lexicon
of memory braided with history
she'll have reflective decades to write down?
Not thinking she'll get old (or not) and die;
thinking: she can, if anybody could.

Cynthia Macdonald

Miriam's Grandmother

Willi and Lotte picked raspberries each summer
to squeeze for Hinbeernsaft. A perfect pair:
Lotte could pick just high enough so Willi did not need
to stoop. Pails and pails of berries, then home
to spread them out on sheets until the kitchen surfaces
were velvet red. Then more white sheets on top
to catch the worms, the tiny green ones nestled
in the berries. They moved up toward the light,
clinging to the sheets where Willi picked them off.

The berries rested thick, ready for the press of morning
when every pink-red titty yielded up its drops of juice.
Lotte got a suck of it each time a bottle filled.
The day she went with Mama on the train to Düsseldorf
to visit Oma and Opa, she carried a big bottle of juice
before her. Like a wise man in a Christmas play bearing
myrrh to the manger. Like a movie where the heroine,
running to escape the vampire, approaches the cliff edge
the audience knows is there but she does not. Her mother

busy with the luggage and the baby, did not see but heard
the bottle crash and Lotte's cry. She stood in streams of red,
her white dress splashed with red. Red dripping
on her best white shoes. Flowers of glass, halos of glass
had formed themselves within the lake of red, and drops
of juice merged with those of blood from slivers stuck into
her legs. Tears. A small catastrophe. All their work was lost.
In grief she hit the air. Red never was the same again. In years
to come she learned much more how difficult deaths are.

Singing Miriam's Lament

It is too late to have breakfast. Blue's Cafe serves from 6 to 8 A.M.
It is too late to touch you when you sleep beside me.
You are not there.
Considering my weak ankles and my middle age,
it is too late to become an Olympic-class skater.
It is too late to have lunch. Blue's Cafe serves from 12 to 3 P.M.
and the sushi is all gone and the halibut dried
till its bones stick out through its flesh.
It is too late to become a World War II spy, and in the next one

there will be no time to assemble spies.
It is too late to be on time for our wedding
which, for some reason even you could not explain,
you wanted in St. Patrick's Cathedral although
you are Jewish. I should have known then.
It is too late to have dinner. Blue's Cafe serves from 7 to 10 P.M.
and the food has become infected with toxins
so all the customers are dead in their seats.
The late Mr. and Mrs. Bixby still hold their wine glasses,
The late Mr. Porter is stiffening, his head resting in
the soup plate which makes a halo round it.
Perhaps being on time is not always a virtue,
as Opa and Oma found out on Kristallnacht.

Maps and Globes

Greece – Ischia, Cumae, cities on the Hellespont and Bosporus,
Al Mina: all colored Violet Red which turned to pink against
the page. We spun the conquests and alliances
with colors of our choice. My Holy Roman Empire was
Lavender. How pleasurable to stay within the lines.

And down one side we made a color key: who hated whom
and why, and then who joined them in their puffy hate –
like faces of the angry winds – to turn another country
Jungle Green or Goldenrod. Al Mina became
Antioch and changed into a lovely Silver Grey.

Each week we had an air raid drill. The Germans and
the Japanese – Spice Brown – might turn our school
and us into a smoky ruin like the ones in London where

the schools had photographs of Churchill, Roosevelt and Stalin,
chair-by-chair, comrades-in-arms. Cerulean.

Now the world is glass, a globe of glass, more fragile than
a baby's skull, and all I know is this: Haiti, Somalia, Bosnia
it's all the same (not motive; outcome) nothing is helped,
O, maybe in the sprint, it is, but not in the long run by war.
I would have died in Dachau or in Bergen-Belsen, had my family

not left Alsace in 1840. Ashes are used sometimes in making glass.
I think I'd fight to save my children, my city; perhaps, myself.
Red and no color: ash, sand, glass and alum tears.
Glass globe. Glass globes, joined like the body of a woman.
An hour glass. I hold it, turn it over and watch
The passionate rush of dispassionate time into my hand.

Casual Neglects

People forget their children in the strangest places.
Crossing Fifth in front of Saks, Little Jane
left behind. In the basket of a bicycle, then out of it,
Little Paul whose absence was unnoticed until
a neighbor brought him home. Little Raylinn of the
Projects left at Burger King while Mama met
her mark in Union City. And Little Hetty home from
school to find an empty house cleared of its furniture.
Her Mom forgot to tell her they were moving.

And then there's What's-Its Name who watches over us,
checking his wrist to see if the time is right, patting
her breast to check the milk run, folding the timetable,

pulling its trunk with its trunk when it moves toward
India. The celestial throne is passing hard and the studded
jewels poke What's-at-the-Bottom of it all. We prod
the godly cheek so It/She/He, He/It/She slides off; the left
behind, to be exact: that's us. The air is absentminded
and the empty sky of Paradise is pocked with small pink shells,
those baby fingernails which couldn't quite keep holding on.

Vermeer's Lady Reading
at an Open Window

The curtain in this delicate work presents a problem.
Is it in the room or in front of the picture?
      – J. M. Nash: *The Age of Rembrandt and Vermeer*

She is standing at the window.
Glints of gold, of gilt in her hair and dress –
on the crumpled paper in her hands,
on the fruit in the blue and white bowl,
on the rug covering the table – are painted
by a light more canny in its choices than
God's light through the open window.

She hangs in Dresden.
Perhaps she is a sibyl reading of the firebombing
three hundred years hence, of the light
that caused flashcars, flashparks, flashpeople
to run, burning through that German city. We read
into event our own pain and destruction even when
it does not fit the calmness of the figure by the window.

Perhaps she holds a letter telling her her lover
has fallen picking up his sword
to fight again in Brabant's field
and will not be coming home.
Is her expression sad? It's difficult to tell.
Her gaze is steadfast but we cannot see into her eyes.
Vermeer's glints transfer transfiguration to each object.

She stands absorbed by March light.
One curtain hangs looped over the window frame
whose leaded rectangles encase diamond panes
and those which look like tall slope-roofed houses.
The houses of the diamond cutters are still in Amsterdam
but not the Jews who lived in them. That window curtain
is inside the room. "Vermeer has a genius for evasion."

And is the other curtain – hanging from gold rings
on a rod that crosses the room
before our eyes, just where we're standing, looking –
inside the room or in front of it?
Any moment it could be drawn to keep her
safe, to keep us out. Pictures were protected by
curtains in Vermeer's time, and so were ladies.

It's difficult to give up such protections. All those
gold rings slide easily across the rod.
Abundant proof that she is married.
Or perhaps not. There is no wedding ring on her left hand.
We cannot see her right where she would wear it if
she is a Catholic. The Diet of Wurms took place
a hundred years before her reading of this letter

All those downy peaches spilling out
of the Delft plate announce that she is ripe.
Yet perhaps it is a poem she's reading,
not from a fallen lover but from herself.
That she can read is clear. In painting,

women reading books were usually Virgins being told
by haloed angels of the hallowed cargo of their bellies.

Or women reading books were almost-banished
sibyls who were feared and sought.
They saw too clearly,
as if those lenses polished by Spinoza – yes,
he was Dutch – for microscopes and telescopes
were lenses in their eyes.
The woman looking down intently

is focusing the meaning of her poem.
How difficult. She cannot get
the last line right.
She wants to reach out of the frame
to pull aside the curtain so she can surely see
the clarifying light that glances off the winter road.
The last line trembles in her hands and heart.

For Jane Cooper on the occasion of her seventieth birthday,
and the publication of *Green Notebook, Winter Road*

Jesus Returns

I am Jesus.
No, I do not think I am. I am. Believe me.
If I must, I will perform miracles for you.
But I never liked that aspect of my earthly visitation –
a bit hokey, don't you agree? I had hoped this time
to do without multiplying the red bream and the loaves.
Perhaps I can. The older broom of earth
sweeping around the sun will tell.
Housekeeping – that's why I'm here. My Father
could not seem to get it right without

my personal appearance. You genuflect?
Have you forgotten I was Jewish?
That made my heavenly Father Jewish,
Mary and Joseph, too. As Jewishness descends
through the maternal line, it means we all are.
The way I argue this is so Talmudic, it proves the point.
Unless when I was Christianized I was a Jesuit.
And then there are the Buddhists whose arguments
are unopposed. One hand makes manifold
the lack of opposition. If you believe me –

I see by your eyes you do – then welcome me:
Christ in my bed on earth again and not a single scar.
The only nails are on my fingers and toes.
Balm of balsam, that's what did it, and juice
of the white heal-all. You still don't seem to understand
however clearly I explain that in the land I visited,
just after B.C. ended, the local populace was Jewish.
Only the intruders, Egyptians from the land of Ptha
and Romans full of Jupiter and Mars, were scattered
through the Judaic mosaic. To keep the tile agleam

use pomegranates sieved of seeds mixed with Mr. Clean.
It's pleasant here in Amarillo, reminds me some of Bethlehem.
Do you imagine Paradise is interesting? Eternal bliss?
How do you think of it? Such bliss as may be had is where
you are. Where we are now. That is my message.
Perhaps that is my message. The time of certainty is past.
Certainty is today's poison. I have to stick the meat thermometer
into the chicken and baste it every fifteen minutes.
Of that I'm certain. You think the way I speak is not poetic,

no sweeping phrases? Remember I must use the language of today.
What can I do to move the world into the paths of generosity
and kindness? How can I know? This is the ending of a century.
And who can tell me what and how? A vision of my father
tells me he is pulling hairs out of his head. The skin he frees of
hair will be a halo for the century to be. Or not. Think about that.
I have to go and mop the floor of Bosnia. I have to trellis
and then train the *Star of Bethlehem* to meet itself.
I have to go and sweep the sky of the spilt milky way.

Dark night ahead.

David Ignatow

Christmas Eve

Smitty, the cop in the booth
at the intersection of two converging streets,
waved us over on Christmas Eve. It was
a silent deserted night. He was standing
in the entrance, holding out a plate,
on it slices of a Christmas pie. Each of us
accepted a slice, thanking him hastily.
My friends gobbled theirs. I held mine,
looking down on it, wanting to eat it.

Smitty, I told myself, was not trying
to convert me to his observances of Christmas,
which I feared, hearing my parents talking
between them as Jews. I was not aware
of the religion of my friends.
It never occurred to either of us to ask.

They gobbled their slices with great relish,
with throaty sounds. If they are Jews,
they were abandoning their identity. I was
sorry for myself in such confusion.
It was not worth the anguish
of losing my friends if as Jews
they were breaking with their beliefs.

I held my slice with thumb and forefinger,
scarcely touching the edge and slowly
lifted it to my mouth. I tried to assure myself
that it was only to discover the taste.
It was sweet. Still, with misgivings,
I nibbled a piece of the crust and swallowed.

I bit off a much larger chunk, with apple in it,
and soon finished the whole with pleasure,
feeling betrayed in myself.

At home, later that night, I did not tell
my parents. I let them be gentle with me,
as always, and I was gentle in return. It was
Christian of Smitty to have done what he did.
It was Christian of me to accept the slice.
I could thank him as a Jew.

For Johannes Edfelt

I once had a religion to turn to.
I listen to a singer singing
the prayer I once sang.

What I have now is myself,
the skeptic,
looking at trees and grass
that live out their lives
never in doubt.

My childhood is in that song.
In contentment with my childhood,
I look skyward with curiosity.

A Brief Biog

Begin from the vacant.
A room unoccupied
I had forgotten
having left to visit
other rooms elsewhere
in adventure. I am back
in mind to this room.
It contains my childhood
where I sat and listened
to voices of my elders
who sat in leather chairs
and talked.

I listened, enthralled with life
for having induced such stories
I too wanted to tell,
hard, complicated, sometimes funny,
of pith, of magnitude, of accomplishment
and resignation, finally to become
the person seated in such a room
as this to tell the story
and be content that it would come
to telling in a room with others
with whom to share a falling short,
to be constrained to telling.
I listened and was curious
that one could talk of failure
with passion, as if to talk
was in itself success.

I became respectful of speech,
I could expect to speak
with that same authority

as could my elders and learn
to give my troubles my respect
for giving me the means
with which to exercise my satisfaction
in speaking to my peers who then
would speak to me in turn
with equal force of having lived;
a gathering as a child I sat
and listened to: a round of happenings
I learned to care about
in my elders.

For Rose

1913–1995

I have a name
a substitute
for the word
infinity

When my name is called
it is not me
you are calling.

The Hebrew Lesson

What I remember is the rabbi's hand
upon my genitals to show what he meant
by ancient Hebrews taking an oath
of faithfulness in God.

I was surprised,
then offended
and then curious
that he should trouble himself,
he a rabbi, a man of learning
and soul, to place his hand
upon the parts from which I urinated.
I was awakened to a double standard
in the role of rabbi.

I was confused.
Did I have to learn from books
when already I knew of being
that I did not know until then?
What then, was superior:
book learning, intellect and soul
or the life and actions
originating in my genitals?

From then on I took my learning lightly,
instead guarding my genitals,
made aware of their sacredness,
of their threat to my body and life,
inhering in an oath.

From then on, when the rabbi came to teach,
I was alert to the movements of his hands.
My genitals were mine to guard,

to keep secure
as a sacred trust
conferred on me.

I was suspicious that he wished
the sacredness of my parts
to be in his possession. Eventually,
I saw less of him,
finally, not at all,
and it never was explained to me.

Daniel Stern

The Man on the Dump by Wallace Stevens: a story

Abrams, a Rabbi on the run, woke to an awful confluence of smells. Ripe, rank odors of garbage, the coppery smell of rust and sweet rotting flowers. There was something soft moving under him giving off an odor he could not place, seaweed, potato peelings, old damp fabric, something he could only hope was still alive; not that there was any reason to assume he'd fallen asleep close to something dead the night before, more like morning when he'd hit the sack, dead drunk at the end on some sweet liqueur, how could he be expected to know what he'd lain on. This was a new low in sacking out, the dump just outside the town limits, Abrams just barely inside his own limits: of loss, of drink, hope, fatigue.

He groped under his legs and felt – legs, small, bony, fur. A quick look and he saw it was a dog. Dear God, he said out of anxiety, out of habit, a little out of irony, not Adonay, not Elohim, just Dear God – don't let it be dead. Don't let me have spent the night and part of the day sleeping with a dead dog. He was not even certain why it would be so much more humiliating to have lain with a dead dog than a live one. Either was a far cry from percale sheets, white or patterned, a far cry from Beth Abrams's perfectly patterned life and home on Water Street, full of elegant touches because she had instinctive taste, but not pretentious, everything in scale, books the center of gravity, the house, like the life, clean, tasteful, inexpensive by necessity: the quintessential Rabbi's home. And why not? Beth meant house in Hebrew, his home was Beth Abrams, his temple was Beth Shalom, house of peace.

The dog who essentially had been lying with Abrams, not beneath him, wobbled to his feet, shook himself weakly and wandered towards a huddle of people cooking something in a large can over an improvised fire. What brought a dog to this lousy end, this place, Abrams wondered, not pursuing it further in thought, what, after all, could bring anybody here?

He stretched his bony legs. He'd lost a fair amount of weight since hitting the road or the skids, whatever it was he'd hit that had landed him here, skinnier but still going, on the dump. He stood up, leaning on an automobile tire for leverage. He stared at the tire; it had the gray, anonymous coloring of discarded parts, of alien animal skin. Abrams didn't care for the thought; all too easy to think of himself as a discarded part, as an alien animal these days.

Oh, bullshit! He'd wanted to surprise his self pity, get rid of it. Instead, he surprised himself by speaking the word aloud. Careful, he thought. Bad enough being on the dump. Once you start being one of those people you see talking to themselves – he shook his head, a cautionary, rabbinic movement. It was a mistake. His head reminded him about pain; his new life, a headache without a medicine cabinet full of aspirin, ibuprofen, Tylenol, Valium. He doubted that any of his willy-nilly companions consoling themselves, a few yards away, with something hot, would be able to offer an aspirin, let alone any more exotic nostrums for his ache.

At his feet were strewn a smattering of objects he'd shared his bed with. A clump of yellow flowers wrapped in newspaper held his gaze, azaleas they were, he could tell because Beth's sister, Rowena, had brought them azaleas and had lectured him, as she lectured everyone, about their care and feeding; Rowena who had, at the end, turned out to be one of his worst mistakes.

Abrams's mouth was dry, yet he felt a desperate need to spit – as if by spitting he could clear his mouth of the mixture of foul tastes, could purify something, at least his miserable, sour breath. He spat into the dust, someplace clear, wanting to spare the azaleas, to spare the scatter of books, mostly paperbacks, sprawling next to where he'd slept, sharing a bed of gravel and ash. God, who would send books to the dump. Books were meant to go from hand to hand, eye to eye, forever, or as long as their bindings held pages together. Abrams knelt and browsed, old habits die hard, even on the dump.

A Complete Guide To The Automobile and Its Parts . . . Forever Amber . . . The Great War and Modern Memory . . . He didn't need a book at the moment. Abrams had brought his book with him, only one book in his flight, stuffed into his jacket pocket. *The Palm at the End of the Mind: Poems by Wallace Stevens.* He pulled it out and ruffled the pages, tempted to add it to the collection in the dirt.

On impulse he did it – tossed it into the filthy, torn collection at his feet. It was the book with which he'd antagonized the Women's Reading Circle at his Temple, suggesting that they introduce poetry into their list – a needed change from Chaim Potok, from Leo Rosten and *The Joys of Yiddish*. They'd nervously agreed, but had thought perhaps of Longfellow, of Edna St. Vincent Millay, then in comes Stevens with his "Notes for a Supreme Fiction," his difficult images, his philosophical references. He'd tried to make it less painful with "Postcard From A Volcano," an easier job, but it was a bad number from the start, the women made to feel foolish, inadequate, the opposite of what he'd had in mind. He'd already been told that some in the congregation were not happy with him using so many references to T. S. Eliot, to Auden and even more obscure poets in his sermons. Don't think just because we're reform – and so on. That might go down in New York at Temple Emanu-el, they said, not here in Hillcrest.

Yet another misstep from Abrams, pretentious, insensitive, according to Beth; trying to make people into what they weren't, instead of meeting them on their own ground – another melody added to their old sweet song of bedtime discord. Useless to tell her again how moving the poems were to him, how consoling in a difficult life, so once again he shut up, sulked, drank. And when he'd started his buried life, the secretive attempt to write stories based on poems that moved him, he'd said nothing to Beth.

Abrams bent and retrieved the Stevens. Why had he grabbed it out of all the possible books for a fugitive journey whose end was dim, obscure? As a reminder of his humiliating failure with the Women's Reading Circle? Or because the poems could be read and read again with Talmudic persistence, giving a different pleasure each time? Both! An action over determined like actions in Freud's dreams.

Abrams brushed dirt and fragments of gravel from the book. It was damp and he wasn't too happy about what the yellowish stains might represent – he'd slept on the ground more than once, his jacket rolled up as portable pillow – had sometimes peed haphazardly. But the pages turned and were readable and he stuck it back into his jacket. He was thus reminded that he had to pee now, but where? Even here modesty made its claim. There were rusted remains of a car a few yards west, the dropping sun behind it, but it looked too low to offer privacy. Closer in was a tree. Gnarled, almost bare as if to spite the spring season, it was like a tree in a Beckett play. It would serve.

Afterwards, he walked toward the trio thinking how lucky for all of them that it was a hazy, warm spring day. The fire was for some kind of food, not warmth. Day? The day was fading. The air had a bluish tinge, the sky would be making a change toward evening soon. How long had he slept – maybe a night and two thirds of a day. His watch was gone, he had no idea where. His worst toot yet.

The presence of the woman surprised Abrams. He was old-fashioned enough to have always suffered a special frisson of horror whenever he'd seen a woman in the street, on the skids. And here, of all places in the good green world. She was pretty, still young, though it was hard to be sure about that, her reddish hair any which way, skin cracked around the mouth, no lipstick, at least not lately. The man next to her was large, he needed a lot of space, even his head was grand. Beside him was a delicate, trembling sort of man, quite old judging by the gray, by the shuffling gait as he rose to poke at the fire.

They made room for Abrams as naturally as if he'd been expected. He came right to the point.

"What's in the can?"

"Soup," the woman said. "Soup du jour."

"The jour is almost over," the large man said, admiration in his voice. "Mary Louise cheers us up with a little French talk now and then."

Mary Louise handed Abrams a Campbell's soup can. She used a cardboard cup to transfer soup from the large can over the fire to the small one in Abrams' hand. It took a long time. It tasted like tomato-flavored water decorated with pepper. By the time he drank the cupful it felt as if he'd been sitting there for a long time and these were people he knew. He thought, and had thought before in his pre-dump life, about how quickly a Rabbi gets to be comfortable with strangers – like his professional siblings, analysts, therapists of all stripes, priests, visible reminders of the strangeness of everyone.

Knowing people's names usually helped and he said, speaking to the fire and thus to all three, "I'm Jack Abrams." Usually followed with "Rabbi of Temple Beth Shalom," but at this moment it seemed more sensible to say, "Thanks for the soup."

Nobody replied to this but a flutter of birds pouring an awful racket from their beaks and coming too close to the small circle around the fire making the old man scramble and wave his arms at them.

"Take it easy, Eddy." Mary Louse said.

"Damned birds," Eddy muttered and subsided. "Godawful noise."

"What kind of birds are they?" Abrams asked and felt awkward at once. Ornithology could not be a great concern on the dump. But Mary Louise surprised him. "Grackles," she said. "These here are grackles. A bird of the south. Quarrelsome sort."

"Like crows," Abrams offered.

"Sort of."

"Mary Louise knows all hell about things," the large man said.

"Oh, please, Rory. Lay off."

Rory addressed Abrams directly. "It's one of the reasons I'm in love with her. "

"Jesus!" Mary Louise looked to Abrams as if for rescue. Her eyelids were either oddly shaded or she carried the remnants of eyeshadow, purplish in the darkening air. "Even here, he carries on. Can you believe it?"

Abrams smiled. He was more comfortable with this moment, was used to a life of generalized discourse. Words he could handle, however obliquely attached to lives and places.

"Yes," he said. "Love happens anywhere, everywhere."

Rory nodded his almost hydrocephalic head in sage agreement. But in the few seconds that passed, Abrams' own words tasted foolish in his mouth, dumb echoes – years of automatic rabbinic response. He would have to stay away from opinions, especially banal, rhetorical ones, trapdoors waiting to send him spinning into a pit of self-disgust.

He remembered the retiring Rabbi Greenwald at Beth Shalom, replaced by Abrams eight years ago. The older man had moved from the residence supplied by the congregation, had taken a house on the not-so-fancy part of Lake Shore Drive and a joke went around:

Question: Does Greenwald have a view of the lake?

Answer: Honey, he's a Rabbi, he has an opinion on everything.

Instead of cheering him, the remembered moment of self-mocking malice triggered gloom. Or had it been the word love spoken here on the dump? He'd loved Beth, had even been in love. But that hadn't prevented his whole enterprise from going south. Years of his uncertainty, his endless retracing of his footsteps, a man always in question, had turned her from a witty charmer into a scold. Love, that solemn, sacred word so beloved of song writers and clergymen, hadn't helped him believe in his vocation, hadn't made him a good teacher – that was all a Rabbi was, a teacher, in spite of all the fancy, ancient reverberations of the word; love hadn't granted him the secret of being a good husband, hadn't resolved the dilemma of children refusing to arrive after years of making love, at first with passionate hope, later with cheerless persistence. How could you *make* love, anyway? An odd phrase, peculiar term of manufacture. Only a God could do that, and if he existed he didn't do it often or well enough.

"Lukewarm! You'll be thinking about what to do with your life when you're seventy. For Christ's sake be a Rabbi or don't – but be something. Don't be a Rabbi with a half-finished novel, a bunch of poems and afraid to adopt a child because it's the last nail in the coffin of having your own kids. Jesus!" He made no mention of the incongruity of Beth's eternal use of Christian imagery in her expletives. She was always a volatile woman; he'd liked that in her in the beginning. His was a more quiet soul, a quiet style. She needed more opposition, more sparks with which to ignite her flame.

They must be going crazy at Temple Beth Shalom . . . He'd not told anybody anything – just vanished. A nasty, cruel thing to do, given all the responsibilities – but it was all he could manage. By now the police will have come up empty and a period of mourning will have begun.

The old man, Eddie, was still standing at the perimeter of the makeshift fire, as if on guard against the return of the grackles. Mary Louise was filling a container with soup and handing it to an adoring Rory. Suddenly Abrams could not sit there one minute more, did not want to hear another word about dump-love. He would have liked a drink but he had no bottle, no glass available to him, not a dollar left in his pocket. He took the book of poems from his jacket pocket and walked away from the group.

Mary Louise looked over at Abrams and said, "What'd you used to do, Mister – I mean before you stumbled?"

"She calls our troubles stumbling" Rory said, marveling. "Isn't she something?"

Abrams paused, wondering how to reply, then from a lifetime of habit came the truth. "I was a Rabbi," he said, surprised at his use of the past tense, as if this was the famed life after death, damned souls introducing themselves, instead of just the worst morning after, in months of mornings after. He kept walking, wanting no more discourse, no more exchange of information. "Thanks for the soup," he called out.

Abrams retreated to the tree behind which he'd pissed and sat down on the other side of it. He was waiting until he felt the strength to get up and out, to go home, apologize to Beth, explain to the Board of Directors, check into Hillcrest Hospital, call an end to his loony flight; or maybe to call Rowena and dry out at her apartment, he remembered how deliciously deep her bathtub was, and he would soak himself clean and ask her not to call her sister until he was ready, which might be never.

To distract himself, to stall, he rambled through the book of poems. Reading had been his reproachable vice; in childhood he read to escape his foolish, all too often unemployed, father, his ailing mother, later he read to put off responsibilities. It was better than drinking. He leafed past the ones he knew – "Post-card From A Volcano," "The Snowman," until he skimmed past page 94 and saw the title "The Man On The Dump."

It was like a moment in a dream, the moment in which every-thing points with portents and signs to some meaning you can feel but not understand, least of all after you've woken up. His skin was shuddery while he read, an eerie sensation, but his headache was gone.

> Day creeps down. The moon is creeping up.
> The sun is a corbeil of flowers the moon Blanche
> Places there, a bouquet. Ho-ho . . . The dump is full
> Of images. Days pass like papers from a press.

Abrams, of course, knew the poem well. Jerry Cardoza, his obsessive roommate at Amherst, had done a major paper on it, had kept Abrams up with his endless interpretations and re-interpretations so that, finally, an exhausted Abrams felt like he'd written the poem himself, would never forget it. It was Cardoza who'd started him on Stevens. Later, when Abrams was at the seminary, he'd amused himself by counting the number of times the word Rabbi appeared in the poems by a New England gentile. More than thirty, as he recalled.

Reading was almost the same as remembering and Abrams laughed aloud, remembering something about last night. He'd left the Scat Bar, deafened by the million decibels of the Rap music juke box where some triumphant Hispanic guy in the wide, brilliant red suspenders had been buying the drinks; had walked past the railroad tracks, had seen what seemed at first to be simply a graveyard for old, rusted automobile parts but which turned out to be nothing less than a dump, perhaps the town dump. He wasn't even sure which town he was in, but he thought it might be Larkspur, only a few miles from his home in Hillcrest.

Giggling to himself, beat, teary with self-pity, Abrams had thought, why not? remembering "The Man On The Dump," the pimply, driven Cardoza and his A paper, both of them nineteen and remembered all the hopes and confusions of the time of Amherst. What the hell, he'd thought, if you could call such dizzy, sodden fragments thought, go ahead, act it out, do it, be it, don't just read and talk and drink, be *something*, if only the rock bottom. That was sort of the way it had gone and he'd lain down in the dark next to something soft, something large, and slept.

Now, that night gone and most of the next day, Abrams skated on the surface of the poem, a better description than reading because the piece was complicated and he was hearing in his dizzy mind both the images on the page and the endless conversations with Cardoza, intent on getting his Ph.D. and setting the academic world on fire.

> . . . The dump is full
> Of images. Days pass like papers from a press. . . .

Then a bunch of what Stevens calls janitor's poems of every day that show up at the dump:

> . . . the wrapper on the can of pears,
> the cat in the paper bag, the corset,
> the box from Estonia: the tiger chest for tea.

Abrams could now have added the piss-yellow paperbacks. But none of this carried the main impression he recalled from the poem, the sense of a tiredness, of a distaste for used things . . . well, yes, maybe used things was more like it . . .

> The freshness of night has been fresh for a long time,
> The freshness of morning . . .

How could freshness be fresh for a long time? Didn't that imply staleness? And then came a passage about dew. As a city boy in summer camp he'd wondered about the evening dew. He'd expected morning dew. But why the evening, too?

> . . . the dew in the green
> Smacks like fresh water in a can, like the sea
> On a coconut – how many men have copied dew
> For buttons, how many women have covered themselves

> With dew, dew dresses, stones and chains of dew, heads
> Of the floweriest dew dewed with the dewiest day . . .

Mocking the nice, fresh dew, of course . . . *copied* a key word
here . . . as tired of the conventional dew in poetry, in people's
minds, as Gertrude Stein was tired of the red, red rose. It was
with such ideas that Cardoza had lectured him with passion – a
passion on behalf of a poet tired of used things, fed up with
living on the dump of old, received images.

Abrams' heart jumped in him, it was like being young again.
Cardoza pacing the room, spewing lines, images and interpretations; Abrams, uncertain of his future: a writer, a teacher, a Rabbi –
his father's goal for him – mostly eager to read, write, get laid. In
this vulnerable state, Cardoza had had him dazzled, confused,
hypnotized.

He'd died still young, poor Cardoza, long after they'd lost
track of each other; the circumstances suggested suicide, but
when Abrams called Cardoza's father he got a stone wall and
he'd had to leave it at condolences. Now, for a moment, he lived
again in Abrams, here on the dump, the daylight going fast.

> Now, in the time of spring (azaleas, trilliums,
> Myrtle, viburnums, daffodils, blue phlox),
> Between that disgust and this, between the things
> That are on the dump (azaleas and so on)
> And those that will be (azaleas and so on),
> One feels the purifying change. One rejects
> The trash . . .
> That's the moment when the moon creeps
> up . . .

Abrams put the book down on his lap. Purifying change . . . Was
that why he'd dashed out of the house, out of his life? To reject
the trash of bad faith, shaky belief, bad luck, bad times. (Two
salary cuts in three years and the pension fund a mess because of
the economy, because of bad management.) *Between the things*
that are on the dump (azaleas and so on) and those that will be on the
dump (azaleas and so on). . . . He knew about that dump, the one all
things come to, finally, el ultimo dump. All those condolence
calls, all those funeral services, one Kaddish after another. A
woman of valor is a jewel beyond price . . . a man of compassion,
of tzedakah, who gave to charity . . . Oh, yes, he was well acquainted with the dump, an expert on the dump, a professional
you could say.

Abrams touched his cheek where a trim, neat beard had once distinguished itself from the rest of his pale face and, of course, from most of his cleanshaven congregation. It had been more than a week since he'd been in combat with a razor. It was all stubble of varying lengths now. Non-rabbinic, anonymous.

The light had changed, become less than daylight but still more than night. Abrams looked up and saw that a batch of mattress-shaped clouds had drifted apart and the moon had unexpectedly risen. He had to laugh. The moon didn't creep up the way it does in poems, at least this moon hadn't. It had arrived, been revealed. Or was it only that Abrams was in the mood, in the market for revelations: tricky things he'd never trusted before?

The moon drifted through clouds, a movie shot. Abrams' gaze drifted up then back to the page.

> . . . That's the moment when the moon creeps up
> To the bubbling of bassoons. That's the time
> one looks at the elephant-colorings of tires.
> Everything is shed; and the moon comes up as the moon
> (All its images are in the dump) and you see
> As a man (not like the image of a man),
> You see the moon rise in the empty sky.

Abrams particularly liked the part about the empty sky. Once the sky was truly empty could you see as a man (not like the image of a man). Portrait Of The Rabbi As A Man. He'd thought that for a long time, had wondered at the completeness of his un-faith, wondered should he quit, play fair with a congregation who had the right to expect, at the least, belief from their spiritual leader.

Once, at an Oneg Shabat, he'd actually tried to shock Weinstein, the President of the Board, with a revelation of unbelief. Only to be greeted by a flood of postmodern bullshit, The Courage To Be, God as the Ground of Being, the kinship with the Buddha, the God Within Us, Doubt As A Form of Belief. Weinstein had read Buber, he'd read Paul Tillich and Teillard de Chardin. You couldn't turn these people off by merely telling them their Rabbi didn't believe in God. This was the end of the twentieth century. If the moon was the only occupant of the night sky, that was okay with them. Nobody wanted whitebearded Gods waiting in the sky any more. Everybody was comfortable with doubt and uncer-tainty. Traditional observance was enough for them, and ulti-mate doubt only made them feel like grown-ups; all they needed was ritual – that and discourse, the endless flood of talk, opinion, interpretation. It was enough to be with other Jews. Only Abrams felt like a fake.

"Excuse me. Don't let me interrupt."

The small old man was standing there, red rheumy eyes staring at Abrams. He kept shifting his weight from one foot to another as if he, too, had to pee. But that was not his mission.

"Excuse me," he repeated. "Mary Louise and Rory and me, we wanted to ask you something."

"Yes?"

"To ask you if you would give us a sermon."

Abrams was wary. He scowled. "What's this, some kind of joke?"

A shake of the skinny head. "No, we wouldn't make a joke about that. Please."

Abrams tried not to laugh. "You're asking for a sermon? Most people just get stuck with them."

"Well, it's kind of weird being on the go. It's Sunday. And you being a clergyman, we talked about it and wanted to ask you if you would."

Abrams was not about to get into the difference between the Christian and the Jewish Sabbath. Amused, and in some odd way, saddened, on the instant Abrams knew he would give them their sermon, and knew what he would use as his text.

They gave him the central seat, an upturned milk can, and sat in front of him. For themselves they pulled some mattresses, stained in various, unthinkable ways, but long since dried out. Mary Louise was central, her long, ragged skirt spread around her like a gypsy queen. On her left Rory hulked. Ed, his endless fluttering stilled for once, waited on her right.

"I thought you were kidding," he began.

"Me, from a Baptist family," Mary Louise said. "Rory, here from a couple of Episcopalian atheists and Ed's adopted but his mother was Lutheran."

"She keeps track of everything," Rory said. I'd be lost without her."

Mary Louise, our lady of Rory's perpetual adoration, ignored him. She said, "Couldn't believe our good luck having a minister fall by like this."

"Not a minister."

"A man of God . . . "

Abrams let it rest there. "Well, " he began. "Since everybody's so different I'm not going to do a usual Rabbi's sermon. I'll use a poem."

"Great," Ed said, as if every Lutheran child had expected a poem for a sermon on Sunday.

He began with the title, "The Man On The Dump," and they seemed to take its utter on-the-nose appropriateness as if he'd tailor-made it for their mutual situation. Preaching – Yes, the dump, the man, here we are. They paid perfect attention, followed him through the moon's rising, the itemization of objects on the dump, even through the slightly surreal section of dresses, stones, chains made of the worn-out dew. Then –

> One sits and beats on an old tin can, lard pail.
> One beats and beats for that which one believes.
> That's what one wants to get near. Could it after all
> Be merely ones' self . . .

They seemed to like that part and Abrams paused for a little commentary, raised the question of one's beliefs being a road to who one is. Ed nodded, Mary Louise murmured something inaudible. Abrams liked the feel of still controlling a congregation, even a rag-tag one of three, like this. He could always tell when a sermon was going well. This one was on track.

> . . . as superior as the ear
> To a crow's voice?

Abrams had written a poem about a crow and then had read Ted Hughes' long poem "Crow" and had torn his own piece up. The right thing to do? Wrong? Just young? It didn't matter. Apparently, once you tore something up it was in pieces forever even if you pasted it back together again.

> . . . did the nightingale torture the ear,
> Pack the heart and scratch the mind?

Abrams wondered, did it bother Stevens that Keats had already done the nightingale? Probably not. Beth used to say, with some contempt, that all poets do is talk to each other. She was probably right, they even talk to the dead ones – and they talk back. And what of his crazy idea of writing stories based on poems, what had made him stop? Fear of ridicule, of feeling foolish. Careful, don't lose your audience, speak to them, about themselves.

> . . . is it peace,
> Is it a philosopher's honeymoon, one finds
> On the dump?

He sees, from the corner of his eye, Rory smile hugely at the notion of finding peace on the dump. Abrams picks up volume and tempo, asking them to join in, to repeat some key words, phrases in responsive reading. They nod.

> . . . Is it to sit among the mattresses of the dead,
> Bottles, pots, shoes and grass and murmur *aptest eve.*

He pauses, inviting the responsive chant.

Mary Louise glances at her two men and they chant in unison: *aptest eve.* Abrams is accustomed to responsive readings in his synagogue, but this is stranger. It comes out like dream-talk, like music, the sermon as abstract art. It is wild. Abrams is high; he is running a revival meeting, chamber music style just for three, and where better.

> Is it to hear the blatter of grackles and say
> *Invisible priest . . .*

They chant in response: *Invisible priest.* Mary Louise's eyes are closed, her cracked lips puckered around the letter p in priest.

> . . . is it to eject, to pull
> The day to pieces and cry *stanza my stone?*

Their voices are louder now, more confident, calling out *stanza my stone* as if they are three poets of the dump who want only to have immortal longings in the shape of poems inscribed on their tombstones when they die. Abrams takes a breath and breathes out the last line of the poem.

> *Where was it one first heard of the truth. The the.*

The the. What a way to phrase the truth – the the. It was like telling all seekers to go to hell. The *the.* A stammer, a passionate bad joke. God!

But the moment is too impossible, too good, to last. When he has read the last line, their interest starts to fade, he can feel himself losing them, their attention drifting off. They think he is stuttering. He tries a commentary on "the the" as truth, but it doesn't work. Mary Louise says she lost interest when the moon rose in the empty sky.

"I don't want an empty sky. Too damned depressing."

"It depends on what skies you're leaving behind. And what you trade them in for." He wants her assent more than he'd wanted Weinberg's, the President of the Board. He has no idea why, but he feels as if he's fighting for his life. With whom, three strangers, an old man and a woman doted on by a loutish lover? All of them brought to the dump by God knows what?

And they don't like "the empty sky." Exactly what will liberate him is what they are afraid of. How can he explain to them that it is only that freshly emptied sky that can free him, get him off the hook, off the dump, back to life?

Abrams is tossed by nausea; he has eaten so little in the past few days it's no wonder he's in some kind of hallucinatory state, finding sermons in iambics, busily ungodding skies.

"Listen," he says, "I'm sorry. That wasn't much of a sermon, using a poem and all."

They gathered around him in a reassuring chorus.

"Did me a hell of a lot of good," Rory said. "I like that part about beating on a tin can for what you believe."

"And I liked the stuff about finding peace on the dump," Mary Louise said. She stood up and shook her long skirt out, brushing away a few pebbles along with something small and crawling. "I don't believe it's true, but I liked believing it."

"Well, for about a minute," Ed said. He poked at the dying fire with a stick, raising a cloud of unhelpful sparks. He spat in the embers, a hiss.

Abrams gazed at Mary Louise, at the swell of her stomach. Is she pregnant? Terrifying thought, here. How he and Beth had slaved at making a child. One final casualty had been his potency. "Too much intensity," Dr. Law had said. "Why not adopt?" Why not, indeed? Pig-headed, bull-headed, pick your animal and put its head where it didn't belong, that was Abrams on the subject. Most awful of all were the moments when he'd tried to rouse his flagging potency by seeking out porn pictures of men making love to pregnant women. He'd not known such startling, extreme sexual things existed, but in some hidden place he understood: it was a matter of touching the woman and also the immanent child; a mixture of shame and wonder, a mad sensuality of becoming.

His three chance encounters were busy rolling up some sort of blanket – getting ready for the night? To move on? Abrams walked quietly back to the stunted tree that served as refuge. His headache was down to half its size. The brief parody of preaching had been somehow settling. But he was not finding peace on the dump. He was ready to get out, to move on, too. To find a homeless shelter, the Salvation Army – did they take Rabbis, he wondered, would he have to sing "Jesus Loves Me" in order to get a meal, a clean bed, a night's sleep? What the hell! He'd given up the fantasy of a Rowena-return. That was over and it had nearly wrecked the two sisters, his marriage. But it was finished. Maybe he'd just go home. The sleepier he got the nicer the idea seemed. He'd walk in, Beth so happy he was alive, no reproaches, only homecoming love.

His half-closed eyes scanned the reaches of the dump and beyond; across the railroad tracks to the shadowy outlines of some kind of stile fence, a house lovely in its simple lines, against the purplish sky, a hint of a garden blurry in the foreground. But to get to it his eyes had to take in all the rusted metal large and small, automobile fenders rusting, tin cans and bottles, greenish, moldy colors, this poisonous beauty making mounds for the eye to cross. He thought he saw the trotting figure of the dog who'd shared his first night on the dump, a tiny figure on the horizon.

Finally, what a gorgeous dump this world was, rotting, taking pleasure in its absolute decaying beauty; old, young, it didn't matter to the dump. If everything came there in the end, then it was a world, a real place, as real as Hillcrest, as his study at Temple Beth Shalom with its rickety piles of books, real as the women's reading group. All you needed was the patience to make everything fresh, young; to reject the trash amid the trash.

Where was it one first heard of the truth? The the. He'd come home from a movie, "The Three Musketeers," a ten-year-old thrilled with honor and courage and sat down and wrote a story he copied from the movie's opening scroll: *A young man from Gascony set out to seek his fortune in Paris as a member of the Queen's Musketeers* or some such. He'd shown it proudly to his sister who'd given it to one of her friends, a pretty, ironic girl who'd laughed and said, "This is from that movie we just saw. You stole this." Terrible mixture of truths and untruths. Honor, courage, and theft. The the. Trying to write stories, his novel-in-the-drawer, all had been a wounded endeavor, somehow tainted with fakery, ever since – as complicated as making children.

Or the moment he'd decided to become a teacher of long-true truths, a Rabbi, calling his father in the hospital to tell him, the old man happy with anything his son would do. Then losing courage, wanting only to sit alone in a room and make up tales to break people's hearts and make them laugh, with no heart left to call his father again, gone to join his mother by then anyway, via the Laocoon tangle of tubes they give you instead of death, instead of honor and courage these days.

Or the moment the moon rose, tonight, in the empty sky. That was a kind of truth. He wished he had a pencil and paper, saw himself writing a story based on a poem as he'd wanted to do for months, maybe years; saw himself doing this in the Salvation Army shelter, or in his comfortable, book-haunted study at home – they seemed oddly interchangeable. Whichever one, it could become one of the places, times, one first heard of the truth, the the. He wanted a lot at the moment: a scotch, a beer, a steak, a soft bed. Still, to trade all of it, God included, for a pencil seemed at this exhausted moment a reasonable exchange.

Abrams was falling asleep, back against the scratchy bark of the tree, his right leg stiff, tingling. His trouser cuffs were unpleasantly wet: the mysterious, ubiquitous evening dew. As waking faded his mother appeared, her usual time for return. His mother, blessed with a witty tongue but cursed with a stammer, would have understood all that had happened to him. Laughing, doomed to a shortness of breath and life, uneducated, unread, she saw through the smooth talkers around her, but said little. Everyone in the world busily talking away, treating those who stammered as unfortunate, sad cases. But underneath the smooth, endless rabbinical discourses, the clever talk, how many hid the stammering of a lifetime, the passionate stuttering search for the moment they first heard of the truth, the stuttering search for the the, the the, the the the the the the the the the the the the the the the the the the the the the the *the*.

Alicia Ostriker

Tearing the Poem Up and Eating It

i
Take this, you said
As if I were a prophet
As if the poem were something healing
As if the poem nourished
Not only itself, the life of language
Which certainly is worth nothing
Next to a biological life –
What are you saying?
Do you think the life of an insect
Is worth more than the life of a poem?

In childhood
I did –
That is exactly what I thought

An ant, a pink-grey worm on the wet sidewalk
Was worth everything.

ii
Cause and effect: yesterday it was raining so that today
This amazement of shallow pools, the beauty the brisk beauty
Of rain slicking the gutters – the sluice
Bearing its running images of buildings
Defeats Plato defeats Descartes
And St. Paul and the Buddha

Culture and anarchy the lifeblood of the poem, of the book
Which can never be killed, tell it to your pink-grey stones
Tell it to the stone of sacrifice
Where the sons finally rise to slay the fathers
Tell it to the assassin's grandmother
Speak the poem to her oranges and fish

iii
Shoot and penetrate me that is what I want
I who in childhood knew the infinite
Without needing to think about it
Azure sky brown dirt red brick gritty gravel
(Infinite worm, infinite living ant)
Because whiteness kept bursting out of me and everything
So obviously I could only smile

(This furious energy, God, when did it stop)

So when T___ bloodied my mouth and her friends
Said Jew Jew how do you do, unable to raise my fist I cried and they
Liked that but I myself could only smile
The way you do at a first snowfall
At the meeting of word and thing, the meaning *evil*
Because I had heard of it with the hearing of the ear
And what a revelation to see to see

iv
Juice and seeds liberated by a shooting!
Winds of spirit flood toward the aperture
Gnats borne into windy throats of birds
Without a plan, a system, an organization, a manifesto
Might as well forget it might as well speak in tongues might
As well vomit up butterflies. Shred the butterflies.

Tearing the poem up and eating it
Will get me nowhere. Better to burn than to marry
What asks to be married. And better to write than to burn.
And best to clear a path for the wind.

v
At the funeral one of the ministers produced
What will obviously be the icon of this martyrdom:
The sheet of paper bearing the words of the peace song
R___ sang at the rally ten minutes before his assassination
The paper was folded into quarters and stained
With an irregular shape of blood from where
It was in his pocket, fire and blood

You wonder at funerals why nobody bursts out laughing

His granddaughter touchingly said to the microphone that she
knew angels would bear him to heaven and perhaps they will, who
Am I
To doubt

vi

Can you understand, you, that this is not what I intended?
Not what any of us intended?
And that ugliness is a form of recrimination?
That by stupidity and ignorance we hope to avenge ourselves?
That to pace magnificently within the bars you have planted, our
        musculature
Rippling and popping and singing beneath warm fur, like
        Rilkean beasts,
Is unacceptable to us, you who have countless eyes,
Whose entire body is eyes, eyes and language,
Do you not see we prefer fleas, excrement, disease,
To fling at the purple fountain of your wild iris
And her yellow streak and her beard?

Will you stop drooling? My God, do you understand nothing?

xiii

For those who believe you chose them
        break the bones of the unchosen
And those who trust in your righteousness
        study death's secret handshake
For those who remember you promised them the land
        sow it with corpses
And those who await messiah
        imagine apocalypse
        in which their enemies burn –
I speak of all your countries, my dear God.

Diaspora

i
The forsythia bush is made of yellow fire,
The daffodils are made of yellow fire,
It is why they are so difficult to look at.

To obtain your attention
They cry shrilly just beyond the capacity of your ears.
Perhaps you feel the discomfort in your sinuses
And guess that if you permitted yourself one glance

They would grip you with the tenacity
Of the wheelchair-bound elderly, or of the mad –

ii
Take the above as an allegory of learning:
Springtime, resurrection, your heritage, death and life,
Each dangerous truth you would almost prefer to refuse –

Neither does it stop here,
For already a row of magnolias holds flesh cups
Like the dead family around a child
Dressed stiffly for a first recital, a row of eyes

And a row of heaving breasts, until you see
You can never learn the routine of truth –
Were you ever wise?
If when you were children you knew, you knew –
More and more will be expected of you.

Norman Y. Harris

Ikey

I weighed ninety-five pounds when I started High School.
I weighed a hundred twenty-five when I graduated.
I got all A's except for typing and freshman gym.
When I was a sophomore, my biology teacher
was the gym teacher, so I got an A in gym, too.
Some tough guys in gym used to call me Ikey.
They never knew any Jews and thought they could
Rile me. But "Ikey" wasn't so bad.
I'd been called "Christkiller" too many times
By Catholic kids in the neighborhood parochial
School. But I knew they didn't know what or why
they were doing it. It made me mad, but I never cried.

Bronchitis

Doctor Potts told my mom to give me bacon.
He said it was full of iron and would help
Me get rid of the bronchitis that made me
Stay home from school for a semester
When I was nine. He used to try to
Cure my earaches, too.
The bacon ended our keeping a kosher home!
And my grandpa had to move back to his own house later.
But I got better, gained weight and
Went back to school in the fall.
While grandpa lived with us, he taught

Me to play casino, to box, and told me
Stories about the old country. I think
he helped me to get well more than the bacon did!

My Hero

My uncle Isadore died when I was six or seven.
I was too young to go to the funeral, or to grieve.
His dad, my grandpa, gave me Isadore's baseball bat,
and his catcher's mitt. I used them for a long time.
But I wasn't as good as my uncle. He was a thirteen-
year-old freshman at Tech High when he died of diabetes.
In later years, I remembered all about him.
I loved him before I knew about loving anybody.
Sixty years later, I still love him.

All Stars

We didn't have a little league or Pop Warner.
Just old taped up baseballs and a beat up football,
The streets, backyards and empty lots.
No coaches, no helmets, no pads, no umps or refs.
Just dirty overalls and torn Keds and lots of heart.
One guy named Jimmy was the best at everything.
I liked him, but his dad was mean. Told me that
The only good thing about Hitler was what he

Was doing to the Jews.
I was okay at softball but no good at football,
Unless we were playing touch. I was fast, but
Little and skinny.
God, did we have fun, and did we learn!

April 1, 1924

My folks moved into our brand new house, on a
High hill, a long way from the old neighborhood.
It was also six blocks from the streetcar line.
I remember my dad carrying me up the hill that
Rainy night. I was four the next day.
I rode that streetcar for years, and always
Wondered how that glass and metal box sorted out
The money and tokens.
When it snowed, we'd sled down that long hill
And trudge back up. But it was worth it.
Those were years between wars, and the only
Problems we had were depression, unemployment,
prohibition, gangsters, segregation, corruption
and the stock market crash.
But my dad had a job, wasn't in stocks,
Didn't drink, and although some neighbors
Didn't think Jewish people were, we were white.
That old new house is still up there on the hill.
The garage behind it is falling apart. The
Little tree we planted in the yard is a monster
Now. The neighborhood is still segregated.
It's all black.
Were those the good old days?

Jerry Mirskin

Bronx Park East

My grandmother gives me a glass of cold water.
I say out loud.
My uncle wants to know if it's a poem.
She's from Russia.
She gives me what I wanted.
Is it a poem?
Did she come here to give you a glass of water?
My uncle is cantankerous.
Seventy years old,
and we're sitting in the kitchen
of the apartment in which he grew up.
I wanted a glass of water,
and I wanted to say something true.
For that you have to open your mouth
and say it, and see how it sounds.
This is the apartment in which my father
and my aunt grew up.
The one from which my father and uncle left
to go into service during the war.
The same they returned to, to find their father gone.
If they wanted a glass of water
they probably got it for themselves.
I know that's what he's thinking.
They didn't wait for Grandma to push by the table.
They didn't watch her shuttle from stove
to refrigerator to sink and back to table.
They just went and got it.
It wasn't a poem.
This has been her home since he was a boy.
His hands on the same table for sixty years.
When my grandmother hands me the glass

I feel that I'm among them.
I'm his brother. She's my mother. She smiles at me.
I should say, "On" me.
The yiddish word is "kvell." You say, She kvells on me.
Though it's not something you say about yourself.

I want to say,
My grandmother gives me a glass of cold water.
And maybe reveal how she smiles at me
with all the light of her kitchen
in her well-traveled eyes.
Eyes that left Russia when she was twelve.
Eyes that left behind her mother and father
the people she loved, the acres and the hours
she spent in her home.
My uncle is cantankerous,
but that doesn't mean anything.
Sixty years in the same apartment,
people ask her how she feels.

My grandmother gives me a glass of cold water.

Happiness

In a dream
I reach into a crib at night,
lean over and lift a blue silk torah
from its bed. And look!
– It is my son.

Asleep or crying, I cradle him
sometimes holding his head,
and rock like an old priest
in love.

As a boy,
I saw the old men pray
wrap weekend arms
around the torah
and carry their stiff baby
around the temple.
If they fell
it would mean weeks
of bread and water.
To me, a small boy,
it seemed such a risk.

Years ago,
sitting with a friend
I saw my father
standing in a field
and my friend said,
Look at that man swing!
And I watched him
in the distance – a life away.

In one of my first efforts
at poetry, I wrote
"too young to buy, I built my strength
running at my father."

It's late summer
and my son runs at me.
I can see by the yellow
and orange glass in his eyes
that he runs blindly
into day's abundant light,

and I can do nothing
but fall, and laugh with him
and hold him
and take this risk.

My son's head rests
sleeping on my shoulder.
And I know
what others have known.
And no one will blame me
if I give everything I have
to him, who runs at me –
who lets me for a while
into his dream.

Early in the book of brothers and sisters

It's early in the book of brothers and sisters.
We're crossing the lawns of the suburbs
traders on a walk through the stars.
The blue waters of dusk part for us.
The grasses turn to Persian rugs.
In one hand I carry a velvet bag
and in the other a prayer book.
Soft body of tallis calmed my small shoulders.
Simple body of prayer book kept me from flying away.

Rosh Hashanah.
I can still hear the shofar on the turnpike
can hear its stipple hit the concrete.
A horny toot sibilance, a chaos in the lives of children
men, boys, women, girls.

My memory is wrapped in that wilderness.
Wrapped in beautiful shawls, wings, drapery
in which each person is no less

than a tree, a cloud, a kind of tossing
a kind of thrown together.

If on some days all we have
is a few words to swing like a knife in the dark
on others we sway in our penumbra shawls.
Swaying in and out of our small circles
out of the small shadows of our lives.

Soon we would be returning home.
Soon we would see our house with its excited lights on.

They're blowing the shofar tonight, I say to myself
looking up at stars' bright vigilance.
Reminded how our prayers fly around like leaves
and how peace comes with anticipation.

Early in the book of brothers and sisters
I crossed the lawns of the suburbs.
In the sky our ancestors were lighting small fires.
The soft body of the tallis touched my shoulders.
The simple body of prayer book
kept me from flying away.

Grace

The hospital bed is a mute hand.
It has nothing to say
and cannot be improved upon.

My grandmother – Grace
was not afraid of death. And said so.
And in response

the grime of my own fear
lit a cold fire, and I shivered,
my light fallen and ashamed.

Earlier, I wondered
what we would do if we had our real work.
If this life and death were truly ours

would we lie down in the bed
in which we are going to live forever
and begin talking?

This is not for some, she said
and for a moment it was like leaning into a candle
until we were completely inside.

And how thick and luminous it is
to be in time . . . and wonderful
but only for a moment.

Later, I went back
into the light
in which we would be separated

and put my hands in hers.
And when they were finally warm, she said
Your hands were cold. You were frightened.

Our real work?
To die is one thing, and to live another.
And how relentless it is to love.

Linda Pastan

A Craving for Salt

Because I don't trust the future,
I look back over my shoulder
wherever I go, like one of those fish
with eyes at the back of its head, or an owl
who swivels its face around full circle.

And though the past is made up
of ordinary things, they smolder
in the heat of afterlight
until memory becomes longing,
as strong as a craving for salt.

Ask Lot's wife who knew
that what she left behind
was simply everything.

Poison Ivy

Even then the leaves shone
in green trios, turning
to red in autumn,

a season which in that garden
was simply a quickening of the breeze
for variety's sake.

Pale flowers grew like shadows
of flowers along the stems,
and from these she made bouquets

for their simple table.
Sometimes untangling the vines
from around a tree

she would weave garlands
to wear around her naked neck
or wrists, to please Adam.

Ivy, they named it, a child
of the sumac clan, mild
and innocent of harm as they were.

The Lost Kingdom

No book is as fictional as the one that begins I remember . . .
— Patricia Hampl

I remember the castle
and the chilly moat where we swam
or in winter skated,

and how on the shiny seat
of the coach an ermine lap robe
casually waited.

And all his courtiers smiled
and thanked him. I knew I was lucky
to be his daughter.

That was before the succession,
before the years had trickled through
my hands, like water.

Marcia Pelletiere

I Visited the King

I visited the elderly and ailing king
of kings. It had snowed that morning
and the roads were slick.
So much snow so near the end of winter.
He lay in bed, paler than the sheets
that held him and twice as damp.
I leaned down, stroked him like a horse
and pressed my hands against his ribs. We kissed.
Between long kisses he told me of his every longing
and regret. As I left he was recollecting each of his creatures;
one by one each beast recalled itself to him.

When I came again he lay alone,
tranquil as a letter in a holy text
soon to be shut away inside a dark tabernacle.
It must have been the nurse who shut the lids,
pressed them together so tightly
that upper and lower lashes, dark and thick,
intertwined like brambles;

and him lost behind them, his wrists losing their last heat,
and his face was empty, windswept, a silent place where I went in.

Under Her Crib

In the Yiddish song a goat danced under
Ehteleh's crib, to rock it gently.

Ehteleh is Esther now; at seventy-nine,
small and frail in her hospital bed,
she recalls a strange feast.
In Lithuania no trace remained of those
who didn't escape. Here, in America,
they'd know where their dead rested.

Twenty immigrants gathered
at the still-barren family plot.
When the first year passed without a death,
they came to celebrate,
walking through cemetery gates
to find the site and set covered baskets
down in high grass, on a slight rise.

The blanket spread on top of empty graves,
Miril and Razel make up plates
so each one gets a little of everything,
roast beef, kugel, beets; even Morris
who hates herring has to have a taste, as Ehteleh,
strong and only small because she's young,
tilts her face to feel the sun and prances
around her parents like a little goat . . .

until Jacob drives them home at dusk
and Miril sings, so the goat will dance her girl to sleep.

Michael Blumenthal

The Silent Synagogue of Köszeg

Köszeg

The silence surrounding it – interrupted only by the occasional chirping of a sparrow or the cawing of a crow from atop one of its forsaken towers – is at least equally heartrending as the sounds of prayers that once filled it. For it, and the ruins like it all over Eastern Europe – in their utter dilapidation and abandonment, their surrounding mini-jungle of overgrown weeds, vines and hedges – are perhaps more poignant, and more melancholy, re-minders of the fate of East European Jewry than even the gas chambers of the concentration camps, the burial pits, and the skeletal, resonating *"Arbeit Macht Frei"* that hangs over the gates of Auschwitz.

As you walk through the neo-Gothic Heroes' Gate and into the historic Belváros (Inner Town) district of the quaint little town of Köszeg in western Transdanubia – sometimes referred to, I can-not help but observe ironically, as the nation's "jewelry box" – you must, in fact, make a certain effort to locate the crumbling, circular brick towers at Várkör 34 that once served one of the oldest Jewish communities in Hungary. You must perhaps, as I did, first knock on the door of Kolnhofer Ernö at Várkör 38 and ask to be allowed into his courtyard and then, graciously enough, onto his second-floor patio in order to stand for a moment and survey what remains of the house of worship that – at the height of Köszeg's Jewish community around 1941 (not long before Köszeg became the headquarters of the Hungarian Arrow Cross) – served some one hundred individuals, a building recently pur-chased by a local former Communist Party secretary named Krug Gusztáv, whose original plan was to turn it into a beer hall (Sörözö).

You must remain here, perhaps, for many moments and listen to the long silence of unanswered prayers, then gaze for a long

time at the scarred and hardly recognizable twin tablets containing the Ten Commandments that are the only exterior evidence
of the building's once-sacred origins, in order to appreciate the
fact that it is not merely yet another "ordinary" ruined building
you are staring at, but an edifice within whose now-crumbling
walls dozens of the soon-to-be-slaughtered millions turned their
eyes toward a seemingly deaf and unsympathetic God and prayed,
unsuccessfully, for their and their loved ones' salvation.

For Köszeg, not unlike many smaller and larger towns and
villages throughout Hungary, is haunted by the sounds and sights,
by the resonant echoes, of Jewish history. Along with nearby
Sopron, it was one of the two cities in western Transdanubia's
Vas County where Jews lived during the Middle Ages. As early
as 1420 – at the time when they were also forced to leave lower
Austria and Vienna – Köszeg's Jews were first forced to flee, not
returning again until approximately 1509, only to be evicted once
more by the Hapsburg emperor in 1565, and to return once more
during the final years of the seventeenth century. According to a
1788 census, there were only two Jewish families residing in
Köszeg at the time, a number that grew to approximately fourteen adults by 1807.

The neo-Gothic synagogue itself, occupying an interior space
of 30.6 x 12.8 meters, was built between 1858 and 1859 with dona-
tions from local Jewish merchant Schey Fülöp, later elevated to
the status of Count by the Austrian Hapsburgs. Inside, its cupola
still displays a rich, Baroque-style painting bearing the German
words *"in Ehre Gottes gebaut von Philip Schey von Koromla"* ("built
in praise of God by Philip Schey von Koromla"). The two crumbling outbuildings – which now resemble, more than anything,
tombstones in an abandoned cemetery – once housed, to the
synagogue's right, a *mikva*, or ritual bath, and, to the left, a
Hebrew school classroom and teacher's apartment. Now, as with
most of Hungary's well over one hundred mostly abandoned
synagogues, they are home only to insects and rats . . . and to the
persistence of memory.

"I myself am Catholic," says Kolnhofer Ernö, a frog-eyed, highly
sympathetic man approximately my own age whose disarrayed
house and thinly-veiled comments suggest he is in the midst of a
certain amount of marital upheaval, "but I think it is disgraceful
that anyone would think of turning such a house of worship into
a beer hall." Others, led by Hungary's surviving Jewish community and its Historic Preservation Law, apparently shared
Kolnhofer's feelings, for it seems that public sentiment ultimately

prevailed over Krug's entrepreneurial vision, though the building's actual future still remains uncertain. According to Kolnhofer, estimates are that it would cost approximately five million forints (roughly $400,000 U.S.) to restore the synagogue to its original state. An American teacher named Bruce, hoping to raise the money, apparently staged a series of concerts and other fund-raising events in Kőszeg several years ago that fell far short of the mark. And the issue – namely, of finding both the collective will and the funds with which to restore and preserve synagogues in towns and villages whose Jewish population consists entirely of ghosts – is, of course, not unique to Kőszeg. The preservation of memory – no matter how tinged that memory may be with guilt and repentance – is, during times of economic crisis and transition, a luxury few, if any, nations can afford to indulge in.

And yet – as I gaze from the innocent patio of Kolnhofer Ernö out at yet another of Eastern Europe's sad, neglected ruins, yet another endangered testimony to history's most unspeakable tragedy and evil – it occurs to me that it may also, ironically enough, be a duty no nation can afford to ignore.

Visit to Majdanek

Lublin, Poland

It is – how else can I say it? – a beautiful day in the south of Poland . . . the air is crisp and clean, crows alight and rise up from the grass-covered, once torture-ridden fields. As I emerge from the "new" crematorium – whose ovens, I am told by a tactfully brief placard inside, could produce (reminding me of Hannah Arendt's description of Auschwitz as a "corpse factory") a "yield" of over a thousand bodies daily – a white and brown fox hastily beats a retreat into a hole just below one of the SS guards' watchtowers. In the not-far-off distance, the new and old buildings of

Lublin, the eerily evocative smokestacks, can be seen, and the morbid thought crosses my mind that – were this another place, were this another life – this might be a good place, a good day, for a picnic . . . or maybe it still is.

On the single day of November 3, 1943 – exactly fifty-one years from the day I am writing this – some 18,400 Jews were shot and dumped into the execution ditches close to the crematorium at Majdanek, just outside of Lublin. In all, between 1941 and its liberation in the autumn of 1944, through a combination of insufferable living conditions and direct executions, some 360,000 persons – many, but not all, of them Jews – lost their lives here. It is a number that encompasses many times all those I have ever known, much less loved, a number so staggering in terms of actual human lives, of unlived human potential, that only the 800,000 pairs of victims' shoes gathered in wire bins at Majdanek – mens' shoes, womens' shoes, children like my own son's shoes – are capable, somehow, of concretizing it, of "giving the tortured person back," in the words of Israeli writer and Holocaust survivor Aharon Appelfeld, "his human form."

I had never before been to a concentration camp, a visit to which has virtually become one of my generation's "rites of passage" into the dark underbelly of twentieth-century Jewish history. Though I am told by the brochure that "the guides of the Polish Tourist Country-Lovers' Association (PTTK)" – a name I cannot help but wince while reading – "are also qualified to take tourists round the Museum," it seems best to do this alone . . . alone, that is, with the ghosts of the past.

The visitor to a place such as Majdanek always asks himself – *must*, I suspect, ask himself – before going, the inevitable questions: *Why go? Why hunt down such evil, go actively in search of it – I who have "escaped," remained, superficially, untouched?* But the answers are also rather obvious – so obvious, perhaps, as to obviate the questions. We are not, none of us, "untouched." We have not, any of us, "escaped." And because it is our destiny in this life to attempt to visit the unspeakable – those regions of beauty and love that defy speech – we must also contemplate that other unspeakable reality of our lives: absolute evil. *Hier*, as a Nazi guard at Auschwitz once told the Italian-Jewish writer Primo Levi, *ist kein warum*, Here there is no why, nothing that needs be explained.

"Go there," the Hungarian writer George Konrad told me in 1993 when I mentioned never having been to a camp. "Go there. I would suggest it to you, and to everyone," he said. "I was not there until '82, and I said 'Why should I go there, I can imagine it?' However, it's good to go there, to touch those walls and to look at those shoes and to look at the hill of hair which is now completely grey, because it was once maybe black and blonde and brown, all kinds of hair. But it became grey, the whole stuff. It's good to be there. And to touch somehow the extremes, to touch the walls of the executions."

To touch the walls of the executions. One likes to think of the concentration camps as, somehow, located "out of sight" (ergo, potentially out of mind), in venues remote, secreted, exempt from the daily gazes and contemplations of the local citizenry. Therefore, from the shocking moment when one first comes upon Majdanek, it jars the senses, shatters one's moral and moralizing boundaries. Located so close to the center of Lublin (once the center of a richly varied and influential Jewish community numbering some 40,000) that, to put it crudely, a profit-minded entrepreneur might well choose the site for a shopping mall or drive-in, the physical fact of Majdanek itself starkly belies the myth of the innocent and unknowing bystander.

And so – even before we step onto its fields of torture and degradation, even before we set foot into its crematoria and barracks – Majdanek confronts us with a primary, only slightly less unspeakable reality: They *knew*, and, being here, we now *know* that they knew, and thus we are forced, not merely to accuse, but to ask ourselves: "What if *we* knew? What is it, at this very moment, that *we* know and remain passive in the face of, preferring not to see, to know, to act? One is forced, in other words, to reconsider one's use of adjectives: Was it purely *Nazi* evil that occurred at Majdanek? Or just *goyishe* evil? Or – that ugliest of possibilities, already considered in great detail and eloquence by Hannah Arendt – merely *human* evil?

This being the information age, here, too, information abounds. And, like all "information," it is easily confused and confusing, threatening to obscure real feelings with mere facts. "The prisoners of Majdanek came from 29 states all over the world (according to the world political map of l938)," says one brochure. "Poles were most numerous, constituting nearly 40% of the total number. Jews constituted 30%." "In the years 1941–1944, some 500,000 inmates of 54 nationalities passed through Majdanek," reads the "official" museum brochure. "It's hard to take in the brutal fact that over 200,000 people of more than twenty nations were murdered here, a significant number of them Jews," says my own guidebook. But what's in a number, when one considers an evil of such magnitude? A fact by any other name is equally harsh.

Hands in my pockets, looking up, down, around, I walk past the Mausoleum, where the ashes of prisoners executed at Majdanek, once used as fertilizer, mingle with the earth. Even here I can't help but notice, half-guiltily, that all the abstract pieties of the human mind – or, at least, of *my* human mind – distanced as they are from the brutal specificities of such events, do not resist the obscuring imperatives of desire and pleasure: The young Polish girl standing staring out at the Mausoleum before me, I still notice, is exceptionally pretty.

I continue past the mass execution ditches, now overgrown with grass; past the overseers' barrack and the barrack houses that also housed several of the camps' gas chambers. I walk past the horrifically named "Field of Roses," the selection square in front of the bathhouses, within sight of which – as if to suggest a universe as indifferent to evil as it is resilient with beauty – roses still grow. I enter the bathhouses and gas chambers of the old crematorium, so silent and eerily clean that hardly the ghosts of the dead seem able to disturb them, open the door of the small cell from which certain SS officers would introduce pellets of Cyclone B gas through holes in the ceiling and then, through a small, grated window opening out into the chamber itself, watch their prisoners die. I remember, as I close the door, Irving Howe's well-known formulation of disequivalence: *In classical tragedy man was defeated; in the Holocaust he was destroyed.*

There is so much to see here – so many photos and facts, so many shoes and rooms, so many hectares of land, so many images of torture and degradation and death. But, in the end, as Peter Davies wrote of Auschwitz, it is *"all these things, cumulatively crushing you, a seeping of evil from every wall and corner of the place, from every brick and block, until you reach your limit and it overwhelms you."* In the end, you are simply left to walk out into the fields and gaze at the nearby hills of Lublin, the grasses and roses and smokestacks of this world. You are left to praise whatever there may be left to praise. You are left to contemplate yourself and your kind.

Michael Blumenthal

Lukács Fürdö: December 31, 1995

Budapest

Why should I not be among them? –
the old man with the face of an angelfish
whose balls sag like overripe apricots
as he glides, the lamed *nagymamas,*[1]
their double chins bellowing out
like frill-necked lizards, the aging professors
still revising their footnotes as they swim,
and the old seamstress, whose left hand
takes on a life of its own as she strokes,
parting the waters like an injured eel.

Why should I not be among them? –
the old Jewish writers whose pens have run dry,
and the squidish satyrs, their ink gone as well,
this floating democracy of back pain and arthritis,
flesh-bedecked former sybarites
who tread and stroke, who will gather,
later, in the sauna like a *kaffee-klatsch*
of cardless bridge players,
where I will relish the grim satisfaction
of being the youngest among them,
a man who, not wanting to resemble
his father, resembles his grandmother.

Lukács Fürdö: One of the many curative mineral baths of Budapest, this one
known for its traditional clientele of elderly Jews, writers, and intellectuals, as
well as for the metal plaques in several languages mounted on its outside wall,
disclaiming as to the curative powers of the waters for arthritis and lumbago.
[1] *nagymama* (Hung.) – pronounced NADG-MAMA . . . grandmother

So why should I not be here? –
anticipating my own destiny,
ontogeny recapitulating phylogeny
as we glide, on impaired limbs,
downward to darkness, scrinching
our balls back into their scrotums,
hoping to rectify these god-given bodies,
cleansing ourselves of earthly pain, trying
to heal ourselves before we are healed.

Harvey Shapiro

Prague

The Gothic half-light
in which moulder
the stones of the Jewish Cemetery,
a tumbled mass of stones
crowded on each other
like the cadavers in the camps
so that you keep sliding out
of one picture into the other.

"The world is a narrow bridge,"
said Rabbi Nachman,
"the important thing
is not to be afraid."

History

They burned the cities because this life is insupportable.
They killed the Jews because this life is insupportable.
They put on leather and chains and fucked in the streets
because they were animals. Pigs they called the others
because they knew *they* were pigs and were searching for
       humans
to kill them too, their books and their buildings.
"He punched her out," they yelled to each other
and grooved on the slop and the blood.

In Tiberius

Rabbi Akiba
measured the distances
of angels, archangels and principalities
from the throne of God.
It was probably on an August
afternoon like this one,
his beard tangled in calculations,
the noise outside his window –
an old man beating his donkey –
making him aware that angelology
is a refuge like any other.

Mark Halperin

The Second Coming

They come looking like Latinos, dark
hair, dark eyes, air of poverty, that
slight build, those stoop-shoulders:
one turns to another, there's a dip,
a shrug and who they are is clear –
or like Native Americans, till one smiles
to another, and in his bewildered eyes,
rheumy with terror you see history –
or like Chinese, clubby, having sneaked
in someplace they don't belong. One
lifts a fist heavenward, pounds his heart
and you've no doubt who's there. They're

a Conga-line snaking, heel-and-toeing
forward toward you, smelling of garlic,
smelling of matches herring, a troop
with dripping noses and wailing babies,
yours. And your house is so clean,
you're sure they'll ask themselves in
for the night because these ones are not
Latinos or Native Americans or Chinese
but your ones, old Jews from the Pale,
Litvoks, Galitzianos, and why they've
come and where they're going, you
don't have the right or chutzpa to ask.

Karaites of Vilnius

i
In Vilnius a woman tells the Germans come to collect her
she's a Karaite, not a Jew, though the dictionary calls Karaites
"a Jewish sect that rejected the Talmud in favor of the Torah."
Forty years pass like breathing in and out and she mentions it
to a friendly visitor who tells me: she said *every Karaite in Vilnius*
was spared – Karaites exotic where Jews were numerous
and rounded up and shuffled off to that gas which blew away.

ii
I always pictured Karaites as a part of Persia's warm downtowns,
streets lined with trees that tremble, and a delicacy
so privileged, people avert their eyes, hum and busy themselves
at any required work. In Vilnius, luck might consist of a ring
or cow, a chicken or a friend, not really close to buy your life with.
It was cold with the chill that follows recognition. People froze
and scales swayed endlessly: who sold whom, sold out, bought
what with who and at what price.

iii
Six years ago when the Soviets turned off the gas in Vilnius
history grew gravid with a shame like the frost that touched
the grapevine outside my house last night. Its bronze-like hands
shone this morning, till my touch shattered them. The Karaites
repudiated demons as "human imaginings." And now
no demons live in Lithuania – or Karaites or their Talmudic
        neighbors,
too poor for gas. What gleams there presently must be the slick,
now blank, now cold, that follows innocence.

The Escape

Amused when she asks, *is your wife Jewish?* and,
    because it's easier, because I don't
want to think, I answer *yes.* It's the first time.
    Later, a pushy man wants to know my
son's birthday. Confused, I make him younger
    and the shift of dates feels so natural

I let it stand. Then it's happening with family
    names, with where I work, how long, with
whom – minor changes in my *vita,* small alterations,
    other lives, one variant for this person,
another for that, as though I were picking out
    ballpoint pens or books, rummaging for

keepsakes to give away, a different self to
    each, each time. Months pass before I
catch on too and admit I've done what I did out of
    caution, an attempt to screen the self,
erase the scent, obscure the trail with a series
    of dead ends until no one could thread

a way ahead through those dense thickets back to
    me, reeking of fear. What did I think I
had worth hiding and who was I trying to deceive?
    Tell me: surrounded by those casual lies
fabricated with disarming aplomb, why didn't I ask
    whose escape I imagined I was fashioning?

Mark Perlberg

The Edge of the Forest

Like the witch in a fairy tale,
she opened the kitchen door
and shoved her small son and daughter
out on the back stoop.
The lock sprang shut behind them.
She turned and walked away
deep inside the house.

It was a chill winter dusk,
the cobalt blue sky
unstained by any cloud.
Limbs and fingers of trees
twisted across it.

In a swamp of rage and fear,
the boy punched his fist
through the glass
and opened the kitchen door,
saving himself and his sister
from the cuttlefish dark.

Confused, angry, loving,
amid the noise and crying
she took the boy to the sink
and teased needles of glass
from his hand.

The blood on that white door
is a sign on his doorpost still,
and the chill of that clear sky
a sliver in his heart.

Nightsweat

The poem I need to write is the poem of rage.
Not the poem of sinking into harmony with wind rhythms,
wave sounds lapping this northern island.
Nor the poem of the round of seasons, effulgent summer
dying into fall. Nor of taking my place
in the cycle of generations.

I need to write how the great wind came on a filthy night,
rammed up the coast, ripped spruce 80 feet tall
and strewed them like straw over a neighbor's
woodlot, a man who built his house deep in those woods
and painted it black.

I need to write of the squire on the crest of my hill,
who left a trail of stumps and ash from his house
clear down to the bay, trashing a woman's land
because her treetops smudged his view of sunsets,
clouds, boats passing.

How my daughters, both, were given
halting, difficult sons.
Of their nightsweats, vigils, sorrows.
But most – how the surgeon split my chest
with a whirling saw and took out my heart.

O blooming world of chaos and decay,
I want my old heart back, not this alien pump
that was pressed, cut, chilled, changed,
and held in hands remote from me
as those of a man on a spacewalk, working
with delicate instruments
in the violent dark.

Ira Sadoff

The Veneer

When I think of veneer, a surface or facade,
I think of the peeling panel on her old bathroom door,
how you could look in as she doused herself with a sponge,
the old train station in Los Angeles, police sweeps

through the skeletal remains of 5 and 10's
(how far apart we are, the private and public sectors)
and closer to home, I watched her forge her lipstick,
shaking before she goes out, rehearsing in the mirror,

assembling the costume she's seen in a department store –
and you know what we think of mannequins –
wondering if she'll make it through the evening downing valium
and Manhattans, the actress carting around her character,

where some fragment, some broken sliver of her
is lodged in her finger, a lipstick smudge, a little blood trickling
            out.
And I might even shift in my seat a little,
knowing how my face absorbs and refracts that light,

and as the camera pans in on the closer yet,
the distance between the surface of that
undeveloped adolescent face and what *it feels like* to me,
seems abysmal, knowing her doctor said *Psychosis is personal,*

how her hand shaking becomes way too personal
as she puts on a string of pearls of water, flour and paste
I made for her, because we've taken a wrong turn somewhere,
(because the "good providers" of the fifties

have driven to the end of the century)
and now I remember the story of my great aunt,
ferreting through the debris of her bombed-out
Warsaw apartment, searching for her dead husband,

hauling on her back a hardback chair, a vanity of oak veneer.

Hassids on the Subway

Shameful and humble, the bearded Hassids
bumble to their seats with their challahs in their shopping bags,
stinking up the subway with their sullen unwashed flesh.

I can see how circumcision might not be necessary,
the way I used to have sex, looking into her face, trying to figure out
what my *shiksa* was missing. If only I'd only washed away

my body scent, a little gym, rind of tangerine,
a sharp tinge of bleach . . . I'm trying to rearrange a sequence,
so I can sit in peace and shut them out, but when he goes on

to the Haitian boy about the Chosen People,
meaning the boy should give his seat to him, I hear
my Cantor mutter as I approach the Torah, the law and story.

Us and *them*. Deep down, I think, we're all one. How deep?
In the pockets? Beneath the Flesh? In the lilting twists
and coils of speech, stalled by lurching guttural exclamations,

in the raw, hypnotic, intoxicating flicker of tunnel light?
They all get out at Forty-fifth, the diamond district.
They all get out in Queens. In the teens, where they peddle furs

and flimsy dresses in the garment district. So thick with entries
and exits, it's hard not to think of them as one.
But to look at the looks, the look of sour milk, lips drawn down

like puppets, when someone pulls a knife – to pry
into one I think – on one who holds a bag of diamonds
to his chest and spits, I feel both sides of the blade

as the *Yid* gets on his knees to beg for his daughter's education.
We don't have to worry about ditches for scatterbrained souls in
      black hats
and flesh-defending dresses. No, for now the diamonds will
      suffice.

In the Dream

We launch from a city wharf an old canoe
through the drab and scabrous waters, water of dented cans
and hypodermics, of old brassieres and shaved hair,
water of dead flesh and fecal stench. My hands are oars

tangled in debris. We're headed for a picnic on a nearby isle
until I strike what must be an animal, because the bow
begins to knife its way down and we hear a high-pitched wail
as the hull takes in water on all sides, soaking our shirts

while my friends float away – the fault, of course,
who else's could it be? Lately I've been dreaming too of tigers
gnawing children as if they were dolls, while I'm in the basement
that serves as their den . . . of course it's all about the sexual
      excitement

of being too close to someone, how I'm consumed by it,
or conversely it's about my friend rowing down the Mekong
with his M-15, shooting into the trees until he hears
the body drop, a little boy, his surmise, by the shrill pitch of
       scream,

and God's in there too, the infant God who'll forgive us our sins
if we go a little hungry, or how I'm taking my mother to the
       hospital
for one of her imaginary diseases before she actually dies,
before thank God I'm only one of a thousand lodgers waking

to sparrows on the hotel ledge, looking down on everyone,
the traces of whatever scent I take with me from the night before,
the year before, from centuries before my birth, the animal
that's my terror and enemy, surfacing here and there and here
       again.

Vesuvius

Frenzied, scatterbrained, worried,
I pace and stare, I squander
the days as if they were infinite.

Oh spirit world, with your fat little cherubs
leaning on their elbows weighing the scales,
flapping away with their feathery wings,

I don't want to join Uncle Matty
and his sequined accordion in the casket,
I don't want to hear Bach's Cantata on the resurrection. . . .

The lilacs are out, and then
there's my mother in me scanning the Frigidaire
for rewards, but you want to hear about

the before and after, the sputtering venom,
the slippages, the molten fluids blackening the town.
The staggering semblance of existence

stirring in the bowels, the sheer magma of it all.
Not today, pal. I'm downright effluvial,
I'm a slick little trellis who loves to be climbed.

Then there's the prolific sweet william,
and irises the color of ivory, tinged with violet
like a bruise, in the century when nature could "cure."

All the while cathedrals charge admission,
and the shops staggering replications, sell disasters
as little comic operas. I have the nagging suspicion

that "to be saved" is all about money, is to save up,
to put on the shelf until maximum value
is accrued. And then what? To become a souvenir:

an autodidact, an old snail coated with char.

Near Van Cortland Park

even the stop lights have their tribulations.
The pileups are placebos and metaphors,
except for the gringo with a tire iron.

Another wasted afternoon, staring out.
I was going to. I was about to.
At least give me that.

They shot her before the jewelry store.
With her purse, they wouldn't have to
enter, menace and appraise, break the glass.

Then there was the two-year-old,
who scuttled out the third-story window,
banged his skull on the air-conditioner

and was, at bottom, still breathing.
The mother was "out," no one kept track
of the dad. So this nuclear, extended, cosmetically airbrushed

family is kind of patchwork, even downright osteopathic.
And doesn't include bodies dumped and torched
in disposals. The man was interred when he couldn't pay the fine

for his highjacked car. Honest. This is a city
scrutinized by a statue, an alabaster sports car
just parking himself. An intern, someone familiar

with the cul-de-sacs of New Jersey
and whose toes were once, on a golf course,
soaked with dew. It's late afternoon, late August,

late in the century, a little late for pronouncements,
until my bookkeeper comes to collect.
I'm splayed out, not bleeding – thank God – on the stoop,

asking grandpa, who's been put on diapers again,
"Tell me about Princeton, the Parthenon,
    the incomparable architecture, the knockout with the pan flute."

The Blue Gum

Mississippi 1964

The Blue Gum stood for nothing.
Like a father. The willow, well,
why wouldn't the wind saw through it?

I fancy the switch as a gift
that passed between them. Father
and son. Servant and master.

In lyric productions, we rely
on stand-ins. The tire on a rope
as a swing, and on the same Blue Gum

the black man who hung from it.
Crow-picked, the anatomy of him,
a skeletal example. A shame, the trellis

inclined toward the mansion, inviting him.
Imagine, if you're white, the mistress's bed.
And now the art part, where we move

freely in time and space, is over.
I went back to chop away at it, to break
the word Blue as fluid oozes from the bark.

I'm tempted to call it bloody, that sweet
bucket of excess. Greenville, Mississippi,
which must have been green long before I got there.

Doris Radin

The Snapped Thread

And will you indeed have known me
Without having known them
Who died before you were born.

Who will have known him
When I am dead
He of the often melancholy face
Who wore frustration like a brand
Between his eyes
He of the shouting angers
He of the made-up words
The nonsense jingles
He playing the violin, sweat
Running down his chest
At the stove concocting soup
Cabbage tomato and everything else
He marking battles on a map
Held to the wall with surgical tape
Medical journals in French
French on the radio
And books, the only passion he fed
Burrowing in bins
Bargains in philosophy history religion
Reading with a pen
Making notes in the margins
                    Here I like him best
In a Connecticut field
Among wildflowers of August
Anxiety's noose loosened
A field guide in his hand
With her

And who will have known her
She of the sun
Who tried to light his feet
Who wore confidence, a crown
She tried to have him share
She of the singing, of the tin ear
Who wanted a bird's song
She bearing with his angers
Her reading aloud Sunday evenings
Like an actress
Her aplomb with pliers and hammer
Her cross-stitches on the trolley
Her fluent Hebrew long before the state
Oh to see the Holy Land
Her using a Ditto to compose exams
Her purple hands
And in a darkroom prints
That never found an album
Foot-and-a-half-wide layer cakes
Hats she assembled from parts
Her forwardness among strangers
A certain spark
Indefinable
That drew you
The whole mouth smile
The space between her two front teeth

Who will remember

Them canoeing Everett's triple lakes
On a dock, the heavens between them,
Following the stars
Them at the Apollo with Raimu and The Baker's Wife
At the Davenport Theater
Butler D. greeting in a Roman toga
Them in the Sculpture Court, them in Prospect Park

Them at the zoo
Sitting at the kitchen table
He in a big round anger, she in tears
Who will have known

My husband, my dear one

My sunshine

Who will remember

The Wedding

Daughter-in-law your sari
your mother brought from India
kept these years
your red sari
woven with threads of gold
daughter-in-law your *bindiya*
perfect red dot on your forehead
daughter-in-law your hands,
yesterday
the women
worked patterns with henna
made you ready
beautiful
    bride of my son
there is painted an auspicious sign
Ganesh's own,
yet what I see (my flesh recoils)
is a Hitler sign
        in your hands

my son's silver *kiddush* cup
his great grandfather's
that he brought from Russia
when he fled the pograms of the czar
that he filled each Sabbath
all his life
he blessed the wine
you sip from the cup
your eyes filled with my son, both your families
      looking on, *Lekhayim*
bride
beautiful daughter-in-law

Liz Rosenberg

Locomotion

Two white clouds puff across the cross-panes of my window, like
slow freight trains, then are gone.

Oh, but my friend the Rabbi's wife lay on her sofa yesterday, her
bald head wrapped in a scarf, her brown eyes shining, telling me
the story of Esther. Suddenly her arm shoots up, "And this is the
most beautiful moment in the whole story. Mordechai tells her, If
you don't speak to the king, the people of Israel will survive
through some other heroine, but you, and the king, and this
kingdom will come crashing down. So, go! This is your moment!"

I look at her, and think, She is dying. I try to keep my eyes
steady on her living face. That moment, her words, her moving

mouth are eternal. I plunge into the next few sounds she utters
thinking, Here, here is forever. Then I fall backward into time.
My son adjusts his small warm body beside me on the loveseat.
Funny, how the station seems to move from the train, when the
train moves away from the station.

Sarasota Sunrise

Calm on the bay, but coming up like thunder
the new light shines in the gray hair
of a man swinging a curled-up Yiddish paper in one arm.
Five water birds skitter off, leaving a lithograph behind.
Old women guard the swimming pool
and the Sarasota Yacht Club rises high in its initials
where the members' names end neither with a vowel
nor with the German-Jewish words for flowers, mountains, stones.
One must forgive the rich
for having all the best views of what is free –
sunrise, and gold-foiled water glimmer,
wildlife creatures that carry no purse
as they fly from paradise to paradise.

Hope

Edith B___ and her mother on a Sunday afternoon. The ancient mother, ill, about to have a biopsy tomorrow, falling asleep in her chair, but plays piano like a brilliant young girl, a snapping light in her blue eyes. There's a portrait of her in 1908 before her "European tour," wearing a blue dress with a lace fichu.

Mother and daughter play a two-handed duet – one thin and lithe, the other broad and bumptious, both wearing paisley print blouses and navy stretch pants, chunky brown shoes. The poodle with his bowed legs lies asleep on the plaid blanket on the floor, a Sunday afternoon silence, the clock with domino pieces for numbers, map of the United States made of a quilt of U.S. stamps. The mother's delight on seeing the chocolates in the box – dark and milk chocolate leaves. But she's left her hearing aid turned off in case we turn out to be dull guests.

Edith, her lonely daughter with the chopped-off hair, her anti-Semitism, arcane references, bitterness about Leonard Bernstein and the Jews, fretfulness and snobbery, standing like a woeful child at the door as we leave and saying in her stilted voice, "I hope I shall come to know you."

My Mother's Arm

My friend stepped on the brakes and threw his arm out in front of my body, protectively, the arm extended like a dancer's; and my Jewish mother's arm came back to me, flung there across me a dozen, no a hundred times, almost at every stop sign, that arm would begin its rapid journey across my upper body, my mother's arm would be there like a royal seal, a barred window, invisible safety shield – I don't remember her ever touching me with the arm – that was a part of its magic property, the way it halted like the railroad crossing bar going down and swinging in midair, red lights blinking, just a caution against disaster, a mime; she'd signal danger, her body erect, alert as a cat's, that silly-looking arm stuck out in the middle of nowhere, her willingness to be a fool, that too was part of the magic charm, like pulling the chain of the attic fan, like turning out the lights goodnight, calling sweet dreams across the hall, the cool fingers pressed against the fever, the face lowered to kiss. Always in the coming-and-going my parents seemed nearest, most solidly there, so when my friend's arm approached my nose at the speed of light, I halfway ducked and half rose up to greet it, feeling in that instant of danger perfectly calm, perfectly safe and happy, remembering my mother's arm.

Peace in the House

To her the memory is always the same: she stands next to the old *zaideh*, where he sits at the deal table, so close she can smell his tobacco and the dried pee drops permeating the front of his heavy work pants. On the table in front of him: halved walnut shells, wrinkled like the tiny balls that hang beneath her baby brother's little thing. "Now watch," her grandfather says, his great bony fingers enveloping the husks. And she tells herself, this time he will not fool me. No matter how quickly his hands fly over the shells, no matter how fast he whirls them under his fingers, this time I will be the winner. Patiently, he lifts the shell to show her the tiny pebble underneath. "Look, now," he says. "Don't be a stupid girl. Don't fall asleep. Are you ready?" And she nods her head, unaccountably cross, far from the fun of the game's beginning. She tastes woodsmoke, dead ashes, sees her grandfather's bottom teeth: kernels of dried yellow corn. Around and around the hands sweep, the shells buried beneath them, her eyes following until suddenly he coughs and for one flicker they leap to his face; she is caught again. Hopelessly, she points to the shell. "Lift it," he says. And always, there is nothing.

Outguessing Grossman is a game, too, with the same inevitable results. Meryl tells herself she is on to his tricks, his *shtik*, and each time, gullible still like the child she once was, she swears the outcome will be different. Today she hears him climbing the stairs to their flat from the Hebrew school. Classes are dismissed early for *Shabbes*; the last bar mitzvah boy has gone home, and Grossman will be wanting his dinner. After almost twenty years with him she can discern the quality of his mood from the sounds his shoes make on the squeaking treads: a certain kind of thump, and she knows that devil Yankel has mouthed off at him again; another thump: Moishe with the snot nose has failed to bring in his tuition for a change. She has even learned the staccato accompaniment to the rare good days when he will mount the stairs full of grandiose plans that never come off: replacing the icebox with a refrigerator, for instance, or enlarging the cheder, or, perhaps, taking them all to Mount Clemens for the baths.

Whatever his mood, Grossman expects to find her in the kitchen, so now she smooths her soiled apron and hurries from the dining room to stand at the stove, stirring the chicken soup gently so as not to break up her feathery *knoedlach*. Daniel and Shirley have the sense to be anywhere that their father is not, especially when the message tapped out on the stairs spells trouble.

"Come, eat," Meryl says. Dealing with him on a good day is like walking on knives, and today the news from the stairs is not good. Don't be a nag, the "Bintel Brief" advises. Keep peace in the house. She will not speak of the overcoat he refuses to put on in spite of the icicles outside the kitchen window. She will not remind him that even the few steps from the door of the cheder to their flat entrance are enough to chill a person to the bone. If he wants to get pneumonia, that is his business, although, God knows, if he does catch cold, it is she who will be running with the mustard plasters and whipping up the *gogol-mogels* for his sore throat.

Perhaps he will notice how pretty the dining room table looks, set with the rose-sprigged china she has collected, piece by piece, on dish night at the movies. She has even placed the silverware, forks to the left and knife and spoon to the right the way Shirley showed her from Home Economics at school. Keep a pleasant atmosphere in the home, the "Bintel Brief" counsels. You would have thought Grossman came from Krakow, the airs he puts on, instead of some muddy village, but fine, let him play that game; what does it cost her? Somehow she has found time, too, to scour away the orange stains in the porcelain sink and carry down the leaking garbage bag herself without waiting for Daniel. Grossman can call her a *shlump* and complain about her housekeeping, but, as she pointed out in one of her letters, who could do more than she does? Without her help, the school would never be able to take on the extra pupils that keep meat in the borscht. Without her to divert Grossman's wrath, what parent, no matter how dedicated to assuring himself of a brilliant bar mitzvah boy, would put up with tales brought home of Grossman's black rages, the wild flailing of the ruler? No, even a man as convinced of his bad luck as her husband must concede she wasn't such a bad bargain after all.

Meryl tells him, "Go wash," hoping Shirley has had the good sense to wipe away the hair combings she is forever leaving in the bathroom sink. More likely she has left the comb there, too, and is mooning around her bedroom as usual. God forbid she should lend her mother a hand, and Daniel, her genius, where is he? Lying prone between the legs of the radio listening to one of his programs. Jack Armstrong, the All American Boy! Even she with the *tsehockteh* English her children constantly criticize, can follow Jack's adventures. The All American goy she calls him, driving Daniel into a rage that would do his father proud. The "Bintel Brief" is filled with letters from mothers like herself whose sons waste their time in America on stupid shows when they should be studying. What does Daniel learn on the radio but "Buy Wheaties?" Corn flakes are not good enough for him any-more, thank you.

"Daniel, Shirley, come," she says, her voice rising. Grossman is already seated, reaching for the seltzer. One more minute and all her work will be for nothing. She slides a plate of chopped herring in front of him as he rises to pour himself a glass of wine for kiddush. Sidling up behind him, she hastily dabs with the corner of her apron at the fat purple drops that have slopped over onto the white tablecloth. "Couldn't you for once take off that *farshtinkener* apron?" Grossman asks.

She is used to him belittling her in front of the children. Better to bite her tongue, she supposes, and refuse to fight back. Peace in the house. Besides, she will not give him the gift of a reaction. As if he needs an excuse to turn on her. Such irony, she had said, far back in her first letter: all the way to America to escape the pogroms, only to go and marry a Cossack. She fumbles at the apron strings, wonders how she could have been stupid enough to leave it on.

Though the letters give her more and more comfort, something else has happened to provide hope, to make her feel less outnum-bered in her own house. In the old days, whenever Grossman went into one of his moods, slamming books against the walls, banging the table with his fist so the water glasses rocked, Shirley would glare at her as if her mother alone were to blame for his anger. Meryl and Daniel would sit, frozen, unwilling to move until the spell passed for fear Grossman would turn on them, and then there was no telling what he might do. Only Shirley chat-tered on, flirting with him, tossing her black curls, sharing tidbits with him from her plate.

Shirley, my pretty girly: That's what Grossman sang to his daughter when she was little, the English R's catching softly in his throat. "Shorely, my pretty gorely." Times like that, his attention deflected, Meryl could almost believe she and the girl were allies, that unlike her mother, Shirley had simply learned the trick to mollify him. The truth was he and the girl had conspired against her almost from the beginning, and for a long time, she felt she had two adversaries to outwit instead of one. But in the end, Dear "Bintel Brief," everyone needs something from someone. The day she came on Shirley at Meyer's Drugs, legs wrapped around the soda-fountain stool, eating ice cream from a long silver spoon, and holding hands with who knows what pimply-faced boy, a subtle shift in balance occurred. Silence is expensive, and one way or another, her daughter must have known she and her mother were now partners in this business of being a woman.

Grossman lifts the linen *challah* cover and cuts slices of bread for all of them after he says the blessing. On Friday nights, he can actually work up tears about the *challah* his mother baked in the old days, but everything changes. Meryl shops for her bread at Ruben's Bakery in the old neighborhood. Like so many things in her life, baking bread demands attention, hours at home she doesn't possess to answer to its needs, the mixing of flour, yeast, oil and salt, peeking under the white cloth to check the rising dough where it sits in a bowl near the hissing radiator, then punching it down till it lies like an old woman's deflated breast before it begins its ascent again. Still, she writes, she misses the kneading: those moments when, her hands dusted in flour, she worked the dough until it answered the pressure of her fingers, until her own shoulders began to grow elastic with the smooth rocking rhythm.

She has described the bakery where women moil and chatter, *yentas,* all of them, written of how steamy shop windows obscure the chill, gray streets; the very clang of the Linwood streetcar, muffled by the rising din inside. But even here – early – plump rounds of coffee cake giving off the scent of cinnamon from between their sweet braids, the clerks reaching into glittering glass cases, still goodnatured, joking – the world is a battleground. Meryl is no match for the grim-faced woman, babushka falling forward on her face, who has elbowed her way to the front shouting, "My next; it's my next!" Or the other *Yideneh* jostling Meryl with her heavy leatherette shopping bag: "I think it's *my* next." In fact, both these women have entered the shop after Meryl, but she is at fault for being such a *shmatte.* She needs to

stop dreaming so much; she needs to keep her eyes on the whirling walnut shells. Meryl is surprised at how near the tears are.
Will it ever be my next?, she writes.

Supper is silent except for the clatter of cutlery against china,
Grossman noisily downing his chicken soup. Meryl sits at the
edge of her chair, ready to leap up to remove the bowls, bring the
plates of roast chicken, mashed potatoes, and canned peas from
the kitchen, replenish the bread, and serve the compote of stewed
prunes and apricots that is their dessert. For a moment, she rests
her chin in the palm of her hand and looks at the man and the boy
and the girl, heads lowered over their plates, and she wonders
how she came to be ministering to the needs of these strangers; it
seems to her she once had other plans. Then, she sees Grossman
has tipped his *yarmelke* over his forehead; he is singing *shabbes
zmires* in a high-pitched tenor, his teaspoon tapping out the rhythm
against her good china cup and saucer. Daniel and Shirley watch
in fascination, waiting for the crack to appear.

Meryl is careful not to spare herself in her letters. She tells the
story of her courtship without smoothing anything over. She
relates how Grossman had been a reluctant suitor and an even
more unwilling bridegroom. She still smarts from overhearing
years afterward that her brother had to shame him into showing
up for their wedding. The guests milled around the house for
hours, waiting, while the roast chickens grew cold and the ice for
the seltzer and pop slowly melted in the zinc wash tubs.

Her sister-in-law, Sarah, Meryl's brother Aaron's wife, had
been the matchmaker. The moment Grossman first walked into
the grocery to buy his bachelor's tinned soup and sardines, Sarah
had spotted him from behind the counter where she stood
wrapped in her white apron. Sarah had no shame. Meryl wasn't
getting any younger, as she was quick to point out, and the truth
was, if she didn't marry soon, Sarah feared her sister-in-law
would end up living with them forever. None of this was a
surprise to Meryl. The apartment was cramped enough as it
was, and no matter how she tried to efface herself, she knew it
rankled Sarah each time she and Aaron had to close themselves up in their tiny bedroom at night so Meryl could strip the
cover off the day bed and go to sleep. After a while, she could
see that even Aaron noticed how Sarah no longer bothered to
muffle the sounds of their lovemaking or their quarrels; the
effect was not to make Meryl feel more at home, but rather as if
she had become such a fixture, her sensibilities didn't matter
any longer.

So, Meryl learned later, Sarah made inquiries, engaged Grossman in conversation, discovered he was indeed single and therefore eligible. What was wrong with the match? The man seemed decent enough; his clothes were clean and in good repair despite his solitary state, and when he put his groceries "on the bill," he never failed to pay up at the end of the week. True, he was a *Galitzianer*; that was a minus, but she knew plenty of Litvaks who seemed less refined than he did. As for looks, well, she would admit he was no Valentino with that belly already riding before him like a wheelbarrow – and his hectic flush: that might mean a temper. So *nu*? Show her a man without drawbacks, and she would show you a cemetery plot. Facts had to be faced: Meryl was no spring chicken. And, most exasperating of all, she hadn't any style. Sarah made no secret of her disdain. Meryl's clothes never seemed to fit right, always a hem crooked or a sweater hiked up in back. Hopeless. Someone else would have made an asset of that thick black hair, but Meryl managed to make even a bob look unfashionable, chopping off the ends herself so they stuck out every whichway. And she was so dreamy, forever pricking her fingers on the sewing machine at the factory where she worked attaching belt loops to men's trousers. The last time she bled on a bolt of gray serge, the supervisor docked her pay and threatened to fire her. "I don't think you have a future in the rag business," Sarah told her sister-in-law. "Grab him!"

Grossman took Meryl to the movies, and afterward, Sarah waited up for her. "So, *nu*?" she said. "Tell me." Meryl can see the scene as she writes: the day bed they sat on, her thighs' flesh still leaping from the December cold, the ice between her shoulderblades refusing to thaw. In a corner, the Philco quietly nattered away. "He's nice enough, but I don't feel anything for him," she confided shyly. "Meryleh, dear one," said Sarah, cracking her knuckles, "You see too many moving pictures. Love takes time, and anyway, you can't live on it." "Well, I don't want to work in a factory all my life," Meryl had replied, "but I'm not ready to get married just yet, either." She wanted to apologize, to say, I know you can't wait to get rid of me, but that would have meant listening to Sarah's denials. Instead, both women sat in silence, so close their knees touched. "This concludes our broadcasting for the day," she heard the Philco say, "This is WJR Detroit." Droplets of steam spritzed from the radiator and fell to the flowered Axminster.

"My God," said Sarah, "It's midnight already. How will I get up for work tomorrow, and even if there are a few hours left, I'll never sleep anyway, you make me so crazy," Meryl's nose was dripping now, from the cold, tears, she didn't know. "I want to go to school and learn more English," she whispered. "Speak up," Sarah said, deliberately raising her voice. "*Now* she worries about her brother waking; believe me, he sleeps like a baby. I'm the one who hears it every time you go to the toilet at night. I could toss like a ship for hours and he'd never know it."

Meryl cleared her throat. "I thought some day I might be a teacher," she said, more loudly, wiping her nose with the small embroidered handkerchief Sarah had tucked in her pocket earlier, just before Grossman was to arrive. "For God's sake, don't thank me," she had said impatiently. "What will you do if you sneeze? Wipe your nose on your sleeve? And stop looking like you're going to a funeral, God forbid." Now Sarah clapped her hands together, and put her fingers to her mouth. "A teacher?" she said, "Old maid, you mean. *Gottenu*, Who do you think you are, anyway – John D. Rockefeller's daughter? How many chances do you think you'll have? Maybe I'm blind, but the last I looked I didn't see a line of suitors knocking down this door." She rolled her eyes as if to say, Give me patience. "Does he want to see you another time?" "Yes," Meryl said, and that is when she knew she had lost again.

Later, after she has done the dishes and the children have gone to their rooms, Meryl lies in bed next to her husband. He is already snoring, the rich smell of fermented Concord grapes filling the air with each rattle. It's her habit to turn her back to him at night, willing her body to let go, hoping he will be fooled into thinking she is asleep. There is always the possibility that he will find waking her not worth the bother after all. Though this is not a subject women often discuss, she knows there are some who actually don't mind that business . . . who even crave it. She's read their letters. "Dear "Bintel Brief": My husband falls into bed like a stone each night. How can I get him to want family relations again? Dear "Bintel Brief": My man deserted me and our young children. I still have thoughts of a physical nature, if you'll excuse me. What can I do to help myself?" Meryl can't imagine feeling that way about her husband. What Grossman did to her: it seemed so far from romance. But that was her own *narrishkeit*. Why couldn't she be content with all she did have? If she has learned anything from life and the letters of others, it is that everyone has her bundle of *tsores*. But still, now that she has begun to write, she feels her particular plight worthy of attention.

The letters she composes in her mind have become so real to her that on the days the "Bintel Brief" column appears in the *Forward*, she can hardly bring herself to open the paper for fear she will find one of her notes there, suddenly materialized for all the world to see, the words scattered like peppercorns over the white page. So powerful have her thoughts become, so driven by yearning, she can almost believe they have found some magical route straight from her heart to New York City.

A small man with delicate bones, refined and learned, only slightly older than herself, a widower, perhaps, or someone who has not yet found a match for his fantasies: this is the "Bintel Brief" adviser Meryl has pieced together from novels and moving pictures. She imagines him in his tiny, cluttered newspaper office, searching for her familiar handwriting in the blizzard of envelopes on his desk. Who else can I turn to, she writes. You know my history. Tell me what to do. Your eyes are so dark and piercing they could read me as if I were a heroine out of Tolstoy. And she blushes. It's her adviser's slender wrists that move her most, emerging from spotless white cuffs to end in long aristocratic fingers with nails as glossy as the leaves of a rubber plant. Once or twice she has allowed herself to consider such hands roaming her body, "a Siberia yet to be explored," she tells him boldly. At this very moment, her husband's great belly rising and falling beside her, she can feel those noble hands on her, grounding the sparks of her electric hair between his palms, absorbing the antic energy that has nowhere else to go.

Such *mishegoss*. It's her sisters she blames for filling her head with foolish expectations so long ago, everyone crowded into one bedroom, she and the older girls, jumping from bed to bed, hiding under the feather quilts, whispering and laughing and shushing. She can still recall the hot cheeks she felt redden even in the dark. They were joking about things she couldn't understand, but it all seemed wrapped in the toss of a braid drawn across her face in the damp, warm blackness or a hand reaching up under her nightgown to scratch her back. The air hung heavy with their scents: Masha, spicy like cinnamon; Itkeh, wild strawberries; Golda even as a girl, reeking of onions and stale sweat. A kiss – on the cheek or the fingertips – even the earlobe, like what her sisters meant, like the movies, she can see that – even at times, the other thing. She isn't entirely the kettle of cold water that Grossman claims she is. What would he think if he could read her mind just now. What does he know of her dreams?

There are nights, after he'd done poking at her, after he'd turned his bare ass to her without the decency to pull down his nightshirt, when she would wait for the ripping snores and then creep gingerly from bed. She couldn't sleep until she washed the smell of him from her body. She would draw a glass of hot water from the tap and sitting on the toilet, soap herself and rinse with the water. It was strange: that rubbing with her fingers and the soothing trickle sometimes made her want to pee even if she had just gone a moment before. Then she would have to do the soaping and rinsing all over again to make sure she was really clean. The rough towel to finish, back and forth between her trembling legs, and she standing there on the black-and-white tiled floor, her head thrown back, neck arched, eyes closed so she would not be caught spying on the stranger reflected in the mirror on the medicine cabinet door.

This night she is following the advice she has gleaned from the "Bintel Brief," though she's not sure she wants to. Peace in the house. She has taken time to bathe and dress herself in a freshly pressed flannel gown. She has smoothed Ponds Cold Cream into her elbows and the backs of her ankles. Like she has seen Carole Lombard do, seated at her dressing table in the movies, she dabs behind her ears from a bottle of toilet water so yellow with age, so concentrated, the smell is overpowering. She cannot remember being this nervous on her wedding night, but what did she have the sense to be wary about then?

For a long time she lies listening to his snoring. She needs something from him, something hard to name, but she has begun to think she will die if she doesn't get it. This time, her adviser has told her, *she* must be the awakener. Tonight she will reach down under his nightshirt, force herself to touch that pink snake sleeping lightly in its dark nest ready to strike. Tonight she will be a Biblical heroine, Queen Esther pleading with Ahashuerus, but she expects no golden sceptre, and the only life she will bargain for will be her own.

In the end, she has to admit the night is a failure. Despite her preparations and the promptings of her adviser, there has been no rousing Grossman from his insistent stupor. Dear "Bintel Brief": she writes, lying awake long after she has given up hope. For years now, I have sensed my soul shrinking until I think sometimes I can actually feel it lodged in my chest, a dried lump shriveled as the shell of a walnut. Shameful as it is, I want . . . I want.

Sunday, Meryl carries an armload of costumes down to the *cheder*. For weeks she has been sewing a rainbow of tunics, sashes, and capes for the *Purim* pageant while Grossman rehearses the older students in the reading of the *Megillah*. Already giddy with the promise of the holiday, the children are wilder than ever. She is a soft touch, and the students know it. She sees spitballs rain like hailstones whenever Grossman turns his back. Even seated in an orderly row with his hands supposedly folded on his desk, a boy will risk a beating to snatch off a *yarmelke* and sap the unfortunate student ahead of him with a walnut knotted in a large handkerchief. Grossman has confiscated a dozen of these makeshift blackjacks in the last few days, and *Purim* is still a week away. After the hard Michigan winter, keeping order won't get easier as spring flirts and then reneges on her promise. In the patch of snow out back of the apartment, black dirt has begun to appear, and with it, the tin cans and bones dropped there before snow fell by slovenly tenants who still think they live on Hastings Street.

Meryl considers which of the youngest pupils she can persuade to take the two female roles. She won't even bother to ask any of the older boys for whom every other word is "sissy." Though she, herself, played at being Queen Esther a couple of nights before, it is Vashti she really identifies with, the stubborn queen who defied the king and refused to dance for his guests. She always wonders if Vashti might have been feeling tired that fateful night; perhaps it had been her time of the month and she just didn't feel up to parading her body in front of a band of rowdy drunks.

Now Meryl indicates the small chalkboard wobbling on its stand. "Bo, Ba, Beh," she says, touching each consonant and vowel with her pointer. "Bo, Ba, Beh," the children repeat. She has appropriated a corner at the back of the classroom for her handful of students, seating them with their backs to Grossman who terrifies them and the older pupils whose bad example they will soon enough follow. "Lo, La, Leh, Mo, Ma, Meh." The warm room, the rhythmic chanting, her own troubled sleep the previous weekend, and Meryl finds herself almost nodding. And then she becomes aware that her voice is the only sound in a room grown suddenly still.

She turns to see one of the bigger boys – Yaacov it is – hunched in his seat, his arms crossed in front to protect his face. Grossman looms over him, cracking the thick ruler down on his head, his shoulders, any place he can land a blow. When the stick breaks,

Grossman brandishes the useless half, pulls the boy to his feet by his sweater, and begins to slap his face, methodically, first one side and then the other. Meryl's children have turned in their seats and watch, eyes large as Gold Eagles. Mottke, her youngest pupil, scarcely five, begins to cry silently, slimy trails running from his nose. The older boys have buried their faces in their Hebrew books, quiet for once.

Meryl has been an actor in this scene before. She knows the role she plays, has studied it hard. Sometimes she improvises, but, as at this moment, she never strays too far from the text. Heart leaping, with both hands outsplayed, she encircles her husband's flailing arm. So wicked is the force of its thrashing that her heels are lifted from the wooden floor. She says, "Grossman, for God's sake, stop it, have pity, the boy's sorry," but now her husband turns on her, his upper lip gone white, his eyes filled with blood. She has time to wonder just whose face he is seeing before him, and then dropping the ruler, he drives his fist into her open mouth.

Later, Meryl sits in the living room holding a blood-soaked dish towel filled with chipped ice to her swollen jaw. Thank God for Shirley who came down and sat with her pupils and told them the story of Purim, though God knows, they knew it word for word by now. They would have another story to tell their parents when they got home, that was for sure. And once in the parents' mouths, everybody in town would soon know that Grossman the Hebrew teacher had beat up on his wife in front of the whole school.

Grossman wanders around the kitchen banging pots and pans for her benefit: an announcement to all that he is getting his own dinner. She is tempted to say, wait, I'll do it, just let me rest here another moment, but she is not quite sure she can find the proper words for him just yet. What she *wants* to say to him about the food and everything else is choke on it.

There will be time, when her pulse stops pounding in her ears, when her mouth is no longer filled with blood, for the old lines, the apologies, an opportunity to explain she was not questioning his authority, only worried about the school, their reputation, on and on. She will say she is sorry to have shamed him in front of the students. She knows she has made it more difficult to control them from now on. And so forth.

Shirley brings her a fresh towel, a glass of water, sits opposite her on the edge of the davenport biting at the nail of her little finger. She has made a show of drawing the water from the bathroom tap so as not to be in the same room with her father. Shorely, my little gorely. "You think he doesn't feel bad?" Meryl says, favoring her swollen lips. "You know those boys – wild animals; they make him *meshugge*. Go, Mameleh, for my sake. Fix him something to eat. Don't be mad."

And when the girl goes, reluctantly, to the kitchen, Meryl writes, What legacy do I leave my daughter?, Dear "Bintel Brief." What is the price of peace in the house? And Daniel? What words for a son who cannot protect his mother? Daniel says, "Ma, can I turn on my programs?" He stands across the room from her, hands in his pockets jingling change, just like his father. He looks away from her, over her shoulder to the framed dimestore photo of F.D.R. hanging on the wall behind her. "I'll make it low," he promises, the only indication he can give her that he knows. She is tired of being the comforter. She wishes they would all leave her alone. In a moment, she will get up, be herself again. Just now, she wants a few more minutes to sit quietly, letting cold spread through the dull ache, writing . . . writing.

Barbara Helfgott Hyett

Wartime

Do roses remember the journey
upward, earth's eyelid opening,
forcing them through? I was
conceived in wartime, in a hospital
bed tented with muslin sheets,
It was spring in North Carolina.
I was content to happen there,
a rosette in the whorl that passes
between cells. By June my mother
recognized the friction in her belly,
climbed into the bathtub, a wire
coat hanger sprung open in her hand,
She wanted to undo me but I clung
to the wall inside her, tucked up,
refusing to be let go. From the sound
of things I knew I'd better not breathe.
After that, birth was an indulgence:
I thrived on ordinary riches: daffodils
in a milk bottle on the sedar table,
a cardboard toybox, my brother's
collection of stones. I grew gregarious,
street-smart, a perfectly aggressive girl.
Sundays we'd all drive to the airport,
watch planes take off, I believed
in the *Book of Knowledge*, everything
there was to know. My father
prayed to the God outside
the sunroom windows. Night
after night he woke me, left
thumbprints on my flowered
taffeta spread. In the living room,

my mother kept a rose under water,
bivouacked inside a souvenir
crystal ball. Waxed and stemless,
that blossom refused to bleed.

On the Edge of
the Twenty-first Century

Even when the ginkgo forsakes its leaves
it stands in the wind that churns them.
A century is closing; the map is redrawn
and no one remembers the landmarks.
In the north, a moose has come out
of the woods to stand each day
at the barnyard, snout bent to the fence
to nuzzle the neck of a Guernsey cow.

All around us, not hidden but bright
and comprehensible, *dura mater*
enveloping us in our rooms as we
undress in the solace before sleep.
From my window I can see the proof –

That half-moon over the city
stays, even after we stop watching.

Henny Wenkart

The Good Girl

Erev shabbes sun bathing the towers across the park,
Gleaming windows, gently blowing branches
All remind me how we sat here at this table

I'd tell you we have tickets Sunday   but we don't have to go
Shall we do something else?

O, you'd say, shrugging on your jacket,
I won't be around this weekend – I didn't want to tell you,
It makes you look so sad.

Why did I never
                    NOT ONE SINGLE TIME
Toss on my coat, ok where are we going?
Or, You are my husband!
You'll stay and spend the weekend with me!
Or even darling, what's happening with us?

Because
If I was a good girl
And kept silent
Surely, surely whatever it was
Would go away

Splintering

Our son has some triumphant news and when he tells me he says
If you talk to Daddy don't tell him, I want to tell him myself
But tell him that he should call me
Right away.

I say mazel tov, mazel tov, no I won't tell
I won't give away your surprise.
And son, by the way, when you tell him
Tell him also that he should call me
So that we can shep naches together and say mazel tov
To each other.

Oh Mommy, he says

You can't do that

You can't tell me
         to tell him
                to call you

Ruth Stone

Uncle Cal on Fashions

Troy New York! Where they made celluloid collars!
Great center for celluloid collars!
Someone might say, "His collar exploded!"
You mean he got hot under the collar?
"Went up like wax! Flammable stuff, celluloid collars!"
Didn't take much to ignite but they were stiff.
They could hold up your chin. Several chins.
I've seen men resting on them.
But the cigar ash, it posed a certain risk.
Of course in the privacy of the bedroom you'd take them off.
It was nothing at a large dinner party to see several exploding.
Of course, it would be after the ladies withdrew.
And if you had a beard – well, it was quite a flash.
This was fine for the tablecloth business.
Table linens moved fast in those days.
But some ladies took exception to the loss of linens,
heirlooms and so forth. Got so an invitation
to dinner might say RSVP and SCC –
sans celluloid collar, you know.
The less bold ones might say, "soft collar requested."
Yep. Some mighty red necks.
Yep. Back then Troy was like a plug of dynamite
with a short fuse. That's where the expression,
"he's a turkey," came from. Then some feller invented starch.
But 'twasn't the same.

So What

For me the great truths are laced with hysteria.
How many Einsteins can we tolerate?
I leap into the uncertainty principle.
After so many smears you want to wash it off with a laugh.
ha ha you say. So what if it's a melt down?
Last lines to poems I will write immediately.

Yes, Think

Mother, said a small tomato caterpillar to a wasp,
why are you kissing me so hard on my back?
You'll see, said the industrious wasp, deftly inserting
a package of her eggs under the small caterpillar's skin.
Every day the small caterpillar ate and ate the delicious
tomato leaves. I am surely getting larger, it said to itself.
This was a sad miscalculation. The ravenous hatched
wasp worms were getting larger. O world, the small
caterpillar said, you were so beautiful. I am only a small
tomato caterpillar, made to eat the good tomato leaves.
Now I am so tired. And I am getting even smaller. Nature
smiled. Never mind, dear, she said. You are a lovely link
in the great chain of being. Think how lucky it is to be born.

Then

That summer, from the back porch,
we would hear the storm like a train,
the Doppler effect compressing the air;
the rain, a heavy machine, coming up
from below the orchard, rushing toward us.
My trouble was I could not keep you dead.
You entered even the inanimate,
returning in endless guises.
And that winter an ermine moved into the house.
It was so cold the beams cracked.
The ermine's fur was creamy white
with the last half of the tail soot black.
Its body about ten inches long,
it slipped through small holes.
It watched us from a high shelf in the kitchen.
In our loss we accepted the strange shape of things
as though it had a meaning for us;
as though we moved slowly over the acreage,
as though the ground modulated like water.
The floors and the cupboards slanted to the west,
the house sinking toward the evening side of the sky.
The children and I sitting together waiting,
there on the back porch; the massive engine
of the storm swelling up through the undergrowth,
pounding toward us.

Light Conclusions

Seven light bulbs burned for seven hours.
Delicate but well made,
their seven eyes stared at the leather-hooded killer.
He moved with the wind outside the black window.
Eventually everyone fell asleep.
The bulbs hissing and trembling sent tender ohms
over the strange lonely woman.
"What sentiment!" they observed,
as they jiggled their fine tongues crafted in Hong Kong.

Relatives

Grandma lives in this town;
in fact all over this town.
Grandpa's dead.
Uncle Heery's brain-dead,
and them aunts! Well!
It's grandma you have to contend with.
She's here – she's there!
She works in the fast food hangout.
She's doing school lunches.
She's the crossing guard at the school corner.
She's the librarian's assistant.
She's part-time in the real estate office.
She's stuffing envelopes.
She gets up at three A.M.
to go to the screw factory;
and at night she's at the business school
taking a course in computer science.

Now you take this next town.
Grandpa's laid out neat in the cemetery
and grandma's gone wild and bought a bus ticket
to Disneyland.
Uncle Bimbo's been laid up for ten years
and them aunts
are all cashiers in ladies' clothing
and grandma couldn't stand the sight of them
washing their hands and their hair
and their panty hose.
"It's Marine World for me" grandma says.

Madison in the Mid-Sixties

Names, can you talk without their mirage?
What was his name . . . that rock star,
the one whose plane went down in the lake?
Trees talked all winter in click language.
It was a long drive from the east.
I arrived penniless;
called the chairman.
"Find a motel," he said.
I could hear the background dinner party.
"Take a motel."
I sat in the Oldsmobile.
The Olds would later drop its front end
on the Interstate,
my mother in the back seat
and the hamster and Abigail.
University, where Roger, the graduate student,
gave me his endless poems to read; all

under the influence of Vosco Popa;
all mediocre.
The futile student protests,
napalm and the Feds.
My brains wadded like the Patchwork girl of Oz;
maced lungs, the National Guard
lined up on either side of the main walk,
rifles cocked just above the passing heads,
a surefire canopy of death.
This montage upon which we write the message
that fails in language after language.

Up There

Belshazzar saw this blue
as he came into the walled garden,
though outside all was yellow,
sunlight striking the fractals of sand,
the wind striating the sand in riffles.

Land changes slowly, the fathoms
overhead accruing particles,
reflecting blue or less blue.

Vapor, a transient thing; a dervish
seen rising in a whirl of wind,
or brief cloud casting its changing shadow;
though below, the open-mouthed might stand
transfixed by mirage, a visionary oasis.

Nevertheless, this deep upside down
wash, water color, above planted gardens,
tended pomegranates, rouged soles of the feet
of lovers lounging in an open tent;
the hot blue above; the hareem
tethered and restless as camels.

This quick vision between walls, event,
freak ball, shook jar of vapor,
all those whose eyes were not gouged out,
have looked up and seen within the cowl
this tenuous wavelength.

Marvin Bell

Sounds of the Resurrected Dead Man's Footsteps #3

1. Beast, Peach and Dance

He couldn't say it or write it or sign it or give it a name.
He was suffering, he was terrible, he had a shape you could see
     in the fire.
He blamed the wine, God, the infamous events of Bethlehem.
Each newborn appeared to him in the air, their gorgeous
     proportions shaping the swaddling cloth each to each.
On the one hand, he felt the galaxies cooling, the gears clogging
     and the old passions frozen into debilitating poses.
On the other hand, it was now April and he had a buzz on
     because some seasons are their own nectar.
He could pick out a jacket and tie if he had to.
He could sit without twitching through the outdoor Mozart, the
     band shell gleaming like a new star.
Around him, the concert-goers sat tight-lipped, their expectations
     rewarded.
Before him, the night took on the sheen of flat glass and he could
     see in it the beacons of the town, and the blue-blackness
     of space just beyond.
His eyes fixed on a small, fuzzy star among many larger stars.
He became obsessed with this star, certain it was a Jewish star.
He felt that, if he could follow it, it would lead him to the true
     story of Jesus.
That night, while Mozart resolved in the air, he began to travel
     through time.
His small star would someday pass close to him but not yet.

2. *Angel, Portrait and Breath*

The hands that were nailed, the ankles that were pierced as if one –
        he had seen such proclamations before, it being common.
The bodies that literally came unglued in the furnace, the bones
        festering in lye – he had seen the piles of coats and
        eyeglasses, there being many.
The same angel who watched over the crucified Jesus passed
        over the cremated Jews, or was that a cloud?
The smokestacks carried away their last breaths.
Then Jesus rose entire to show the power of belief.
The dead Jews disintegrated into earth, air and water to show
        the lasting effects of evil.
He could not give it a name but felt that night as if, whatever it
        was, it lived on a small star, encircled but apart.
Thereafter, ordinary objects displayed a consciousness of the
        presence of men and women.
The blackened pots and ladles of the kitchen appeared changed.
They shone from long years of sustenance, from soups and sauces.
And in the shop he felt it also in the saws and sawhorses, in the
        dropcloths and bent nails, each encrusted with the years.
In this manner, he came to see in common objects the shine of the
        angelic.
The divine and horrific were linked by things and their
        descendants.
It was possible to see the good and bad in a needle and thread, in
        a pencil and pad, in a spoon, in a shoe.
The cloud appeared to him by day and the little star by night.

Sounds of the Resurrected Dead Man's Footsteps #6

1. Skulls

Oh, said a piece of tree bark in the wind, and the night froze.
One could not have foreseen the stoppage.
I did not foresee it, who had expected a messiah.
No one had yet dared say that he or she was it – target or savior.
In the slippage between time and the turning planet, a buildup
    of dirty grease made movement difficult.
Time slowed down while events accelerated.
The slower the eye moved, the faster events went past.
The raping and pillaging over time became one unending
    moment.
Nazis, who would always stand for the crimes of culture,
    clustered in public intersections, awaiting deliveries.
The masses would turn in the Jews.
From the officers' quarters could be heard the beautiful Schubert.
And in the camp there was the grieving tenor of the cantor.
The one rose and the other sank.
Today, one can stroll in the footsteps of those who walked
    single file from this life.
Often I stand in the yard at night expecting something.
Something in the breeze one caught a scent of as if a head of hair
    had passed by without a face.
Whatever happens to us from now on, it will come up from the
    earth.
It will bear the grief of the exterminated, it will lug itself upwards.
It will take all of our trucks to carry the bones.
But the profane tattoos have been bled of their blue by the
    watery loam, additives for worms.
Often I stand in the yard with a shovel.

2. *Skulls*

I am the poet of skulls without why or wherefore.
I didn't ask to be this or that, one way or another, just a young
    man of words.
Words that grew in sandy soil, words that fit scrub trees and
    beach grass.
Sentenced to work alone where there is often no one to talk to.
The poetry of skulls demands complicity of the reader, that the
    reader put words in the skull's mouth.
The reader must put water and beer in the mouth, and music in
    the ears, and fan the air for aromas to enter the nostrils.
The reader must take these lost heads to heart.
The reader must see with the eyes of a skull, comb the missing
    hair of the skull, brush the absent teeth, kiss the lips and
    find the hinge of the tongue.
Yes, like Hamlet, the Jew of Denmark before Shakespeare
    seduced him.
It is the things of the world which rescue us from the
    degradations of the literati.
A workshirt hanging from a nail may be all the honesty we can
    handle.
I am beloved of my hat and coat, enamored of my bed, my troth
    renewed each night that my head makes its impression on
    the pillow.
I am the true paramour of my past, though my wife swoons at
    the snapshots.
Small syringe the doctor left behind to charm the child.
Colorful *yarmulke* that lifted the High Holy Days.

Mark Rudman

Approach of High Holy Days

1

That season's coming around again.

The old questions rear . . .

I'm no longer of two minds.
About this one thing.
You won't see me again
in the guise of a hummingbird
hovering at the entrance
with a borrowed yarmulkah
squished in my jacket's side pocket.

Which doesn't mean I've turned my back
on prayer.

I still place prayer in my pantheon.

Prayer is like the Pantheon.

There was a time when I was inside the Anche Hesed synagogue
every day of the week to fetch my son from day care.

What makes you

mention it now? Walking home from our ritual Wednesday night
dinner at the local Cuban-Chinese I saw Mary Faith, the saint who
runs that institution, The Magical Years, eating alone in the rear of
the Metro Diner (which intersects with Broadway and our cross
street).

You're conflating ancient Italy and modern America: there are no more
saints, only martyrs. Mary Faith is a selfless, hardworking woman who
has devoted her life –

what we know of it

at least her later, white-haired years, to the lives of children. But to call
her a saint is inaccurate.

It's not for her labors; it's my sense that she's spiritually there.
That she answers to a higher order.

(Pause)

I wonder if she's a churchgoer.

Would knowing that bring you closer to the heart of her mystery?

I just wonder if her belief includes formal ritual.

Go on, wonder, no one can stop you. But please don't say "her belief" as
if it went without saying. Stay secure in your unknowing until the
door – opens of its own accord.

2

BACK STAIRWELL

I've chosen to take the stairs.
It's harder, but quicker

than waiting for the elevator
which seems eternally stuck on R – Roof.

And I'm late, the last of the parents
who don't send a stand-in.

I'm running, propelled by a kind of demon
– and embarrassed by my lateness –

up the back stairs of the synagogue,
when a window appears in the shaft,

on the wall of the stairwell;
a real window, like a painting on a wall

through which you can see the sky.
The shattered blue leans in, breaks

through the wall; it leaves
an opening, a sudden shudder, a frisson

like a rustle of eternity
shattered in the vista of receding

clouds, antennae, water towers . . .
and I think we are not far from ecstasy

even in the interior.
I can't get my son to hold the banister

as we descend the stairs;
a look of sheer defiance clouds his face,

the same boy who, the other night
I watched shuffle and backpedal and nearly fall,

down the escalator, over
the rapids of the raw-toothed

edges of the blades;
his hands, his attention, occupied

by a rabbit samurai Ninja turtle
and Krang, the bodiless brain.

I gauged the dive I would need
to catch him if he fell:

a flat out floating horizontal grab
I couldn't even have managed in my youth.

3

It's my deal.

I think you think more about prayer
when you're in foreign countries
and you find yourself

veritably surrounded
by churches, cathedrals actually
and that makes one hell

of a difference, ups the ante
of going in considerably
even if it's to see some work of art,

whose content, most likely, is religious,
– Christian religious –
and more sober and solemn

than any ceremony you're likely to hear
from any living
priest or Rabbi.

You've dealt me a good hand.

You did say one-eyed Jacks were wild?

Why you chisler . . .

4

(WEEK OF YOM KIPPUR: THE DENTIST'S OFFICE)

My lips and tongue are slow to get numb.

"What I like about Yom Kippur . . . is that half of it . . .
                takes place . . . inside the temple.
The other half . . . is between
        you and others."

I groan agreement.

"Your pact with your . . . fellow man . . .
                is just as important . . .
atonement means . . .

        are your lips numb?"

Uh uh; tongue.

"I'll take care of that."

Reaches for hypodermic.
"You won't feel this one at all."

"To atone you have to contact
the people you've wronged."

I groan disagreement: "What, on the phone?"

"On the phone or when you next . . . "

"What? Show up at the door? Collar someone on the street . . .

You do remember that I grew up in a Rabbi's house? And I never
heard anything like this."

"Was he orthodox or reform . . . ?"

5

Appalled.

"You must be numb by now."

2

Don't interrupt.

You couldn't control me when I was alive and now that I'm alive in
another way you have even less power over me.

I submit.

Well you are sitting in that damned dentist's chair 37 stories high over
Manhattan and you had to move your tongue while he was drilling –
I bring this up
because you feel compelled to talk about atonement with your dentist

who isn't exactly a Talmudic scholar . . .

no matter how often he flies off to Israel,
spends an hour among the stones
"getting in touch with his ancient past"
and for the rest of the time might just as well be in

Vegas.

Now stand back a minute
from your experience.

Prior to the impalement of your tongue by aforesaid drill,

and the blood he sopped up while making a face that said,
if you weren't such a nervous guy, if you had just kept still,
none of this would have happened

you and he were discussing the coming of Yom Kippur,

which, it's true, I can't think of without thinking of you –

only he had the advantage, when it came to talking,
or m o n o l o g u i n g because your mouth was entering
post-Lydocaine pre-numbness limbo;

and now I must confess that he woke me
from a most powerful slumber – ;

and so, forgive me if my bursting in like this from heaven
(I thought you'd like it if I threw that in)

caused your tongue to move at an inauspicious moment.

    After a life spent, squandered, wasted,
among American jews of the
                  high holy day holiday variety,
the hordes who never set foot in a temple
    except on Rosh Hashanah and Yom Kippur,
I could not let his remark pass unremarked.

Where do these heathens get the nerve to prophesy,

these fools who know no Torah,

who when you say Scholem hear shalom . . .

I can see from your attempt to smile with your lips
stretched to their physical limit and your mouth

like that silent scream in the expressionist painting
you dragged me to see – and I always did what you

told me to do –
that you liked that one.

(Pauses. Clears throat.)

No one should tie practical strings to prayer.

You atone alone, in your heart.

And then, when you're done
        with what is never done,
with what exists only through
        purification,

a continual
        beginning again
with nothing, you can

        reclaim

something of value no one
        can put a price on,
take away, or burn:
        poverty

And begin – wandering?

It is the nomadic way.

Trackless wilderness.

Wavelike ripples on the sand.

(Pause.)

Why did you never sing this particular song
when you were among the living?

Maybe you weren't listening.

Can I go on, your time in this altitude
is dwindling fast.

Put aside those Freudian notions
everyone treats as sacred scripture now

and forget the small stuff,
the unintentional slights,
the gaffs and faux pas.

It's wishing others ill that does you in.

They come back to me now,
the boiling red faces of your congregants.
The vehemence of their tirades,
denouncing others, never dreaming
the problem could lie within themselves.

Innocent of any complicity.

They lived as if there weren't a price.

I took you along so you could learn something, see how people really are
when they unload . . . on the Rabbi . . . as if asking me also to forgive
them for their petty adulteries embezzlements and backfiring calcula-
tions.

And at Yiskur services you raised the ram's horn to your lips,
took a deep
breath and let it bleat, rapid, staccato,
like a jazz player's opening
gambit on the trumpet, to the rhythm of

Ma nishtanah halilah hazeh shemecal halelot

מה נשתנה הלילה הזה מכל הלילות

I know it cost you to blow the shofar. I tried and couldn't get it to
release a sound other
than my own   blowing   and spittle.

So why aren't you in shul?

No other Rabbi's good enough for me.

A friend just called upon returning from services in London,
a bit like Ascot, a fashion show, the women
wearing enormous designer hats.

"Positively smashing."

*That's not reason enough. Would it please you if they came in rags, or
bent double like that poor homeless woman you're about to espy passing
the shut-down bodega on Broadway.*

I can't justify recoiling from praying in synagogues here.

My friends scattered across America say they go
for the sense of community.
Maybe I would too if I lived in Phoenix or Salt Lake.

I tried to lift you out of the mud. No use.

It is – almost – an element.

The Sin of Elijah

Somewhere during the couple of millennia that I'd been commuting between heaven and earth, I, Elijah the Tishbite – former
prophet of the Northern Kingdom of Israel, translated to Paradise in a chariot of flame while yet alive – became a voyeur. Call
me weak, but after you've attended no end of circumcisions,
when you've performed an untold number of virtuous deeds and
righteous meddlings in a multitude of bewildering disguises,
your piety can begin to wear a little thin. Besides, good works
had ceased to generate the kind of respect they'd once commanded in the world, a situation that took its toll on one's self-
esteem; so that even I, old as I was, had become susceptible from
time to time to the *yetser horah*, the evil impulse.

That's how I came to spy on the Fefers, Feyvush and Gitl, in
their love nest on the Lower East Side of New York. You might
say that observing the passions of mortals, often with stern disapproval, had always been a hobby of mine; but of late it was
their more intimate pursuits that took my fancy. Still, I had
standards. As a whiff of sanctity always clung to my person from
my sojourns in the Upper Eden, I lost interest where the dalliance
of mortals was undiluted by some measure of earnest affection.
And the young Fefer couple, they adored each other with a love
that surpassed their own understanding. Indeed, so fervent was
the heat of their voluptuous intercourse that they sometimes
feared it might consume them and they would perish of sheer
ecstasy.

I happened upon them one miserable midsummer evening
when I was making my rounds of the East Side ghetto, which in
those years was much in need of my benevolent visitations. I did
a lot of good, believe me, spreading banquets on the tables of the
desolate families in their coal cellars, exposing the villains posing
as suitors to young girls fresh off the boat. I even engaged in

spirited disputes with the *apikorsin*, the unbelievers, in an effort to vindicate God's justice to man – a thankless task, to say the least, in that swarming, heretical, typhus-infested neighborhood. So was it any wonder that with the volume of dirty work that fell to my hands, I should occasionally seek some momentary diversion?

You might call it a waste that one with my gift for camouflage, who could have gained clandestine admittance backstage at the Ziegfeld Follies when Anna Held climbed out of her milk bath, or slipped unnoticed into the green room at the People's Theater where Tomashevsky romped au naturel with his zaftig harem, that I should return time and again to the tenement flat of Feyvush and Gitl Fefer. But then you never saw the Fefers at their amorous business.

To be sure, they weren't what you'd call prepossessing. Feyvush, a cobbler by profession, was stoop-shouldered and hollow-breasted, nose like a parrot's beak, hair a wreath of swiftly evaporating black foam. His bride was a green-eyed, pear-shaped little hausfrau, freckles stippling her cheeks as if dripped from the brush that daubed her rust-red pompadour. Had you seen them in the streets – Feyvush with nostrils flaring from the stench, his arm hooked through Gitl's from whose free hand dangled the carcass of an unflicked chicken – you would have deemed them in no way remarkable. But at night when they turned down the gas lamp in their stuffy bedroom, its window giving on to the fire escape (where I stooped to watch), they were the Irene and Vernon Castle of the clammy sheets.

At first they might betray a charming awkwardness. Feyvush would fumble with the buttons of Gitl's shirtwaist, tugging a little frantically at corset laces, hooks and eyes. He might haul without ceremony the shapeless muslin shift over her head, shove the itchy cotton drawers below her knees. Just as impatiently Gitl would yank down the straps of her spouse's suspenders, pluck the studs from his shirt, the rivets from his fly; she would thrust chubby fingers between the seams of his union suit with the same impulsiveness that she plunged her hand in a barrel to snatch a herring. Then they would tumble onto the sagging iron bed, its rusty springs complaining like a startled henhouse. At the initial shock of flesh pressing flesh, they would clip, squeeze, and fondle whatever was most convenient, as if each sought a desperate assurance that the other was real. But once they'd determined as much, they slowed the pace; they lulled their frenzy to a rhythmic investigation of secret contours, like a getting acquainted of the blind.

They postponed the moment of their union for as long as they could stand to. While Feyvush sucked on her nipples till they stood up like gumdrops, Gitl gaily pulled out clumps of her husband's hair; while he traced with his nose the line of ginger fur below her navel the way a flame follows a fuse, she held his hips like a rampant divining rod over the wellspring of her womb. When their loins were finally locked together, it jarred them so that they froze for an instant, each seeming to ask the other in tender astonishment: "What did we do?" Then the bed would gallop from wardrobe to washstand, the neighbors pound on their ceilings with brooms, until Feyvush and Gitl spent themselves, I swear it, in a shower of sparks. It was an eruption that in others might have catapulted their spirits clear out of their bodies – but not the Fefers, who clung tenaciously to one another rather than suffer even a momentary separation from their better half.

Afterwards, as they lay in a tangle, hiding their faces in mutual embarrassment over such a bounty of delight, I would slope off. My prurient interests satisfied, I was released from impure thoughts; I was free, a stickiness in the pants notwithstanding, to carry on with cleansing lepers and catering the weddings of the honest poor. So as you see, my spying on the Fefers was a tonic, a clear case of the ends justifying the means.

How was it I contrived to stumble upon such a talented pair in the first place? Suffice it that, when you've been around for nearly three thousand years, you develop antennae. It's a sensitivity that, in my case, was partial compensation for the loss of my oracular faculty, an exchange of roles from clairvoyant to voyeur. While I might not be able to predict the future with certainty anymore, I could intuit where and when someone was getting a heartfelt shtupping.

But like I say, I didn't let my fascination with the Fefers interfere with the performance of good works; the tally of my *mitzvot* was as great as ever. Greater perhaps, since my broader interests kept me closer than usual to earth, sometimes neglecting the tasks that involved a return to Kingdom Come. (Sometimes I put off escorting souls back to the afterlife, a job I'd never relished, involving as it did what amounted to cleaning up after the Angel of Death.) Whenever the opportunity arose, my preoccupation with Feyvush and Gitl might move me to play the detective. While traveling in their native Galicia, for instance, I would stop by the study house, the only light on an otherwise deserted street in the abandoned village of Krok. This was the Fefers' home village, a place existing just this side of memory, reduced by pogrom and expulsions to broken chimneys, a haunted bath-house, scattered pages of the synagogue register among the dead leaves. The only survivors being a dropsical rabbi and his skeleton crew of disciples, it was to them I appealed for specifics.

"Who could forget?" replied the old rabbi stroking a snuff yellow beard, the wen on his brow like a sightless third eye. "After their wedding he comes to me, this Feyvush: 'Rabbi,' he says guiltily, 'is not such unspeakable pleasure a sin?' I tell him: 'In the view of Yohanan ben Dabai, a man may do what he will with his wife; within the zone of the marriage bed all is permitted.' He thanks me and runs off before I can give him the opinion of Rabbi Eliezer, who suggests that, while having intercourse, one should think on arcane points of law . . . "

I liked to imagine their wedding night. Hadn't I witnessed enough of them in my time? – burlesque affairs wherein the child bride and groom, martyrs to arranged marriages, had never set eyes on one another before. They were usually frightened to near paralysis, their only preparation a lecture from some doting melamed or a long-suffering mother's manual of medieval advice. "What's God been doing since He created the world?" goes the old question. Answer: "He's been busy making matches." But the demoralized condition of the children to whose nuptials I was assigned smacked more of the intervention of pushy families than the hand of God.

No wonder I was so often called on to give a timid bridegroom a nudge. Employing my protean powers – now regrettably obsolete, though I still regard myself a master of stealth – I might take the form of a bat or the shimmying flame of a hurricane lamp to scare the couple into each other's arms. (Why I never lost patience and stood in for the fainthearted husband myself, I can't say.) Certainly there's no reason to suppose that Dvora Malkeh's Feyvush, the cobbler's apprentice, was any braver when it came to bedding his own stranger bride – his Gitl, who at fifteen was two years his junior, the only daughter of Chaim Rupture the porter, her dowry a hobbled goat and a dented tin kiddush cup. It was not what you'd have called a brilliant match.

Still, I liked to picture the moment when they're alone for the first time in their bridal chamber, probably some shelf above a stove encircled by horse blankets. In the dark Feyvush has summoned the courage to strip to his talis koton, its ritual fringes dangling a flimsy curtain over his knocking knees. Gitl has peeled in one anxious motion to her starchless shift and slid gingerly beneath the thistledown, where she's joined after a small eternity by the tremulous groom. They lie there without speaking, without touching, having forgotten (respectively) the rabbi's sage instruction and the diagrams in *The Saffron Sacrament*. They only know that the warm (albeit shuddering) flesh beside them has a magnetism as strong as gravity, so that each feels they've been falling their whole lives into the other's embrace. And afterwards there's nothing on earth – neither goat's teat nor cobbler's last, pickle jar, poppy seed, Cossack's knout, or holy scroll – that doesn't echo their common devotion.

Or so I imagined. I also guessed that their tiny hamlet must have begun to seem too cramped to contain such an abundance of mutual affection. It needed a shtetl, say, the size of Tarnopol, or a teeming city as large as Lodz to accommodate them; or better: for a love that defied possibility, a land where the impossible (as was popularly bruited) was the order of the day. America was hardly an original idea – I never said the Fefers were original, only unique – but emboldened by the way that wedded bliss had transformed their ramshackle birthplace, they must have been curious to see how love traveled.

You might have thought the long ocean passage, at the end of which waited only a dingy dumbbell tenement on Orchard Street, would have cooled their ardor. Were their New World circumstances any friendlier to romance than the Old? Feyvush worked twelve-hour days in a bootmaking loft above the butcher's shambles in Gouverneur Slip, while Gitl haggled with fishmongers and supplemented her husband's mean wages stitching artificial flowers for ladies' hats. The streets swarmed with hucksters, ganefs, and handkerchief girls who solicited in the shadows of buildings draped in black bunting. Every day the funeral trains of cholera victims plied the market crush, displacing vendors crying spoiled meat above the locust-hum of the sewing machines. The summers brought a heat that made ovens of the tenements, sending the occupants to their roofs where they inhaled a cloud of blue flies; and in winter the ice hung in tusks from the common faucets, the truck horses froze upright in their tracks beside the curb. But if the ills of the ghetto were any impediment to their ongoing conjugal fervor, you couldn't have proved it by the Feyvush and Gitl I knew.

They were after all no strangers to squalor, and the corruptions of the East Side had a vitality not incompatible with the Fefers' own sweet delirium. Certainly there was a stench, but there was also an exhilaration: there were passions on display in the music halls and the Yiddish theaters, where Jacob Adler or Bertha Kalish could be counted on nightly to tear their emotions to shreds. You had the dancing academies where the greenhorns groped one another in a macabre approximation of the turkey trot, the Canal Street cafes where the poets and revolutionaries fought pitched battles with an arsenal of words; you had the shrill and insomniac streets. Content as they were to keep to themselves, the Fefers were not above rubbernecking. They liked to browse the Tenth Ward's gallery of passions, comparing them – with some measure of pride – unfavorably to their own.

Sometimes I thought the Fefers nurtured their desire for each other as if it were an altogether separate entity, a member of the family if you will. Of course the mystery remained that such heroic lovemaking as theirs had yet to produce any offspring, which was certainly not for want of trying. Indeed, they'd never lost sight of the sacramental aspect of their intimacy, or the taboos against sharing a bed for purposes other than procreation. They had regularly consulted with local midwives, purchasing an assortment of bendls, simples, and fertility charms to no avail. (Gitl had even gone so far as to flush her system with mandrake enemas against a possible evil eye.) But once, as I knelt outside their window during a smallpox-ridden summer (when caskets the size of bread pans were carried from the tenements night and day), I heard Feyvush suggest:

"Maybe no babies is for such a plenty of pleasure the price we got to pay?"

You didn't have to be a prophet to see it coming. What could you expect when a pair of mortals routinely achieved orgasms like Krakatoa, their loins shooting sparks like the uncorking of a bottle of pyrotechnical champagne? Something had to give, and with hindsight I can see that it had to happen on Shabbos, when married folk are enjoined to go at their copulation as if ridden by demons. Their fervent cleaving to one another (*dveykuss* the kabbalists call it) is supposed to hasten the advent of Messiah, or some such poppycock. Anyway, the Fefers had gathered momentum over the years, enduring climaxes of such convulsive magnitude that their frames could scarcely contain the exaltation. And since they clung to each other with a ferocity that refused to release spirit from flesh, it was only a matter of time until their transports carried them bodily aloft.

I was in Paradise when it happened, doing clerical work. Certain bookkeeping tasks were entrusted to me, such as totting up the debits and credits of incoming souls – tedious work that I alternated with the more restful occupation of weaving garlands of prayers; but even this had become somewhat monotonous, a mindless therapy befitting the sanatorium-like atmosphere of Kingdom Come. For such employment I chose a quiet stone bench (what bench wasn't quiet?) along a garden path near the bandstand. (Paradise back then resembled those sepia views of Baden-Baden or Saratoga Springs in their heyday; though of late the place, fallen into neglect, has more in common with the seedier precincts of Miami Beach.) At dusk I closed the ledger and tossed the garlands into the boughs of the Tree of Life, already so festooned with ribbons of prayer that the dead, in their wistfulness, compared it to a live oak hung with Spanish moss. Myself, I thought of a peddler of suspenders on the Lower East Side.

I was making my way along a petal-strewn walk toward the gates in my honorary angel getup – quilted smoking jacket, tasseled fez, a pair of rigid, lint-white wings. Constructed of chicken wire and papier-mâché, they were just for show, the wings, about as useful as an ostrich's. I confess this was a source of some resentment, since why shouldn't I merit the genuine article? As for the outfit, having selected it myself I couldn't complain; certainly it was smart, though the truth was I preferred my terrestrial shmattes. But in my empyrean role as Sandolphon the Psychopomp, whose responsibilities included the orientation of lost souls, I was expected to keep up appearances.

So I'm headed toward the park gates when I notice this hubbub around a turreted gazebo. Maybe I should qualify "hubbub," since the dead, taking the air in their lightweight golfing costumes and garden party gowns, were seldom moved to curiosity. Nevertheless, a number had paused in their twilight stroll to inspect some new development under the pavilion on the lawn. Approaching, I charged the spectators to make way. Then I ascended the short flight of steps to see an uninvited iron bed supplanting the tasteful wicker furniture; and on that rumpled, bow-footed bed lay the Fefers, man and wife, in flagrante delicto. Feyvush, with his pants still down around his hairy ankles, and Gitl, her shift rucked to the neck, were holding on to each other for dear life.

As you may know, it wasn't without precedent for unlicensed mortals to enter the Garden alive. Through the ages you'd had a smattering of overzealous mystics who'd arrived by dint of pious contemplation, only to expire outright from the exertion. But to my knowledge Feyvush and Gitl were the first to have made the trip via the agency of ecstatic intercourse. They had, in effect, shtupped their way to heaven.

I moved forward to cover their nakedness with the quilt, though there was really no need for modesty in the Upper Eden, where unlike in the fallen one innocence still obtained.

"I bet you're wondering where it is that you are," was all I could think to say.

They nodded in saucer-eyed unison. When I told them Paradise, their eyes flicked left and right like synchronized wipers on a pair of stalled locomobiles. Then just as I'd begun to introduce myself ("the mock-angel Sandolphon here, though you might know me better as . . . "), an imperious voice cut me off.

"I'll take care of this – that is of course if *you* don't mind . . . "

It was the archangel Metatron, né Enoch ben Seth, celestial magistrate, commissary, archivist, and scribe. Sometimes called Prince of the Face (his was a chiseled death mask with one severely arched brow), he stood with his hands clasped before him, a thin gray eminence rocking on his heels. He was dressed like an undertaker, the nudnik, in a sable homburg and frock coat, its seams neatly split at the shoulders to make room for an impressive set of ivory wings. Unlike my own pantomime pair, Enoch's worked. While much too dignified to actually use them, he was not above preening them in my presence, flaunting the wings as an emblem of a higher status that he seldom let me forget. He had it in for me because I served as a reminder that he too had once been a human being. Like me he'd been translated in the prime of life in an apotheosis of flames to Kingdom Come. Never mind that his assumption had included the further awards of functional feathers and an investiture as full seraph; he still couldn't forgive me for recalling his humble origins, the humanity he'd never entirely outgrown.

"Welcome to the Upper Eden," the archangel greeted the bedridden couple, "the bottommost borough of Olam ha-Ba, the World to Come." And on a cautionary note, "You realize of course that your arrival here is somewhat, how shall we say, premature?"

With the quilt hoisted to their chins, the Fefers nodded in concert – as what else should they do?

"However," continued Enoch, whose flashier handle I'd never gotten used to, which insubordination he duly noted, "accidents will happen, eh? and we must make the best of an irregular state of affairs. So," he gave a dispassionate sniff, brushing stardust or dandruff from an otherwise immaculate sleeve, "if you'll be so good as to follow me, I'll show you to your quarters." He turned abruptly and for a moment we were nose to nose (my potato to Enoch's flutey yam), until I was forced to step aside.

Feyvush and Gitl exchanged bewildered glances, then shrugged. Clutching the quilt about their shoulders, they climbed out of bed – Feyvush stumbling over his trousers as Gitl stifled a nervous laugh – and scrambled to catch up with the peremptory angel. They trailed him down the steps of the gazebo under the boughs of the Tree of Life, in which the firefly lanterns had just become visible in the gloaming. Behind them the little knot of immortals drifted off in their interminable promenade.

"What's the hurry?" I wanted to call out to the Fefers; I wanted a chance to give them the benefit of my experience to help them get their bearings. Wasn't that the least I could do for the pair who'd provided me with such a spicy pastime over the years? Outranked, however, I had no alternative but to tag along unobtrusively after.

Enoch led them down the hedge-bordered broadwalk between wrought iron gates, their arch bearing the designation GANEYDN in gilded Hebrew characters. They crossed a cobbled avenue and ascended some steps onto a veranda where a thousand cypress rockers ticked like a chorus of pendulums. (Understand that Paradise never went in for the showier effects: none of your sardonyx portals and myriads of ministering angels wrapped in clouds of glory, no rivers of balsam, honey, and wine. There, in deference to the sensibilities of the deceased, earthly standards abide; the splendor remains human-scale, though odd details from the loftier regions sometimes trickle down.)

Through mahogany doors thrown open to the balmy air, they entered the lobby of the grand hotel that serves as dormitory for the dead. Arrested by their admiration for the acres of carpets and carved furniture, the formal portraits of archons in their cedar of Lebanon frames, the chandeliers, Feyvush and Gitl lagged behind. They craned their necks to watch phoenixes smoldering like smudge pots gliding beneath the arcaded ceiling, while Enoch herded them into the elevator's brass cage. Banking on the honeymoon suite, I took the stairs and, preternaturally spry for my years, slipped in after them as Enoch showed the couple their rooms. Here again the Fefers were stunned by the sumptuous appointments: the marble-topped whatnot, the divan stuffed with angel's hair, the Brussels lace draperies framing balustraded windows open to a view of the park. From its bandstand you could hear the silvery yodel of a famous dead cantor chanting the evening prayers.

Inconspicuous behind the open door, my head wreathed in a Tiffany lampshade, I watched the liveried cherubs parade into the bedroom, dumping their burdens of fresh apparel on the canopied bed.

"I trust you'll find these accommodations satisfactory," Enoch was saying in all insincerity, "and that your stay here will be a pleasant one." Rubbing the hands he was doubtless eager to wash of this business, he began to mince backward toward the door.

Under the quilt that mantled the Fefers, Feyvush started as from a poke in the ribs. He looked askance at his wife who gave him a nod of encouragement, then ventured a timid, "Um, if it please your honor," another nudge, "for how long do we supposed to stay here?"

Replied Enoch: "Why, forever of course."

Another dig with her elbow failed to move her tongue-tied husband, and Gitl spoke up herself. "You mean we ain't got to die?"

"God forbid," exhaled Enoch a touch sarcastically, his patience with their naiveté at an end: it was a scandal how the living lacked even the minimal sophistication of the dead. "Now, if there are no further questions . . . ?" Already backed into the corridor, he reminded them that room service was only a bell pull away, and was gone.

Closing the door (behind which my camouflaged presence made no impression at all), Feyvush turned to Gitl and asked, "Should we have gave him a tip?"

Gitl practically choked in her attempt to suppress a titter whose contagion spread to Feyvush. A toothy grin making fish-shaped crescents of his goggle eyes, he proceeded to pinch her all over, and together they dissolved in a fit of hysterics that buckled their knees. They rolled about on the emerald carpet, then picked themselves up in breathless dishevelment, abandoning their quilt to make a beeline for the bedroom.

Oh boy, I thought, God forgive me; now they'll have it off in heaven and their aphrodisiac whoops will drive the neutered seraphim to acts of depravity. But instead of flinging themselves headlong onto the satin counterpane, they paused to inspect their laidout wardrobe – or "trousseau" as Gitl insisted on calling it.

Donning a wing collar shirt with boiled bosom, creased flannel trousers, and a yachting blazer with a yellow Shield of David crest, Feyvush struck rakish poses for his bride. Gitl wriggled into a silk corset cover, over which she pulled an Empire tea gown, over which an ungirded floral kimono. At the smoky-mirrored dressing table she daubed her round face with scented powders; she made raccoon's eyes of her own with an excess of shadow, scattered a shpritz of sparkles over the bonfire of her hair. Between her blown breasts she hung a sapphire the size of a gasolier.

While she carried on playing dress-up, Feyvush tugged experimentally on the bell-pull, which was answered by an almost instantaneous knock at the door. Feyvush opened it to admit a tea trolley wheeled by a silent creature (pillbox hat and rudimentary wings) who'd no sooner appeared than bowed himself out. Relaxing the hand that held the waived gratuity, Feyvush fell to contemplating the covered dish and pitcher on the trolley. Pleased with her primping, Gitl rose to take the initiative. The truth was, the young Mrs. Fefer was no great shakes in the kitchen, the couple having always done their "cooking" (as Talmud puts it) in bed. Nevertheless, with a marked efficiency, she lifted the silver lid from the dish, faltering at the sight of the medicinal blue bottle underneath. Undiscouraged, however, she tipped a bit of liver brown powder from the bottle onto the plate, then mixed in a few drops of water from the crystal pitcher. There was a foaming after which the powder assumed the consistency of clotted tapioca. Gitl dipped in a finger, gave it a tentative lick, smacked her lips, and sighed. Then she dipped the finger again, placing it this time on her husband's extended tongue. Feyvush too closed his eyes and sighed, which was the signal for them both to tuck in with silver spoons. Cheeks bulging, they exulted over the succulent feast of milchik and fleishik flavors that only manna can evoke.

Having placated their bellies, you might have expected them to turn to the satisfaction of other appetites. But instead of going back to the bedroom, they went to the open windows and again looked out over the Garden. Listening to the still warbling cantor (to be followed in that evening's program by a concert of Victor Herbert standards – though not before at least half a century'd passed on earth), they were so enraptured they forgot to embrace. Up here where perfection was the sine qua non, they required no language or gesture to improve on what was already ideal.

Heartsick, I replaced the lampshade and slunk out. I know it was unbecoming my rank and position to be disappointed on account of mere mortals; after all, if the Fefers had finally arrived at the logical destination of their transports, then good on them! What affair was it of mine? But now that it was time I mounted another expedition to the fallen world – babies, paupers, and skeptics were proliferating like mad – I found I lacked the necessary incentive. This is not to say I was content to stay on in Paradise, where I was quite frankly bored, but neither did a world without the Fefers have much appeal.

It didn't help that I ran into them everywhere, tipping my fez somewhat coolly whenever we crossed paths – which was often, since Feyvush and Gitl, holding hands out of habit, never tired of exploring the afterlife. At first I tried to ignore them, but idle myself, I fell into an old habit of my own. I tailed them as they joined the ranks of the perpetual strollers meandering among the topiary hedges, loitering along the gravel walks and bridle paths. I suppose that for a tourist the Garden did have its attractions: you've got your quaint scale reproductions of the industries of the upper heavens, such as a mill for grinding manna, a quarry of souls. There's a zoo that houses some of the beasts that run wild in the more ethereal realms: a three-legged "man of the mountain," a sullen behemoth with a barnacled hide, a petting zoo containing a salamander hatched from a myrtle flame. But having readjusted my metabolism to conform to the hours of earth, I wondered when the Fefers would wake up. When would they notice, say, that the fragrant purple dusk advanced at only a glacial pace toward dawn; that the dead, however well-dressed and courteous, were rather, well, stiff and cold?

In the end, though, my vigilance paid off. After what you would call about a week (though the Shabbos eve candles still burned in the celestial yeshivas), I was fortunate enough to be on hand when the couple sounded their first note of discontent. Hidden in plain sight in their suite (in the pendulum cabinet of a grandfather clock), I overheard Feyvush broach a troubling subject with his wife. Having sampled some of the outdoor prayer minyans that clustered about the velvet lawns, he complained, "It ain't true, Gitteleh, the stories that they're telling about the world." Because in their discourses on the supernatural aspects of history, the dead, due to a faulty collective memory, tended to overlook the essential part of being alive: that it was natural.

Seated at her dressing table, languidly unscrolling the bobbin of her pompadour, letting it fall like carrot shavings over her forehead, Gitl ventured a complaint of her own. He should know that in the palatial bathhouse she attended – it was no longer unusual for the couple to spend time apart – the ladies snubbed her.

"For them, to be flesh and blood is a sin."

She was wearing a glove-silk chemise that might have formerly inspired her husband to feats of erotic derring-do. Stepping closer, Feyvush tried to reassure her, "I think they're jealous."

Gitl gave a careless shrug.

At her shoulder Feyvush continued cautiously, "Gitl, remember how," pausing to gather courage, "remember how on the Day of Atonement we played 'blowing the shofar'?"

Gitl stopped fussing with her hair, nodded reflexively.

"Do you remember how on Purim I would part like the pages of Megillah . . . " here an intake of air in the lungs of both parties " . . . your legs?"

Again an almost mechanical nod.

"Gitl," submitted Feyvush just above a whisper, "do you miss it that I don't touch you that way no more?"

She put down the tortoiseshell hairbrush, cocked her head thoughtfully, then released an arpeggio of racking sobs. "Like the breath of life I miss it!" she wailed, as Feyvush, his own frustrations confirmed, fell to his knees and echoed her lament.

"Gitteleh," he bawled, burying his face in her lap, "ain't nobody fency yentzing in Kingdom Come!" Then lifting his head to blow his nose on a brocaded shirtsleeve, drying his eyes with same, he hesitantly offered, "Maybe we could try to go home . . . "

"Hallelujah!"

This was me bursting forth from the clock to congratulate them on a bold resolution. "Now you're talking!" I assured them. "Of course it won't be easy; into the Garden you got without a dispensation but without a dispensation they won't never let you leave . . . " Then I observed how the Fefers, not yet sufficiently jaded from their stay in heaven, were taken aback. Having leapt to their feet, they'd begun to slide away from me along the paneled walls, which was understandable: for despite my natty attire, my features had become somewhat crepe-hung over the ages, my rheumy eyes tending toward the hyacinth red.

Recalling the introduction I never completed upon their arrival, I started over. "Allow me to present myself: the prophet Elijah, at your service. You would recognize me better in the rags I wear in the world." And as they still appeared dubious, Gitl smearing her already runny mascara as if in an effort to wipe me from her eye, I entreated them to relax: "You can trust me." I explained that I wanted to help them get back to where they belonged.

This at least had the effect of halting their retreat, which in turn called my bluff.

"You should understand," I began to equivocate, "there ain't much I can do personally. Sure, I'm licensed to usher souls from downstairs to up, but regarding vicey-versey I got no jurisdiction, my hands are tied. And from here to there you don't measure the distance in miles but dozens of years, so don't even think about starting the journey on your own . . . "

At that point Gitl, making chins (their ambrosial diet had endowed her with several extra), planted an elbow in Feyvush's ribs. He coughed once before speaking. "If it please your honor," his listless tone not half so respectful as he'd been with Enoch, "what is it exactly you meaning to do?"

I felt a foolish grin spreading like eczema across my face. "What I have in mind . . . ," I announced on a note of confidence that instantly fell flat, because I didn't really have a clue. Rallying nonetheless, I voiced my determination to intercede with the archangel Metatron on the couple's behalf.

Who was I kidding? That stickler for the letter of the Law, he wouldn't have done me a favor if his immortality depended on it. Still, a promise was a promise, so I sought out his high-and-mightiness in his apartments in the dignitaries' wing of the hotel. (My own were among the cottages of the superannuated cherubim.)

Addressing him by his given name, I'm straightaway off on the wrong foot.

"Sorry . . . I mean Metatron, Prince of the Face (such a face!), Lesser Lord of the Seventy Names, and so forth," I said, attempting to smooth his ruffled pride. It seemed that Enoch had never gotten over the treatment attending his translation, when the hosts mockingly claimed they could smell one of woman born from a myriad of parasangs away. "Anyhow," putting my foot in it deeper, "they had a nice holiday, the Fefers, but they would like already to go back where they came."

Seated behind the captain's desk in his office sipping a demitasse with uplifted pinky, his back to a wall of framed citations and awards, the archangel assumed an expression of puzzled innocence. Did I have to spell it out?

"You know, like home."

"Home?" inquired Enoch, as if butter wouldn't melt on his unctuous tongue. "Why, this is their home for all eternity."

Apparently I wasn't going to be invited to sit down. "But they ain't happy here," I persisted.

"Not happy in Paradise?" Plunking down his cup and saucer as if the concept was unheard of.

"It's possible," I allowed a bit too emphatically. Enoch clucked his tongue, which provoked me to state the obvious. "Lookit, they ain't dead yet."

"A mere technicality," pooh-poohed the archangel. "Besides, for those who've dwelt in Abraham's Bosom, the earth should no longer hold any real attraction."

Though I was more or less living proof to the contrary, rather than risk antagonizing him again, I kept mum on that subject. Instead: "Have a heart," I appealed to him. "You were alive when you came here . . . " Which didn't sound the way I meant it. "Didn't you ever want to go back?"

"Back?" Enoch was incredulous. "Back to what, making shoes?"

That he'd lowered his guard enough to mention his mortal profession made me think I saw an angle. "Feyvush is a cobbler," I humbly submitted.

"Then he's well out of it." The seraph stressed the point by raising his arched brow even higher, creating ripples that spoiled the symmetry of his widow's peak. "Besides, when I stitched leather, it was as if I fastened the world above to the world below."

"But don't you see," I pleaded, the tassle of my fez dancing like a spider in front of my eyes till I slapped it away, "that's what it was like when Feyvush would yentz with his bride . . . " This was definitely not the tack to have taken.

"Like I said, he's better off," snapped Enoch, rising abruptly from his swivel chair to spread his magnificent wings. "And since when is any of this *your* business?"

Conversation closed, I turned to go, muttering something about how I guessed I was just a sentimental fool.

"Elijah . . . ," the angel called my name after a fashion guaranteed to inspire maximum guilt.

"Sandolphon," I corrected him under my breath.

" . . . I think it's time you tended to your terrestrial errands."

"Funny," I replied in an insipid singsong, "I was thinking the same thing."

You'll say I should have left well enough alone, and maybe you're right. After all, without my meddling the Fefers would still be in heaven and I pursuing my charitable rounds on earth – instead of sentenced for my delinquency to stand here at this crossroads directing traffic, pointing the pious toward the gates, the wicked in the other direction, not unlike (to my everlasting shame) that nazi doctor on the railroad platform during the last apocalypse. But who'd have thought that, with my commendable record of good works, I wasn't entitled to a single trespass?

When I offered the Fefers my plan, Gitl elbowed Feyvush, then interrupted his diffident "If it please your honor – " to challenge me herself: "What for do you want to help us?"

"Because," since my audience with the archangel I'd developed a ready answer, "I can't stand to see nobody downhearted in Paradise. This is my curse, that such *rachmones*, such compassion I got, I can't stand it to see nobody downhearted anywhere." Which was true enough. It was an attitude that kept me constantly at odds with the angelic orders, with Enoch and Raziel and Death (between whom and myself there was a history of feuding) and the rest of that coldblooded crew. It was my age-old humanitarian impulse that compelled me to come to the aid of the Fefers, right? and not just a selfish desire to see them at their shtupping again.

Departing the hotel, we moved through whatever pockets of darkness the unending dusk provided – hard to find in a park whose every corner was illumined by menorahs and fairy lights. Dressed for traveling (Feyvush in an ulster and fore-and-aft cap, Gitl in automobile cape and sensible shoes), they were irked with me, my charges, for making them leave behind a pair of overstuffed Gladstone bags. Their aggravation signified an ambivalence which, in my haste to get started, I chose to ignore, and looking back I confess I might have been a little pushy. Anyway, in order not to call attention to ourselves (small danger among the indifferent immortals), I pretended I was conducting yet another couple of greenhorns on a sightseeing tour of the Garden.

"Here you got your rose trellis made out of what's left of Jacob's Ladder, and over there, that scrawny thing propped on a crutch, that's the *etz ha-daat*, the Tree of Knowledge . . . "

When I was sure no one was looking, I hauled the Fefers behind me into the shadows beneath the bloated roots of the Tree of Life. From a hanger in their midst I removed my universal luftmensch outfit – watch cap, galoshes, and patched overcoat – which I quick-changed into after discarding my Sandolphon duds. Then I led the fugitives into a narrow cavern that snaked its way under the Tree trunk, fetching up at the rust-cankered door of a dumbwaiter.

I'd discovered it some time ago while looking for an easier passage to earth. My ordination as honorary angel, while retarding the aging process, had not, as you know, halted it entirely, so I was in need of a less strenuous means of descent than was afforded by the branches of the Tree of Life. An antique device left over from the days when the Lord would frequent the Garden to send the odd miracle below, the dumbwaiter was just the thing. It was a sturdy enough contraption that, notwithstanding the sponginess of its wooden cabinet and the agonizing groans of its cables, had endured the test of time.

The problem was that the dumbwaiter's compactness was not intended to accommodate three people. A meager, collapsible old man, I'd always found it sufficiently roomy; but while the Fefers were not large, Gitl had never been exactly svelte, and both of them had put on weight during their "honeymoon." Nevertheless, making a virtue of necessity, they folded themselves into a tandem pair of S's and allowed me to stuff them into the tight compartment. This must have been awkward for them at first, since they hadn't held each other in a while, but as I wedged myself into the box behind them and started to lower us down the long shaft, Feyvush and Gitl began to generate a sultry heat.

They ceased their griping about cramped quarters and began to make purring noises of a type that brought tears to my eyes. I felt an excitement beyond that which accrued from our gathering speed, as the tug of gravity accelerated the dumbwaiter's downward progress. The cable sang as it slipped through my blistering fingers; then came the part where our stomachs were in our throats and we seemed to be in a bottomless free-fall, which was the dizzy, protracted prelude to the earth-shaking clatter of our landing. The crash must have alerted the cooks in the basement kitchen of Ratner's Dairy Restaurant to our arrival; because, when I slid open the door, there they were: a surly lot in soiled aprons and mushroom hats, looking scornfully at the pretzel the Fefers had made of themselves. I appeased them as always with a jar of fresh manna, an ingredient (scarce in latter-day New York) they'd come to regard as indispensable for their heavenly blintzes.

If the plummeting claustrophobia of the dumbwaiter, to say nothing of its bumpy landing, hadn't sufficiently disoriented my charges, then the shrill Sunday brunch crowd I steered them through would have finished the job. I hustled them without fanfare out the revolving door into a bitter blast of winter barreling up Delancey Street from the river.

"Welcome home!" I piped, though the neighborhood bore small resemblance to the one they'd left better than three-quarters of a century ago. The truck horses and trolleys had been replaced by a metallic current of low-slung vehicles squealing and farting in sluggish procession; the pushcarts and garment emporia had given way to discount houses full of coruscating gadgetry, percussive music shuddering their plate-glass windows. Old buildings, if they weren't boarded up or reduced altogether to rubble, had new facades, as tacky as hoop skirts on dowagers. In the distance there were towers, their tops obscured by clouds like tentpoles under snow-heavy canvas.

Myself, I'd grown accustomed to dramatic changes during my travels back and forth. Besides, I made a point of keeping abreast of things, pumping the recently departed for news of the earth, lest returning be too great a jolt to my system. But the Fefers, though they'd demonstrated a tolerance for shock in the past, seemed beyond perplexity now, having entered a condition of outright fear.

Gitl was in back of her husband, trying to straighten his crimped spine with her knee, so that he seemed to speak with her voice when she asked, "What happened to the Jews?" Because it was true that, while the complexions of the passers-by ran the spectrum from olive to saffron to lobster pink, there were few you could've identified as distinctly yid.

I shrugged. "Westchester, New Rochelle, Englewood, the Five Towns they went, but for delicatessen they come back to Delancey on Sundays." Then I grinned through my remaining teeth and made a show of protesting, "No need to thank me," though who had bothered? I shook their hands, which were as limp as fins. "Well, goodbye and good luck, I got things to do . . . "

I had urgent business to attend to, didn't I? – brisses, famines, false prophets in need of comeuppance. All right, so "urgent" was an exaggeration. Also, I was aware that the ills of the century had multiplied beyond anything my penny ante philanthropies could hope to fix. But I couldn't stand being a party to Feyvush and Gitl's five-alarm disappointment. This wasn't the world they knew; tahkeh, it wasn't even the half of what they didn't know, and I preferred not to stick around for the heartache of their getting acquainted. I didn't want to be there when they learned, for instance, that Jews had vanished in prodigious numbers from more places on the face of the planet than the Lower East Side. I didn't want to be there when they discovered what else had gone out of the world in their absence, and I didn't want to admit I made a mistake in bringing them back.

Still, I wouldn't send them away empty-handed. I gave them a pocket full of heaven gelt – that is, leaves from the *Etz ha-Chaim*, the Tree of Life, which passed for currency in certain neighborhood pawnshops; I told them the shops where you got the best rate of exchange. The most they could muster by way of gratitude, however, was a perfunctory nod. When they slouched off toward the Bowery, drawing stares in their period gear, I thought of Adam and Eve leaving the Garden at the behest of the angel with the flaming sword.

I aimed my own steps in the direction of the good deeds whose abandonment could throw the whole cosmic scheme out of joint. Then conceding there was no need to kid myself, it was already out of joint, I turned around. Virtually invisible in my guise as one more homeless old crock among a multitude of others, I followed the Fefers. I entered the shop behind them, where a pawnbroker in a crumpled skullcap greeted them satirically: "The Reb Ben Vinkl, I presume!" (This in reference to Feyvush's outdated apparel and the beard that had grown rank on his re-entering the earth's atmosphere.) But when he saw the color of the couple's scrip, he became more respectful, even kicking in some coats of recent vintage to reduce the Fefers' anachronistic mien.

There was no law that said Feyvush and Gitl had to remain in the old ghetto neighborhood. Owing to my foresight they now had a nest egg; they could move to, say, the Upper West Side, someplace where Jews were thicker on the ground. So why did they insist on beating a path through shrieking winds back to Orchard Street via a scenic route that took them past gutted synagogues, shtiblekh with their phantom congregants sandwiched between the bodegas and Chinese take-outs, the talis shops manned by ancients looking out as from an abyss of years? Answer: having found the familiar strange enough, thank you, they might go farther and fare even worse.

As luck (if that's the right word) would have it, there was a flat available in the very same building they'd vacated a decades-long week ago. For all they knew it was the same paltry top floor apartment with the same sticks of furniture: the sofa with its cushions like sinkholes, the crippled wing chair, the kitchen table, the iron bed; not that the decor would have meant much to Feyvush and Gitl, who didn't look to be in a nostalgic mood. Hugging myself against the cold on the fire escape, I watched them wander from room to room until the windows fogged.

Then someone rubbed a circle in a cloudy pane and I ducked out of sight below the ledge. But I could see them nonetheless, it was a talent I had: I could see them as clearly in my mind as with my eyes, peering into a street beyond which there was no manicured pleasure garden, no Tree.

They went out only once. Despite having paid a deposit and the first month's rent, they still had ample funds; they might have celebrated. But instead they returned with only the barest essentials – some black bread and farfel, a shank of gristly soup meat, a greasy sack of knishes from the quarter's one surviving knisherie. Confounded by the gas range that had replaced her old coal-burning cookstove, Gitl threw up her hands; Feyvush hunched his shoulders: Who had any appetite? Then they stared out the window again, past icicles like a dropped portcullis of fangs, toward a billboard atop the adjacent building. The billboard, which featured a man and woman lounging nearly naked on a beach, advertised an airline that offered to fly you nonstop to paradise.

Hunkered below the window ledge, I heard what I couldn't hear just like I saw what I couldn't see – Feyvush saying as if to himself, "Was it a dream?" Gitl replying with rancor: "Dreams are for goyim."

At some point one of them – I don't remember which – went into the bedroom and sat on the bed. He or she was followed soon after by the other, though neither appeared conscious of occupying the same space; neither thought to remove their heavy coats. The sag of the mattress, however, caused them to slide into contact with one another, and at first touch the Fefers combusted like dry kindling. They flared into a desperate embrace, shucking garments, Gitl tugging at her husband's suspenders as if drawing a bowstring. Feyvush ripped Gitl's blouse the way a Cossack parts a curtain to catch a Jew; he spread her thighs as if wrenching open the jaws of a trap. Having torn away their clothes, it seemed they intended to peel back each other's flesh. They marked cheeks and throats with bared talons, twisting themselves into tortured positions as if each were attempting to put on the other's skin – as if the husband must climb through the body of his wife, and vice-versa, in order to get back to what they'd lost.

That's how they did it, fastened to each other in what looked like a mutual punishment – hips battering hips, mouths spewing words refined of all affection. When they were done, they fell apart, sweating and bruised. They took in the stark furnishings of their cold-water flat: the table barren of the fabric flowers that once filled the place with perpetual spring, the window overlooking a street of strangers and dirty snow. Then they went at it again hammer and tongs.

I couldn't watch anymore; then God help me, I couldn't keep from watching. When the windows were steamed, I took the stairs to the roof, rime clinging to my lashes and beard, and squinted through a murky skylight like a sheet of green ice. When they were unobservable from any vantage, I saw them with an inner eye far clearer than my watery tom-peepers could focus. I let my good works slide, because who needed second sight to know that the world had gone already to hell in a phylactery bag? While my bones became brittle with winter and the bread and knishes went stale, and the soup meat grew mold and was nibbled at by mice, I kept on watching the Fefers.

Sometimes I saw them observing each other, with undisguised contempt. They had both shed the souvenir pounds they'd brought back from eternity. Gone was Gitl's generous figure, her unkempt hair veiling her tallowy face like a bloody rag. Her ribs showed beneath breasts as baggy as punctured meal sacks, and her freckles were indistinguishable from the pimples populating her brow. Feyvush, always slight, was nine-tenths a cadaver, his eyes in their hunger fairly drooling onto his hollow cheeks. His sunken chest, where it wasn't obscured by matted fur, revealed a frieze of scarlet hieroglyphics etched by his wife's fingernails. So wasted were they now that, when they coupled, their fevered bones chuckled like matches in a box. Between bouts they covered their nakedness with overcoats and went to the window, though not necessarily together. They rubbed circles, looked at the billboard with its vibrant twosome disporting under a tropical sun; then satisfied they were no nearer the place where they hoped to arrive, Feyvush or Gitl returned to bed.

Nu, so what would you have had me to do? Sure, I was the great kibbitzer in the affairs of others, but having already violated divine law by helping them escape from *der emeser velt*, the so-called true world, was I now to add insult to injury by delivering them from the false? Can truth and deception be swapped as easily as shmattes for fancy dress? Give me a break, the damage was done: human beings were not anyway intended to rise above their stations. The Fefers would never get out of this life again, at least not alive.

So I remained a captive witness to their savage heat. I watched them doing with an unholy vengeance what I never found the time for in my own sanctimonious youth – when I was too busy serving as mighty mouthpiece for a still small voice that had since become all but inaudible. I watched the mortals in their heedless ride toward an elusive glory, and aroused by the driven cruelty of their passion, achieved an erection: my first full engorgement since the days before the destruction of the Temple, when a maiden once lifted her tunic and I turned away. At the peak of my excitement I tore open the crotch of my trousers, releasing myself from a choked confinement, and spat my seed in a peashooter trajectory over Orchard Street. When I was finished, I allowed my wilted member to rest on the frigid railing of the fire escape, to which it stuck. Endeavoring to pull it free, I let loose a pitiable howl: I howled for the exquisite pain that mocked my terminal inability to die, and I howled for my loneliness. Then I stuffed my bloody putz back in my pants and looked toward the window, afraid I'd alerted the Fefers to my spying. But the Fefers, as it turned out, were well beyond earshot.

I raised the window and climbed over the sill, muffling my nose with a fingerless mitten against the smell, and shuffled forward to inspect their remains. So hopelessly entangled were the pair of them, however, that it was hard at first to distinguish husband from wife. Of course, there was no mistaking Feyvush's crown of tufted wool for Gitl's tattered red standard, his beak for her button nose, but so twined were their gory limbs that they defied a precise designation of what belonged to whom. Nor did their fused loins admit to which particular set of bones belonged the organ that united them both.

My task was as always to separate spirit from flesh, to extricate their immortal souls, which after a quick purge in the fires of Gehenna (no more than a millennia or two) would be as good as new. The problem was that, given the intricate knot they'd made of themselves, what was true of their bodies was true as well of their souls: I couldn't tell where Gitl's left off and her husband's began. It took me a while to figure it out, but ultimately I located the trouble; then the solution went some distance toward explaining their lifelong predicament. For the Fefers had been one of those rare cases where a couple shares two halves of a solitary soul. Theirs had indeed been a marriage made in heaven such as you don't see much anymore, the kind of match that might lead you to believe God Himself had a hand in it – that is, if you didn't already know He'd gotten out of the matchmaking racket long ago.

Scott Coffel

God's Double

What if God's double is a rhesus monkey
in the emergency room, his mask bunched at the throat?
What if he smells of witch hazel and plays
the doctor-priest to a floor of registered sisters?
What if, with the lives of millions hanging fire,
he uses his otherness as an alibi, refusing
to wear the requisite tattoo?
What if he bares his teeth and points his lewd finger
at the table where you lie unvexed by life?

Should I kill him at close range,
dish out the brains with a spoon?
Will my stomach acids make short work of his sadism?
Will I have satiated one of the three human hungers?
Will the voice of God whine inside the elevator shaft?
Will snow blanket the peninsula?
Will I cease being a Jew?
When his constellation rises over the Rockaways,
will the Bear be Catholic? Will I forgive the monkey?

Mountain Jews

When the lampshade revolved clockwise
its handpainted snowstorm
buried a family of mountain Jews
and froze their emaciated horses.

And when it revolved counterclockwise
the snow returned to the clouds
and the Jews drove their horses
into the teeth of an ancient disaster

any number of times until the game
grew tiresome or the bulb exploded.

Ann Z. Leventhal

Oh Abraham

What kind of father
ships his oldest son
into a desert to begin
the Muslims, then trusses

the one other, the kid that took
him a century to produce, and lays
the boy on kindling he should
make of him a burnt offering?

To whom? If some *macher*
ordered me to sacrifice my son,
you better believe I'd find some
place Mr. All-Knowing neglects

to visit, cut and color our
various hairs, join the others –
the boy and I now National Riflers
and living as if we never didn't

in one of the Springfields –
that is, if I didn't slaughter
a stand-in, say that white gorilla
in the Barcelona zoo. If God

never moves in for a close-up,
He won't catch on. And if He does,
let him feel against His own
back as I do, the cold slab,

above us the killing gleam, and
everywhere that spilled blood odor
that always comes with being shot
into life, oh God, to such a Father.

The Day I Watched Dead Guys Dancing

Oh Ginger, how could you
and your Fred, tappity tap,
not be here when I am

and you look like you are, too,
"The way you wear your cap"
tappity tap on the lam

with the other souls un-
coupled from transportation,
shadows waltzing in my fen

of phantasy, marabou film fun
the real transubstantiation
me less here than when

you're "puttin' on my white tie"
in my head whirling about
that white Hollywood light

and we dance the dance and fly
our swoop-swirl that is no doubt
a ta-ta to flesh, a tra-la to life?

Lisa Yanover

Shtetl Life

Watercarrier under the Moon

The watercarrier might
just as easily suspend
two wooden
houses from his pole,
curved as if he carries
the hill, the whole
landscape like that
across his shoulders,
his own orange-red
shadow spilling over,
pooling behind him and a little
to his right, the moon
in its muddy sky, too big
like his own face, half
in shadow, staring up at him,
refusing to be ladled
into cupped hands, into clay jars.

The watercarrier sells
his water for a few
coins, and for a few moments
he carries on the water's
surface: the lovers,
who are not
silhouetted in the blue
doorway but stand beside
it, hidden,
as if they have always
stood like that, face completing face,
like two halves of the moon,

who recite, "We, too,
were slaves in Egypt," remember
forty years
in the wilderness; who now act
like strangers as they turn to face
the watercarrier with only
the taste of their own
salt as they pay and drink;

The fruitseller in her print
skirt, dotted as if with leaves,
with fruit, her basket ready
to catch what falls, already
half-filled with what should be
pears but are only green
lemons for the *Feast of Booths,*
and she thirsting hesitates,
watches the coin ripen
in her hand and hands
it to the watercarrier
as if it is the moon
she cradles, its skin
freckling, silver,
growing loose and she too old
to nourish anything more, even
her own skin, her hand
now flimsy like paper, cupping
the shimmer of water, she drinks;

The baker himself is gibbous,
shining more than half
his face to his wife,
keeping his back turned
away from his customers.
He imagines kneading
the moon, the dough clammy
and luminous, pressing his fingers

into it like into taut leather
gloves, the color and fit of his own
skin. He imagines stretching
the dough, braiding some into Sabbath
loaves, rounding the rest
in his own image, the profile
he keeps so much to himself, turns
only to the watercarrier
who also turns and walks away.
The baker, left with only water
and the moon, still gibbous
and low behind him as if it, too,
might somehow be carried on his back,
imagines himself turning, able
to see the reflection of what
he eclipses, wonders
which of the two moons
he would drink;

The fishmonger and his fish-
wife peddle mostly herring to be
smoked, salted, pickled, creamed, and they wrap
a fish or two, whatever they can
set aside, in paper, but sometimes
one fish is all they have
to sell and must decide sell
or eat, but that's how it goes,
one will always tell
the other, each wanting the silver
skin, he for himself, she for her,
and each will settle,
in the end, selling, spending all
on water for the next day's fish,
and so they start again,
dreaming of what they've given up,
looking into their now full trough

of water, at the moon, its silver
skin beckoning them to drink;

The rabbi clasps *etrog* and *lulav*
between two hands, shaking the green
lemon and palm branch like a warning,
and innocently fingers a button
strapped to his forehead and another
to his left forearm. Buttons are
like eyes, he mouths, and his song
is fragrant, not like the town
drunk's. Only his disciples taste
the onion in his lessons and praise
him for such clarity. He takes
a coin like snuff, like a flea
between two fingers, squeezing it
to extract its few
secrets, those intimacies
of logic he already knows,
demands to know. Only the moon
eludes him as he drops his coin
into the watercarrier's hand
and drinks;

The drunkard carries his few
possessions folded inside his coat
against his chest. He takes out a glass
bottle, fills it, he thinks, with white
wine. He wouldn't pay
for water and doesn't
drink it except when it rains or now
as he sits on a low wall
by the road, pouring the water
into a bowl, stirring it
with the herring he thinks is
a knife and sharpens

against the cobbles or a strand
of his hair. Steel against steel, he thinks
out loud, lifts the bowl
to blow on the water,
and notices the moon. How cold,
he says, how like an eye half-
closed, and he half-closes his own
right eye, dipping his finger, grazing,
then piercing the moon, wanting nothing
more in that instant than to drink;

The tailor, having worked
so long with gray wool, watches himself,
his hands turn gray, working
bolt after bolt of cloth
into vests, coats, trousers. Last he sews
on buttons. Like eyes, he hears
the rabbi say, pinching the crease
of his trouser leg. Too long
like the sleeves, the tailor
answers, still with the coat,
not looking up. Like eyes, like eyes,
the rabbi insists, and it is this
the tailor says like prayer
as he works, pausing only
long enough to buy water,
losing the coin in the gray
of his hand, in the sound of it
dropping into the water
like a cock crowing as it swallows
the moon, the cracked shell and silver
yolk spilling from its beak,
and it is this the tailor drinks;

The marriage broker walks
away, walks over the hill,
his cane, its neck curved out,

cupped in his hand like a child's
face, his fingers curling together
and apart every other up-
step as if it is his own
face he considers, perhaps lighting
a cigarette, pulling his bound
notebook and inevitable
umbrella closer under his wool
coat sleeve, splitting under the arm.
Is it the fruitseller? he might
almost ask himself, Is she the one
he would marry? almost
smelling the citrus and farther
away the palm branch, the wind chirring
from all four directions, even
the moon reduced to a smell
of musk, he with his free
hand fingering a coin, growing drunk;

The innkeeper's wife is always
in need of wood and water,
keeps two pots boiling, and the fire burns
down to the coals but never out
as if it is always Sabbath.
Even on Sabbath, her husband
reminds her, there are laws and strangers.
Who knows but Elijah
himself might come in search of a meal?
So he, doubling as woodcutter,
brings more wood, and she sends
the watercarrier twice
to the river. Being so much
inside, perhaps she has forgotten
the moon, does not see it
lean against her shoulder.
Even her face in the black
pot seems new, hidden

behind its own shadow. Later
there will be time enough to drink;

The poet reclining in his black
velvet suit and lace
collar has nothing
to consider except how like
a white cow the moon appears
behind the forest and lilac
sky, how liquid it all
seems, but he, of course, cuts
right to the heart of a matter,
notices his thirst, turning
to face the watercarrier,
that porter of the moon
and other sorrows, glimpses
of the real world, how
in the months that follow
this one, the poet, too,
will be called, and thinking
of that duty, he drinks;

The butcher, too, falls in love
with the moon, sees the same
white cow in profile, paints
it in blood and fat
on his apron, but he sees beyond
this canvas, considers
the first time holding the knife,
his hand inside his father's,
the white throat of the cow
in the end he alone slaughtered,
the prayer and tears
they offered together,
or maybe this last
he only imagined, both of them
crying, cleaving together

because now as he bends,
looking down at the moon, he sees
only himself, the knife
put away, the cup filling
with water, and he,
opening the slit of his mouth, drinks;

The rabbi's wife waits
for the Sabbath. Certainly
she has plenty between now
and then. Isn't there
the feather bed to be turned, the clothes
to be washed and beaten
dry, the floors and all the meals
to consider? What has she to do
with the moon, even as she waits
for the watercarrier, rattling
the few coins in her hand to keep
the child, the last she still carries
in her arms, still and close at her side
because won't he go chasing
his own sad reflection
soon enough, poking fingers
into eyes and mouth to see them crinkle
and smooth, and won't she simply
let him, carrying in her arms
instead the now full jars of water,
and won't the moon be for her now
a reminder of all that
she's carried and sees in her own face
as she bends down to drink;

The beggar, having studied early
about the world-to-come, fears
what he has in this life will be
denied him in the next and quickly
recites the morning

prayer, listing at the end
those pleasures he would keep
for paradise: the smell of citrus,
a feather bed, a plate of fish
or meat. The poorest townspeople
offer him a meal, a coin,
calling him the pious
one when he refuses,
the gracious one when he
accepts. Imagining paradise
of honey, milk, and wine, he turns
to face the watercarrier,
bending, eyes closed, cupping
the moon in his hands like a coin
until all that is left him
as he opens his eyes
is to drink;

The bookseller, though
he does not know how to read,
knows the stories in books
and in people as if reading
were all divining and fragrance,
holding the book open and close
to his face, the people just
at arm's length. He knows everything
they might say or dream,
so that though he can't tell
a page of Yiddish
from a page of Hebrew,
books for women, from books
for men, still the townspeople come
to hear their own sorrows, their lives
retold. So, the watercarrier
listens, and his buckets are just
buckets, buoyed up by the landscape,
and he, standing with them again, feels

the sudden weight of the moon
as the bookseller pauses to drink;

The painter to the moon is all
in blue and leaning back
impossibly, or so
he paints himself, liquid,
arms, legs ribboning out
above the black and white
landscape in miniature,
a curtain of black-
and-white flowers rising to the right.
Everything is a river
flowing away from touch. The painter
reaches for the unseen
moon as if it were capable
of flight and he only
of illumining its course,
every movement, away from him.
In the painting, his brushstroke
is implied, is a pursuit,
leaving the painter and the moon
always the same distance
apart. Only his brush reaches
beyond the canvas where he now looks
to the watercarrier.
This landscape, too, is doubled,
the water too much like a canvas,
and he, mistaking the moon
for his own face, doubles over
in laughter, declines to drink;

The fiddler holds the violin,
thinking to himself it is the moon
he embraces like a lover,
like a child. Really
it is a white cow whose neck

he cradles, arms bent
under and around, and still
he plays beautifully, always
in white face, an exile like the moon,
circling, arriving in places
he's been and forgotten. People,
turning to see who's come, see only
the violin and white face. They think
he is the moon. Really
they are the ones who wander. He plays
to lure them back, and sometimes
the moon is drawn from wandering
to its own likeness as the fiddler
himself is drawn to the white face
and water, never close enough
to drink;

The boy, doing handstands
against the side of the house,
uprights himself, drawn
to the sound of the water
like feet and wheels and dust,
the whole town gathering
in that sound like a wedding
procession, like rejoicing
in the new month, everything
suspended
from the watercarrier's pole,
carried through the village,
from mouth to mouth. The boy,
leaning over the near-empty
buckets, searches for coins,
gleaning the bottom, cutting
his hand on the blade
of the moon, which itself shimmers
and recoils from human
touch. . . .

Exodus

See, the boy would say,
looking back, Wasn't the promise
fulfilled?
        Aren't we now
like stars, the fruitseller nods
to herself.
        Like dust, the poet
agrees, Wandering for another
forty generations, one wilderness
fading into the next and we,
like perfume.
        As if the rabbi
holds us, *lulav* and *etrog*,
shakes us, the marriage broker continues,
to the four winds.
        We were once slaves
in Egypt, the lovers repeat
to each other.
        Go there,
the rabbi chants, Go
even there.
        So, didn't we
follow the moon? the tailor asks.

Like stars, the drunkard
echoes.
        Like seeds, the innkeeper
answers, falling and hiding –

(After all, isn't it the same
landscape, the same moon? the innkeeper's
wife asks her husband) –

behind the sun.

                        Aren't we
the same? the rabbi's wife would almost
ask.
                        Even with our backs turned,
the baker says to his wife, don't we see
the moon's deception, how
constantly it spies
on us?
                        And the bookseller
asks, Isn't it God who told
the moon, 'Go, make yourself
smaller'?
                        God who said when the moon
protested, 'Go then and rule
by day as well as by night,' the beggar
replies.
                        The fishmonger asks
his wife which half
of the moon she prefers, and she,
misunderstanding, slices the herring
down the middle with her thumb,
says, They are the same.

Aren't we, then, like stars?
the butcher asserts, and the moon
like a bride.
                        The fiddler,
who is used to wandering, says, The moon
is a white cow we can neither lead
to slaughter nor leave
behind.
                        The watercarrier fills
his buckets, sets them down
at the edge of the town, just under the moon,
and walks away.

Solitude: The Watercarrier Alone

Does it surprise you
                    I've grown old?
                                        No doubt you will ask
me why this return
                    to the village.
                                        You will argue,
Did Moses
                    return to Egypt?
                                        Did Joshua?
Moses died
                    in the wilderness.
                                        God left him
there. No matter.
                    He was too old,
                                        and Joshua followed
the sun, led his people
                    into battle.
                                        He was young
and too busy
                    to remember,
                                        all that rebuilding.
This is not what
                    you expected,
                                        an old man
wrapped in a white shawl,
                    telling tales,
                                        no walls, no bench,
no prayer.
                    Were you expecting
                                        someone else
or something more?
                    Maybe you will say,
                                        nodding,
I am more
                    like a white cow
                                        than anyone

you have ever met,
                    standing always
                                        yoked, as if
in an embrace,
                    indistinguishable.
                                        You do not want to hear this.
Rather, look
                    at the moon,
                                        how it is
in its white robes
                    like an angel,
                                        how it hovers
as if snagged,
                    incapable
                                        of loosing its hem
any more
                    than we are
                                        capable
of letting it go.

NOTES

Watercarrier under the Moon, Exodus, and *Solitude* are also titles of paint-ings by Marc Chagall where this poem had its start.

The Feast of Booths, also known as Sukkot or the Feast of Tabernacles, celebrates the fall harvest and commemorates the forty years of wander-ing in the desert following the Exodus from Egypt.

At the Passover Seder, "We were slaves in Egypt" is recited because in every generation each individual must regard himself as though he personally has been liberated from slavery.

Etrog is a green lemon and *lulav* is a palm branch, both used in the celebration of Sukkot.

Buttons here refer to phylacteries, which, though now box-shaped, once were button- or coin-shaped leather cases holding slips inscribed with passages of Scripture. These are worn, fastened with leather thongs, one to the forehead and the other to the left arm, during morning prayer on weekdays.

Elijah the prophet, in Jewish folklore a figure of comfort and aid, wanders incognito village to village on his missions of mercy. It is only after he's departed that his true identity is discovered. Jews, therefore, (traditionally) have been instructed to act fairly and generously toward all people who seek food, shelter, or assistance, as though each wanderer were Elijah.

The promise referred to in the second part is God's promise to Abraham: "And I will make thy seed as the dust of the earth; so that if a man can number the dust of the earth, then shall thy seed also be numbered" (Genesis 13:17); and "I will multiply thy seed as the stars of the heaven, and as the sand which is upon the seashore" (Genesis 22:17).

Rebecca Goldstein

Gifts of the Last Night

That the winds had taken possession of Manhattan on this last night of Chanukah; that they were roaming the wide avenue, snarling and hissing like a pack of demons unloosed from Gehenna: this was not the way *she* would ever have described the situation. Pearl Pinsky had little use for metaphor and none at all for old-world hocus-pocus.

The simple facts: It was late December, early dusk, and cold. Devilishly cold. Those winds.

Pearl had been waiting for almost an hour at her bus stop, not far from Columbia University. Classes were suspended for the winter recess, and the neighborhood felt eerily emptied. She stood on the corner all by herself, as the savage evening deepened around her into demented night. Her eyes, streaming cruelly from the cold behind her bifocals, were the lone eyes fixed on the dimming west, from where she expected to see, momentarily, the bright headbeams rounding the corner from Riverside Drive.

Meanwhile it only got darker, and the imps of the air were whooping it up with the ends of the long knitted scarf Pearl was vainly attempting to keep wound across her face, breathing openmouthed into the woolly fluff to generate some warmth.

It was an incongruous scarf to be seen on a middle-aged woman of an otherwise serious cast. Splattered with primary colors, it was like something a little child might have worn, or perhaps even have painted. So that he knew at first glance that this was a woman who gave little thought to appearances.

Beyond the point at which Pearl had given up all hope of seeing her bus tonight; at exactly the moment at which she had even despaired of finding a taxi on this lonely stretch of Broadway, abandoned to godless gusts; just then she turned and noticed a little plain restaurant. Nothing fancy, nothing trendy. To say it was modest is already to overdo it. Not a glance of the brilliance of the festive season fell upon it. Not a single colored lightbulb glimmered, not a glitter of a word had been hung to wish a patron or a passerby a merry this or a happy the other. Squeezed in as it was, between the corner and a dazzlingly done-up Gap store, aglow with a white star and a sentimental message, a person might almost not have noticed it at all, but Pearl had noticed. The winds themselves had taken hold and almost lifted her bodily from the pavement – she was, after all, not so much to lift, a short woman, full-figured, but still, not weighing more than maybe 115 pounds – and had ungently nudged her through the door, slamming it shut behind her, so that again all was calm within the ill-lit establishment, where a lone customer sat eating his apple sauce.

He looked up, his spoon poised on its way to his open mouth, and stared intently at the bedraggled female suddenly deposited before his gaze. The intelligent high forehead, black-framed glasses, and slightly sagging jowls; the bulging book satchel, incongruous scarf, and unravelling skirt drooping from beneath her coat: he took note of all the telling details, but of the scarf most of all. He was a writer.

Pearl endured the writer's scrutinizing unaware. The over-heated air of the restaurant, hitting the frozen lenses of her bifocals, had completely misted them over. She took them off and began to rub them vigorously with one end of her woolen scarf, taking care to do a thorough job of it, since she hated for obscurity of any sort to come between her and the world. So the writer had a few good long minutes in which to arrange his observations and hazard his deductions.

Her age he guessed exactly. It was what she looked, and a woman who wore such a scarf would have taken no pains to disguise the truth.

Years ago, when the writer had been a man in all his vigor, he used to feel a certain mild outrage with such a woman as this, who took so little care to acknowledge and augment the feminine principle within her. This had been a great theme for him, both in his work and in his life: namely, the feminine principle. With him, it had never simply been a matter of a love affair, of which he had had a not insignificant number. Rather it had been a matter of paying homage to the feminine principle, wherever he had happened to find it realized, and available, in this or that particular lady of his acquaintance.

He had been born to a woman who had known, even while he had not yet vacated her womb, that her firstborn would be a boy-child of remarkable genius, destined to transform, at the least, the century. Nothing in his childhood had dimmed his mother's certainty, which had, quite naturally, been duplicated in him. The consequence was that he had been the sort of man who couldn't feel the insistent urgings of his manhood without at the same time endowing them with universal themes and erecting them into a theory of art and of life.

The exact details of this theory we can forget, because even the writer had by now forgotten them. They had gone the way of the urgings. So that now he could examine this woman and take in the telling details with nothing of his old outrage.

All evening long he had been acquiver with anticipation, since tonight was the very last night of Chanukah, and he could not suppress his sense that the universe was not altogether indifferent. It had been the tradition, when he had been a boy, that each successive night of Chanukah his presents from his parents had gotten progressively more wonderful, a practice grounded in sound theology. After all, the ancient miracle of the little holy lamp that had continued to burn on such meager fuel: this miracle had gotten better and better with each passing day.

He couldn't remember now whether his sisters, too, had received gifts of mounting extravagance. His parents had been overworked immigrants, their circumstances cramped. Maybe the sisters had received joint presents, as would have suited what had seemed to him to be their joint existence. He, the supremely only son, had simply thought of the three – Ida, Sophie, and Dorothy – as "the sisters."

But the presents that it had been his to receive on those last nights of the magical Chanukah of his childhood: these he could recall in loving detail until this day. When he had been five years old, he had received a tiny violin, sized just right for his little cheek and shoulder. When he had been six it had been the entire set of the *Book of Knowledge* encyclopedia, all of whose twenty-five volumes, with appendix, he had read by the time he was eight. In fact, it had been of his beloved *Book of Knowledge*, with its many magnificent pages of full-colored plates, that he had only now been thinking, when the restaurant door was flung open and his attention diverted. So that when Pearl Pinsky finally returned her de-fogged bifocals to the bridge of her nose – not a bad nose, he had noted, though a little wide – she found an old man's watery, red-rimmed eyes avidly fixed upon her.

By this time, the writer knew what he knew, and he closed his mouth around a smile as if he and this woman were on old familiar terms with one another.

"Do I know you?" asked Pearl.

"Such winds," responded the writer, with a sympathetic little shiver. "Snarling and hissing like a pack of demons unloosed from Gehenna."

"Gehenna!" the woman gave a short little hoot of a laugh. She had a high-pitched voice, more girlishly sweet than he would have anticipated, with just a hint of the plaintive to curdle it. Without any ceremony, she came over and sat herself down opposite the writer at his little formica table against the wall. "Gehenna!" she repeated as she placed her bookbag and purse on the floor between her feet. "I thought it was supposed to be hot in Gehenna!"

"You thought wrong," the writer answered, and at last took the spoonful of apple sauce into his mouth.

Pearl was inclined to hoot once again, but she only snorted, and rather gently at that. The man across from her – palsied and bent, with only his imperious nose and vivid eyes still undiminished – was about the same age that her own father would have been, although her father would have had even less use than she for the quaint choice in metaphor just voiced. Simon Pinsky had been all sorts of things in his lifetime, including the editor of a Jewish anarchist newspaper, which had had its heyday when Pearl had been a child. She and her anarchist father had been comrades till the end, and Pearl had always felt most comfortable with men of Simon's generation.

"You know, it's a funny thing," she confided, after she had given her order for tomato soup to the young waitress. "I wait at this corner almost every evening for my bus, and I never once noticed this restaurant."

"You're probably preoccupied. You strike me as a very preoccupied person."

He stared at her for some moments more.

"I wonder," he began slowly.

"Yes?" Pearl prompted.

"I wonder if you even realize what tonight is."

She looked at him blankly.

"It's the eighth night of Chanukah – the very last night – the best night!" He finished on a high note, almost a squeak. A spray of spittle punctuated his excitement.

"Well, you're right there," Pearl answered, frankly taken aback.

The old man was leaning toward her, his striped tie in his apple sauce, his eyes, protuberant to begin with, gazing into hers with strange meaning. "I mean you're right that I wasn't aware."

"I knew it! I knew you had forgotten!"

"It doesn't mean all that much to me."

"You think you have to tell me that? You think I can't figure that out for myself?" he demanded in an aggrieved tone. He sat back in a sulk.

"So why's the last night the best night?" Pearl asked him. Her father had also had a quirky temper, as had many of the men of his generation whom Pearl had known, so she was an old pro when it came to this kind of appeasement. "I never heard that one," she threw in for good measure.

He didn't want to admit to her that the source of his pronouncement was only the order in which he had received his Chanukah presents as a boy. She was clearly a very intelligent woman. He wouldn't be surprised to learn that she was a lady professor. But still she was also, just as clearly, a person completely ignorant on the subject of Jewishness, so that he could lie to her if he wanted, which he did want.

"It's part of the religion," he said, and took another spoonful of his apple sauce.

"So, if this is the best night, you should at least have some potato latkes to go with that apple sauce," she said, smiling so girlishly sweet that he immediately repented. It was a mean trick to mislead a person about her own religion.

"You know what, Miss?"

"Pearl," said Pearl.

"Pearl. I have a little something for you."

He reached down into his pants pocket, fumbling around until he pulled out a little black book and handed it across the table to her. It was cheap imitation black leather, embossed with gold Hebrew letters.

"It's a Jewish calendar," he said, smiling with the sudden pleasure of his own generosity. "Organizations are always sending them to me, whether I send them back a donation or not. This one happens to be the nicest, but I have others. Take it, it's hardly even used. One or two appointments I had in September, I penciled them in, but I'm not so much in demand as I used to be. It's almost as good as new, Pearl. And all the Jewish holidays they've got printed up, even the exact moment of the sunset when they start. This way you'll at least know when you're not observing."

"Well, thank you," Pearl said, her voice gone more girlish than ever. "Will you inscribe it for me?" she asked, a little shyly.

"With pleasure," he answered. He was, after all, a writer. It wasn't the first time in his life his autograph had been shyly requested. Women, young and old, single and married, used to flock when he had given readings, and then they would line up afterwards to have him sign copies of his stories that they had clipped out from the Jewish dailies.

Pearl began to fish around in her purse for something to write with, but he quickly produced his own beautiful silver fountain pen, a gift he had received many years ago from one of his wealthier girlfriends.

"Chanukah, 19—," Pearl read. "With my best wishes on the last night – I. M. Feigenbaum."

Pearl looked up, her intelligent high forehead creased into wondering disbelief, her bifocals slipping down to the very tip of her short wide nose. "I. M. Feigenbaum? Are you *the* I. M. Feigenbaum? I. M. Feigenbaum, the *writer?*"

"You know me?" the writer whispered, barely able to control his quivering voice. "You know me?"

Did Pearl Pinsky know I. M. Feigenbaum? And how she knew I. M. Feigenbaum! His brief heyday had coincided with the brief heyday of her father's paper, and sometimes Simon would receive a manuscript of a short story from the young author. Pearl's father had *detested* the writer I. M. Feigenbaum. It was not simply that this upstart was a sentimental bourgeois, whose writing did not even acknowledge the great class struggles of the day. It was far worse. His stories wallowed in superstition and obscenity, unnatural lusts alternating with old-world hocus-pocus, and Simon Pinsky had regarded each and every page from the pen of I. M. Feigenbaum as a profound and personal insult.

"Don't defile our trash cans with it!" Simon Pinsky would command his wife, who helped out with the editing. Our garbage is too good to be associated with it! Flush it down the toilet, Hannah!"

Simon Pinsky, as radical as he had been in his politics, had also had an almost rabbinical aversion to vulgarity. To hear him utter such a word as "toilet" was painful for his wife and daughter. (A secret: Hannah Pinsky, an otherwise dutiful wife, had saved each and every one of those rejected manuscripts.) In any case, such was the effect that the writer I. M. Feigenbaum used to have on Simon Pinsky.

Pearl's was a forthrightly truthful personality. When she knew something, her procedure was to come right out and say it. It was in her nature, therefore, to explain precisely how it was that she came to know so well the name of I. M. Feigenbaum.

But for once in her life, she held her tongue. Staring across the little formica table at the trembling old man, whose face was luminous with the wonder of this extravagant gift, Pearl Pinsky blessedly held her tongue.

Roger Weingarten

An American *Bubbe-mayseh*

The real question is this:
from what can a Jew earn a living?
                    – Shalom Aleichem

The chartreuse sunroof of the red Bug
appeared up the street before
it skidded through the plate glass
of Feigel's Cut'N'Curl, where –
in a raven-haired pageboy caught
in the low beams admiring her cameo
appearance in the sheen of a customer's
nail – Feigel looked up at her movie
about to shatter in the *fartootst*
grin shimmering across the driver's
kisser. As he drove her through coiffure
catalogs ejected from laps, Feigel
appeared transported by this *tummler* who,
in less than the customary flash, saw
his life and new wife pass through another
window into the future, where he glimpsed
the graven boils of time travel that
covered her, *ongepotchket,* from head to toe.
Her comely skin was more than skin to him
and – giving a *geshrai* that could be heard
from the fleshpots of Egypt to Volcano,
Hawaii – he swore he'd undo the flaw
in their fate or bust. *Bopkes,* she replied.
He repaired the Bug, anointed her wounds
and drove her back and forth from the Bay
of Fundy to Lake Superior. In Buffalo, they
got lucky pulling up to a specialist in a '59
custom Merc with red and white realfur dice

swinging from the mirror, who, unrolling
his window, said, Well, *kinderlach,* a glass
of tea and a *shmooze* would be nice, but I've
got to catch the red eye to Martinique, where
I'm performing my latest technique on a sci fi
plosher who swore a cancer on his mother if
his master bedroom wasn't a Buddhist monastery
from Mars. So what's all the *kvetching?* Was I
kvetching? Can I save my Feigellah – a beauty
mavin no less, a *baleboosteh* and a virgin –
from this *chozzerai? Shmo,* he advised, find a
schmuck who'll give suck to the boils or lower
your own lips to the poison and pretend you're
blowing her *shofar* in reverse. Better yet, say
a *broche* over her blintzes, *Nu?* – and that's
my bottom line. The light and the man
turned green. Self-hate and nausea roiled and
screamed in his ear like customers crowding
the meat counter of a delicatessen. But Feigel
got this gleam in her eye like she could see
to the other side of appearances. They took
a suite overlooking Niagara Falls, where a
seagull-studded aquamarine sky illuminated
a heart-shaped hot tub. The bride eased
her way into churning waters. The groom
followed suit, puckered, hummed a little Rumanian
wedding dance, then dived for another. Breaking
the surface, he praised her reemerging beauty,
but just as he pulled away to admire his
handiwork, she vanished. He *chlopped* tears and
cursed her absence until, looking down at his
shrivelled macaroons floating on the suddenly
still waters, he had an epiphany: That he
had swallowed her in a driving passion, that he
loved his work, like a scholar, more than life,
and that she was his first customer. Thanking
Feigel for her sacrifice, he wrapped himself

in a valentine coverlet. That night,
she returned in a dream. They were taking it
slow in the Bug's dashboard glow across
the bridge between the States and Canada when
Feigel lowered her window and jumped. He woke
in a sweat, drove back and forth between
borders until a customs officer issued him
a jar of spirits, reminding him that when
shnapps goes in, the secret comes out. He raved
in a rest area while Feigel floated out
of the corner of his vision, *utzing* him
to publicize his new profession. Enough
already!, he croaked when wind and the day
broke in the manner of a late eighteenth-century
Romantic landscape. Liking *shmutz,* so to speak,
between his toes, he became an itinerant
boilsucker, his Bug decked out in decals
that boasted his finesse. Customers from
Painesville to the headwaters of the Mississippi
kvelled over his hydraulic sunroof that popped
like the swollen flesh he attended. He floated
downriver on a barge to the costumed wildlife
of the French Quarter to open a custom shop
for an even more specialized practice. Raven-haired
Feigel rematerialized at the breakfast table,
where he was teasing an egg over easy
with the tip of his fork, while Reba LaSadnik
poured Slivovitz into the cookie jar.
I've come back with a boil between the Blue Hole
of Sandusky and the La Brea tar pits, Feigel
blushed. Hush, my little *kreplach,* said the man
in white patent leather and string tie. We'll
drive to Le Bon Temps Roule Professional Plaza,
where, with your permission, I'll take a peak.
A *mitzva,* said Reba, a stringer for *The Hadassah
Flash* – I'd love to assist, but I've got an itty-
bitty deadline. He helped Feigel out of the Bug,

not rushing her through his elegantly appointed
waiting room's wall-to-wall elite clientele. Reba
will grow on you, he whispered under the operating
theater's recessed light. I've missed you,
Feigel moaned. His nostrils flared. Pulling back
from the long-forgotten beauty-parlor vapors
exhumed from the humid time capsule of her wound,
he called her name and there they were, hair
dryers akimbo and hairdos *farpotchket* beyond
repair, holding hands through the windshield
of the red Bug, the sound of glass splintering
into a Milky Way still in their ears. But how
would they get by, Feigel wondered. The more she
eyeballed his chartreuse sunroof, the angrier
she waxed, until, biting into his *shnozzle*
to render him helpless, she used sign language
to secure the name of his insurance agent. Agent
shmagent. I'll make it up to you with caresses
and a bowl of prunes *shmeered* with honey. Did she
let go of his *shnoz?* Did he touch her cheek?
Would her *mishpoche* bless
such a union? Wouldn't you like to know.

Collaborator

Not unlike the Hungarian long
distance runner who never

competed but only ran
to honor the State, I

bathed before tiptoeing
down the hall to scrub

oats out of the pot
I never ate from, not only

sacrificing my writing
time for the greater

good of the family core, but so,
when you bent to open the double

doors of our post-war formica
and chrome cabinet looking

for the missing pot, you
would find it swaying

like a banner in the lap
of your warm-blooded mate,

throw off your robe, crawl in
and collaborate.

Paradise

There it is before you . . . always mute
with an air of whispering.
                            – Joseph Conrad

Running, like a startled miniature
English ship around the bovine

Holier-than-thou, cud-chewing
Armada, a pig will never –

Scratching a merry dance of cork screw
Tail against grass –

Piss like an ungrateful
Child in the wind or on a cousin

If it can help it. Mother Mary help me
Say the sow, tireless and heaving

On her side for suckling pigs,
Has a look in her eye emulated by all the great

Religious figures of the Holy Mysteries. A cloud
Covers the moon and God's squealing mob wakes

In the still brooding chill of an inscrutable
Intention that never said you must

Dine on the pink
Tapestry of flesh or thumb your nose

At those that do. Skip to
The nineteen ninety-two Italian Conference

On International Jewish Pig Farming, where,
Over a loudspeaker, a Peruvian Jewish

Pig farmer claimed Israelis had lost
Their moral beauty, because, like all other

Farmers working in mud from Peking to Oskaloosa,
They now owned swine and acted like it.

You can bet your paycheck the Israeli
Contingent gnashed their teeth, swearing

On their ancestors only
An Israeli could raise an authentic

Jewish hog near the Sea of Galilee and wouldn't
Budge from that position. Nevertheless, International

Jewish *charcuteries* and smokehouses evoke a fear
So deep in the nostrils of the enemy, their memory

Brings dread after years have obliterated
Every trace. Even if J.P.F. isn't the most

Controversial of all vocations, it is
Hard in the extreme for the naked eye

To capture. One specialist, crossing
His heart and hoping to die after a thousand

Nights of Jewish Pig farming, was inhaling
A mixture of holy water

And a rare gas, when a cloud began
To materialize over his small

Brazier. He dropped a pinch of fragrance
Onto the fire. An apparition

Appeared, lying on its side, more
Exquisite in hue and beauty, Selah!, than any

Living thing he ever laid eyes upon. Only
Words could describe the barely

Visible turn of her cloven foot, the ruby
Flare of her nostril. So *boychik?* she said

without saying it, holding
A nosegay of iridescent blue

And fragrant flowers that vanished
And reappeared at her desire . . . He woke

In a private sanitarium in the alps, a bouquet
Of alpflowers cradled in his arms, swaying

On a porch swing above the cool
Meadow of clouds, looking down, halleluyah,

Over the green blanket rustling in the light
Jabber of breeze

And then his eyes glazed over.

Richard Chess

First Day

In the afterglow of what was given
In *Sivan*, they walk
On a scroll of land until the scroll ends,
Where they wait and gaze
Ahead, just beyond the tip
Of the tongue, at that which is
Called not *Israel*, exactly, or *ease*.
Why not settle here, where
One world dissolves
Into another and what one
Loves is not the crown
Once worn, briefly, but the knowledge
That *deserve* has no say
In what one receives?
They have not been chosen
To lay their burden down
Here. Beneath their feet, the scroll
Has been wrapped around
Again to *bereshit*. It's the first day
Of school, roll is being
Called and they are accountable
For what the teacher marks
Beside their names: present, absent.

Sivan: a month on the Hebrew calendar. *Shavuot,* a holiday celebrating the giving of the *Torah,* is celebrated during this month.

Correspondence

A woman who lost a son to the Land
Writes letters daily to the Land.
She addresses the envelope to the Land
With no return address. She lives
At No Return Address where she waits
For the Land to return her son.
Her letters reach the Land
Of Dead Letters and lie in a box
With letters from other mothers
Of No Return Address. When the box is full,
The letters are burned to empty the box
For new letters. Even if the Land could write,
What would it write to the woman who lost her son?
So many mothers have lost children to the Land.
The Land attends to children
Who find their way home. For the children
Of the Diaspora, it has no time.
The Diaspora must care for them, protect them
From the Land that has taken in
The children of so many women
Who devote their lives to composing
Letters to which they receive no reply.

Between Wars

When it's over, we skin the war
And study its skeleton.
An archeologist brushes dirt from a bone
She turns in her hand.
She and the man to whom she comes
Between wars turn over and over
In a cold bed. A student turns
A tall page of *Talmud.*
Interrogated, a suspect from the territories
Turns over names of his neighbors.
Then he is turned out to the desert
Where he is lost until a veil
Lifts and reveals a road.
God turns to observe the familiar world
Hosing blood off its surfaces.
An hour passes, a season
Passes, a cycle of holidays
Completes its turn. A visitor turns
To his host, a woman who lost
A son in the last war.

Ball

At the end of his youth, he kicks
    a ball as hard and as high
        as he can into the air.

It rises over the roof of the brick
    building where his grandfather rocks,
        and rises

over his grandmother frying slices of
    eggplant for breakfast, her body
        a wire soon to be cut. Tomorrow,

he leaves the neighborhood
    for basic training. Today he kicks
        the ball harder and higher

into the air crowded with ancestors
    to whom they appeal, his superstitious
        grandparents, for comfort, a shield

for their grandson, a few extra shekels
    for lamb. *Empty sky,*
        he says to himself. There's no one

to keep score, the children in school,
    the men who have recently finished
        their service asleep or rebuilding

a carburetor or working on a deal,
    the mothers waiting with their pink-
        eyed, rheumy babies to see

a doctor. No score to be kept.
    The ball's covering is scuffed
        from hard use, Friday afternoons

while chickens boil and ammonia-water
    dries on the swept steps
        in each unit of this complex of low-

income housing. It's a black sun
    rising, a beaten face
        falling to the street.

S. Ben-Tov

How Your Father and I Built Israel's First Rocket

This poem is dedicated to Professor Meir Birk.

"Well,
    when shots stopped the spring
        physics lecture, the class turned

into soldiers and I was one.
    The army gave me its book,
        Principles of Rocketry,

a hand-me-down from some GI,
    his signature on the flyleaf;
        and ten sections of Shell's

abandoned oil line, standing
    like armored panpipes.
        Home became the workshed

where scientists machined
　　ideas to halt tanks
　　　　thirty miles away. But how

could I, untried at everything
　　except chalk and blackboard,
　　　　build rockets? One day,

your father stopped the doorway
　　with winged-looking arms
　　　　that shone, fresh off the kibbutz,

like a mechanic who had flown.
　　He flung down his knotted sack,
　　　　and lifted out an ugly flute:

lo retta means *no recoil,*
　　so I named his recoilless gun
　　　　for the beautiful Loretta

Young . . . yes, the 'heart of civilization'
　　beat close, in each café
　　　　where actresses' famous backs

wore lace, and poets' hands
　　debated lightly over cream cakes!
　　　　Tel-Aviv was loved.

But many nights, our bulbs glared
　　when the only other light
　　　　was a bomb, falling . . . Well.

Have you seen Mount Calvary?
　　Bare rock behind gilded glass
　　　　inside the Holy Sepulchre?

It stands no higher than that hill
over whose buried ruins
a dense vine rolled like smoke;

your father dug a launching-pit
and hit the outright stones.
Positioned, our sealed pipe

trailed a fuse like kite string.
Then it soared ten meters.
We danced in the air, crying

'The first Jewish rocket!'
Now the empty site is all
tight-lipped sandwich buildings

and floodlights,
surrounded
by a very sensitive wall.

My dear, you could drive by,
but not enter. No one
will believe you want to see

the base because of poetry.
Imagine a wild gully where
the rocket rests, a branch of rust,

and its cordite fuel a stain.
That stolen British cordite –
I recall how it came packed

in small magenta bags
charming the hand, stiff and silken,
like a gift."

The Last Minute

I asked for my father's help,
the last time we were alive

together. He jimmied
the door with his credit card,

and the latch unstruck.
I had lost my keys. He let me

into my apartment; a sunned
windowshade was rattling.

His usual rushed hug
and shy kiss, full of eyeblinks,

brought close the mystery
of his shrinking pupils,

brought close the surprised
irises, like crumpled jade,

brought close the terrain
of his gaunt, light-stained face

that felt, like his hard chest,
made of tested materials.

For seconds, the windowshade
paused off the sill,

like a page,
sunlight filled the doorway;

we stood holding each other
face to face, a simple tree

that bore father and daughter,
our shared look

a colloquy of leaves;
face to face like capital Y

we stood,
the penultimate letter;

and a smile dazzled,
I cannot remember whose.

The string shade-pull
dangled its plastic lily,

the room breathed newly-
thawed turf and budded trees,

while behind us, in oak
shadow, the back stairs

scored black
by shoes,

descended from my door
around the brown, spiral

interior of the turret-shell
in my recurrent dream.

Before that smile faded,
waiting had replaced him;

before the shade sighed shut,
he hurried downstairs.

Ashes

On old wood scarified with knots,
the strong dark planks of that garret,
I sat like a squaw of the Pequot,
pale telephone to my ear, crosslegged,

and listened to my father's widow hiss
that I had no rights in respect to his
cremated body. I had not known
anything was saved after his plane went down,

I had believed no mote of him was left,
(I whispered) till a strange bill came today;
after twelve months of breathing the false air
that had lifted, then gulfed in fire my father

in plain view of O'Hare
airport, nine hundred feet from the runway.
Even the child of a divorce may feel bereft
of a mourner's rites? Her rightful

wife's voice rose with assured spite,
"The will gives me his material assets.
That means his things. Things includes ashes."
I stroked the mountain ranges folded

through oak grain. I sat on killed wood
and took the law like blows until I understood
later, the bright brass box his ashes
were assigned, and the pigeonhole, glassed-in

and locked, where they sit like cash –
paternal cinders, whose own parents plunged
out of chimneys into the deathcamp's lungs.
And with my storied skeleton, I stood.

Steven Schneider

Joseph

Joseph is a fruitful son. In the late afternoon
In the garden, in summer, the skin
Of raspberries is deep red. When you bend to pick them,
The neighborhood girls, in their white cotton summer dresses,
Run up to the fence to catch a glimpse of you.
In the heat of the day, they want to burst into flower.

But you never step out of yourself.
You collect your berries and sit in the shade of a plum tree,
Just out of sight, dreaming of your brothers.
You can see their arrows passing over you.
When Pharaoh's wife tried to seduce you,
You did not lift your eyes to look at her.

In the dark, in the cellar of the prison,
You practice your art of interpretation.
The sun's radiant yellow light pierces
The butler's and baker's stories.
You read them as clearly as spring water.
The hard rock of knowledge composes you.

Zebulun

Two blue fish swim inside
The red waters of your window.
The letters of your name, Zebulun, hover above.
Their sounds rumble inside the mouth's cove,
Spill out from the palate like bounty
From within the belly of a ship.

Your tribe's members are merchants and sailors,
Buying and selling precious gems,
Shipping oranges and dates from the plains.
To rehearse the distance between ports
You walk the shore line
Accommodating vision to changes in weather and sky.

Freely, you share your wealth with Issachar.
His eyes hover over squiggly black lines of text
Inside the tent of learning,
While you work the seas.
He breathes in, you breathe out –
Suspended together in the light of this world and the next.

Asher

Chagall bestows upon you the greatest gifts.
Doves, bouquets, and a menorah
Fill your window with light.
And what is Asher but light –
The inner light of happiness,
The outer light of the body.

Happy is he who dwells in the tribe of Asher.
He will eat black olives, halvah
And rich sweet breads that rise high.
It will be *Shabbat* all week long.
The wings of the dove are flowers,
a twig of peace pursed inside its beak.

The green in your window
Is the tint of olive trees lining your fields.
The menorah is filled with oil.
Happiness wafts like incense in the air –
It pulls the viewer deep and far in
To taste the bliss on her tongue.

Norman Finkelstein

from Passing Over

Neither remembered nor forgotten
but remembered and forgotten
with an uncanny simultaneity,
an image chosen at random
from the constant course of a life
or an image smuggled in,
stolen from the life of another,
takes on inordinate weight,
an illegitimate density,
frustratingly conditional
in the context of a poem
that claims nothing for itself
and everything for the image
it is compelled to withhold.

The poem as servant of memory
is notoriously unreliable.
The poem serves two masters:
an image chosen at random
means untold numbers of images
have been consigned to oblivion.
There were ten stores on the block
and a shul on the corner.
They may be gone now
nor could they be preserved
if they appeared in the poem.
It would be pointless to describe them
from such a great distance
after so many years.

Remembrance serves the rememberer
and never the thing remembered.
No one would deny the images
and the stories which belonged to them.
No one would turn his back
on the narratives that return,
that make it across the border.
But who will take them seriously,
peering out of the half-light,
searching for the familiar spots
which have disappeared long since?
It's as if a deal had been cut
with the bosses of history:
to listen and to forget.

But if this were a prelude
to a ritual of remembrance
performed around the spaces
which oblivion has seized;
if this were an introduction
to a thesis on forgetting,
a study of the ways of images
clinging to their existence;
then its pages would be interspersed
with indecipherable signs
and it would be bound in silence
and passed from hand to hand
to be read out at the table
all in one night.

yermiyahu ahron taub

a house calling

in a mansion of nineteenth-century medicine,
site of unimpeachable respectability and folly,
an old game is replayed.
it's far away, of course, where it has to be,
where it can only be. under the eaves,
in the attic, maybe. only you know.
there, two children move into a vision of taut transformation.
unravel go polyester pants
and white stringed cotton and smooth pale
harps and clavicle are revealed.
sister, come with me.
help me with the folds of this impossible
turban, careful with the rhinestones. tell me
what you would do with silk tunic: are its
long yellow lines enough for tonight,
this one and only night?
and of this skirt, when the men return
from *shul*, what will they know?
all the babies in the world
and still such a woman. tonight,
they'll have to see for themselves.
will it be clear, big sister?
come on, this once, let's go down and see
what mother thinks.

father grocer

it was on the corner, where he
enacted our livelihood,
literally.
in jars of cane and rows of cans, days were painted.
not in muted sepia, as today, but in tones of
necessity. flour poured forth from endless wells
of dust, boxes sighed in ancient knowing,
and the forearms of hardworking men gleamed
in fast power. women came to arrange feasts
for the most attentive of lords and
girls to study.
presiding over all, ensuring the surest transaction
he stood in creases of welcome.
in a time of rumor, he made certainty,
in days of destruction, he brought the driest of goods
to incandescence.

tsholnt

you must note the perfect pallor of
those potatoes, the
persistent wink of the yam,
the round green of the outer onion,
the cloves that traveled far from
caves of former colonies
to seduce the most elusive of flanks,
the list that cannot explain the way
the chef was driven,
the whimsical grin of the divine.

tsholnt (Yiddish): a stew served on the Sabbath

Naomi Feigelson Chase

Gittel's Fast

At dinner, when she cuts
the black radish,
its hairs pull her to the ground.

The fish jumps from the plate.
Gittel puts her fork down.
"Poor radish," she says, "poor fish."

Her mother fries an egg in butter,
sprinkles cheese.
"Gittel, darling, eat."

On Gittel's plate, the chick breaks the yolk,
its feathers like her doll's hair.
"Just water, mother."

That night the voice tells her,
Eat
what your mother gives you.

"The radish tugs me. The egg gives birth.
The fish weeps when the fork pricks.
Its eyes punish me."

The fish has a short life.
You give it purpose.
A hungry fool hears what isn't said.

"An empty stomach sharpens ears.
I hear the Rabbi guess his wedding price;
the sheep bleat, roasting

for the bridal meal; I hear
wheat spring from seed,
the babies' cry in Joseph's breath."

Empty mouths, empty heads.
You'll get small from hunger
big from Joseph.

"So what do I do with a fool's love?"

Give it to me.

The Interrogation

Cold like devil's cold, men like shadows.

"How can an ignorant girl
speak to the Holy One,
Blessed Be He?"

"An ignorant girl cannot speak to rabbis.
I want my parents here,
a lawyer, if this is a trial."

"Your father may come.
We cannot look at women
and talk of holy things."

"You're looking at me.
My mother and I are made alike."
They call her parents in.

"Before seeing God did you fast like Rabbi Isaac,
    head between your knees, mouth to the ground,
    whispering God's other names?"

"I never saw God,
    and some books say
    all Rabbi Isaac saw was floor."

"How did God make Eve?"

"Midrash says that God created Eve from the rib,
    not from the head lest she be vain
    not from the eye lest she flirt
    not from the ear lest she eavesdrop
    not from the heart lest she be jealous
    not from the hand lest she be thievish
    not from the foot lest she be a gadabout.

    But I say God made Eve from dust, like Adam.
    Some one else made second Eve."

"Your books tell you this?"

"At the beginning, why would God give Adam,
    with so much work to do, a woman
    half as good as he?

"This is a witch pretending
    a bootmaker's daughter."
"Or a demon, pretending a girl."

Emily Warn

Raking the Gravel

All August, the empty lot fakes being a garden.
Pink and white sweet peas tangle in a trellis
of rusted wire, ripe pods swaying like wind chimes.
The blackberries ripen and nod above plumes
of dried grasses. And in the tough, spindly gorse bushes,
spiders string delicate nets to capture yellow flowers,
petals closed like the folded wings of moths.

Each morning I sit still here,
a stray cat in my cave of weeds,
and listen to Esther tell me
about the lot's higher purpose,
how it became holy by being quiet in the sun.
I don't believe her. But I want her to talk
as she does in August when all her gardens
rattle with flowers and gourds. I know she knows
my inner calm is dumb and blank from playing safe
with an old god. She used to doven like crazy, too,
she tells me. She'd rock back and forth
words looped together in a moan sent to heaven
like smoke from racetrack cigars.
No place, no thought, no hunger safe
from God's anger, unless she mouthed the lucky prayers.
She knew them all: the blessing for meat, for milk,
for fruit, for rain, for tears, for wine.
She wore sackcloth and ashes, shaved her head,
beat her breast, and turned her back
on summer to pray in the windowless synagogue.
And God, she said, never answered
like wind in the dried pods.
I sit there silent, letting Esther's words

clear a safe place in broken glass
and blackberry vines. She reads my silences
as first growth, thin grass that grows
after they cart off rubble and backfill
the foundation with dirt. Soon, she promises,
I'll talk tough, thorny and bristled,
lush and clamoring as her tangled lot.

Solitary Date Orchard

Yes, I wrestled
with pillars of light,
of dust. Yes, I solved
oracles, proverbs, parables.
A bell rings in a palm tree.
(I am not making this up.)
I climb into its nub,
sit under ribbed green fronds
that sift through trinkets
the wind hoists. Iridescent
pigeon feathers, eucalyptus quills
land in my lap. I spill my gleanings
into the roses, scattered seeds.
Who needs angel blessings,
the obedience clause
in fine print? Why work
at descendants? Soon people
will outnumber pollen.
Just this digit of earth,
this slow pendulum ride,
swinging from shadow
to light to shadow,
this small plot hatching
Egyptian bottle flies,
red ants, Anna's hummingbirds.
No chiseled covenants. No fixed source.

I'm Telling! Secrecy and Shame in One
Jewish-American Family

1

When I was twenty-five years old my mother informed me, in a letter, that she'd been married before she married my father. I had a slew of questions to ask her, though she'd made it clear in her concluding sentence that she did not want to discuss the marriage with me. I tried, anyway, on several occasions, to talk with her about her first husband and their lives together. She refused to speak. I read and reread the letter. My mother wrote that they had eloped to California. Her parents, she explained, did not approve of this man, and her mother begged her to come home. She felt increasing remorse for running away. She had an illegal abortion. She found her husband irresponsible. Eventually she decided to leave him and returned – determined to do the right thing – to her parents' house. Her parents managed to get the marriage annulled. Shortly thereafter, my mother met my father, a man who was willing to have her, though she was, in her own words, *soiled goods.*

Today, seventy-five years old, my mother is famous, among my friends, for her stubbornness, her *refusals* to eat more, to exercise, to take a trip. When I ask myself why she held herself back from a happier life, I turn up one answer: she would not explore or adventure without my father's participation and assent. Because he did not want to travel, she never traveled. Because he had no interest in the world of ideas, she did not venture there. Seeing her marriage as the center and centerpiece of her life, she allowed herself only compatible thoughts and activities. Thus, any discussion of her romantic/sexual life before my father had to be annulled, like the marriage itself.

I told my parents that I was a lesbian at the end of graduate school. Though I had had women lovers for years, I feared that my parents would cut off my financial support, so I postponed the inevitable *telling*. I knew that my lesbianism would rupture the family, cause suffering, and end the mostly-stable relations we enjoyed. I was also queasy about the intimacy any discussion of sex involved. Our satisfactory relations rested upon our living in different cities, our speaking about pre-approved topics (no politics, drugs, hitchhiking), and our agreeing to "accept" my substituting a *Jay* for a *Jane* and an *Andrew* for an *Andrea*. If they suspected, I didn't know about it. When the second wave of the women's movement broke over college campuses, I jumped. Into the revolution. Suddenly, I had the structure in which to rethink heterosexual coupling, the workplace, childrearing. Conscious-ness-raising deepened my commitment to myself, to a life as an artist, to loving women, to my own voice. Thus, historical acci-dent propelled me into a powerful sense of my own possibilities. By twenty-five, I had a very different self-concept than my mother had at the same age.

I learned of my mother's nose job when my sister, Jill, thirteen years old, met with the surgeon to discuss the shape and style and structure of the nose she was getting. "All of us had nose jobs," my mother said, referring to herself and her two sisters. She laughed, "Your Bubbie thought they would help us get husbands."

In a clear memory, I am dragging a kitchen chair to the cupboard in the kitchen that contains my sister's medication. I am con-vinced that I will uncover the secret of my sister's illness, if I can only see the box in which the large amber capsules come. Inside the box is a folded paper with very small print. I am seven years old, a good reader, but most of the words are unfamiliar to me. In a paragraph subtitled "Side Effects," I understand almost noth-ing. One word occurs in every section: *epilepsy*.

These four memories focus on particular arenas in which secrecy flourishes: marriage arrangements, sexuality, the commodification of women, and health/illness. Ghosting them all is the economic master narrative of European immigration at the beginning of this century: the progress from Russian *shtetl* to North American urban ghetto to American suburb. This overdetermined story is marked by anti-Semitism, the history of Jewish expulsion, the pressure to assimilate and resettle. (An analogous labor narrative reflects increasing education, wealth, privilege.) In the instance of my own family, I feel the proximity of the *shtetl*, I see the dirt roads that led to my great-grandmother's home and animal barn, to the study house to which my grandmother's brothers went each day. And though the social/economic strictures of that culture prevented my grandmother from getting the education (secular or religious) she wanted, the narrative predicts that two generations later I might become the first grandchild in my family to get a college degree. Although Czarist Russia lived on in my imagination, it represented, to my grandmother, an old world relinquished for the new. While she spoke with love for her own parents and grandparents, she held Russia in contempt for the social, class, and religious persecution that forced her family to flee.

2

Transgress: to go beyond or over a limit or boundary; exceed or overstep; to act in violation of the law; to commit an offense.

A second-generation American, I grew up in a clannish, Yiddish-speaking household. I was aware, throughout my childhood, of the tension between allegiance to kin and to *outsiders*. My parents wanted their children to be well-educated, "cultured," and "refined"; at the same time, they wanted us to remain loyal to our aunts, uncles, and cousins, to the forms of American Judaism (Seders and synagogue attendance on High Holidays) that held meaning for them. My parents belonged, for thirty-odd years, to a Jewish country club, created, I was told, in reaction to the exclusivity (read anti-Semitism) of the local clubs. Club membership presented a paradox. Though the world grew bigger with membership (new people, new landscape), my parents remained inward-looking, more focused on sameness than difference. In this context, I've come to construct my mother's secrecy about her previous marriage. The social world to which she belonged required, in her view, obedience to a prescribed set of images of marriage and family. Her immigrant parents had a vision for her future that she thwarted by eloping with an "inappropriate" man. When she left him and returned to her parents' house – having tried to break out once – she rededicated herself to her parents' goals and purposes. But, as life would have it, "transgression" surfaced, unable to remain repressed. In a cruel twist of fate, my convention-seeking mother got an outspoken, Jewish-identified lesbian daughter. On good days, I feel that I represent the part of my mother that she dutifully learned to shut out, the part that she agreed to deny.

Any consideration of secrecy has to consider its twin sister: shame. When a person has understood the social and moral conventions of her group and chooses against them, shame is born. Belonging precedes shame. In the case of my own lesbianism, the fantasy of belonging (to heterosexuality, to the nuclear family model as I saw it) deterred me from exploring my own sexuality. When that exploration became inevitable, the fantasy of belonging silenced me. Subsequently, when I could no longer deny the truth of my own feelings, when the fantasy of belonging no longer protected me, I experienced the shame of *choosing against belonging.* Secrecy and shame hold hands in the night. They are the sisters who, despite their exile, never leave the family. They are tied to it despite their outcast status and rejection. Begotten by those who belong, secrecy and shame are obsessed with *belonging*, the contested ground of their birth and being. Thus, *belonging* becomes the subject of their lives. Any radical social dislocation (choosing to be gay or lesbian, for example) can reformulate the ostensible "subject," but the " – longing" of "belonging" remains, like a nimbus.

Twenty-odd years have passed since I told my parents I was a lesbian. In that time, I've worked hard (and so have they) to redefine "family" to include the circle of friends, lovers, and ex-lovers essential to my life. Most important, I've trained myself to speak, to welcome (as much as possible) the secrecy *and* shame that I know hover just outside the door. Once invited in, secrecy and shame unmask, disarm, trade stories. The stories are sometimes painful, disturbing, sad, egregious; nevertheless, they are always bearable, preferable to silence.

3

Too Jewish

You'll be more yourself, my Bubbie argued.
I already am myself, I shouted.
She turned away. *I'll pay,* she cried,
hurling her last old woman's weapon.
In the Depression, her three daughters marched
before the knife, the gleam of good marriages
in her prescient eye.
My sister only wanted a date.

Years later, in Jerusalem, I bought a Star
of David and hung it around my neck.
Why so big? she asked. *The whole world
has to know you're Jewish?*

When the bandages came off
my sister's nose still lacked perfection.
Look, he did the best he could,
Bubbie snorted, always a defender of doctors.
I was their child: half my life
I believed I could fix a problem
by cutting it away. In the name of love
we draw a blade across the beloved's face.

(*All-American Girl,* University of Pittsburgh Press, 1996)

The nose job as an economic action; the nose job as an aesthetic
act; both explanations interest me. Both require surgical intervention in a reconstruction of female identity. In our post-mod-
ern times, when any understanding of identity is fragmented and
partial, it's possible to dismiss the nose job as a sartorial gesture,
like body piercing. Why politicize it? 1) Because Jewish cultural
identity has been marked (in hegemonic cultures) by particular
signs: clothing, wig-wearing by Orthodox women, ethnic physi-
ognomy. 2) Because stereotypical images of the beaky-nosed mi-
ser have come to us from Shakespeare and from children's books
produced in Nazi Germany. 3) Because the demonization of the
Jew as *other* is as familiar to us as the swastika scrawled on a
garage door, 1993, in Brookline, Massachusetts.

In 1495, the Spanish Inquisition issued an edict of expulsion
requiring Jews to convert or leave the country. (Riots in Spain
against Jews began as early as 1391.) Thus, the Inquisition created a population of *conversos,* Jews who escaped scrutiny (and
certain persecution, sometimes death) by converting or appearing to convert to Catholicism. Many maintained secret Jewish
practices. Sometimes called "New Christians," these crypto-Jews
invented ingenious ways to disguise their practices – from circumcision to koshering of meat. Enmeshed in state-supported
Catholic doctrine, many Jewish children assimilated or practiced
a Judaism that incorporated Christian ideas of sin and salvation.
Others distanced themselves from their parents. Inquisition docu-
ments are filled with detailed accounts of family betrayals, pun-
ishments, sudden departures.

Over the next one hundred years, *conversos* left for New Spain (Mexico) where they sought tolerance. However, by the 1590s, Jews in Mexico were burned at the stake for being "bad Catholics." An article by Michael Haederle in the summer 1993 issue of *El Palacio* explores the emergence of "crypto-Jews." Today in contemporary *New* Mexico, four hundred years after this persecution in Mexico, "hidden" Jews are coming forth. These individuals, raised as Catholics, are discussing "secret" family practices that appear, to some historians, to be vestigial remnants of a Judaism carried into the new world by crypto-Jews.

Why this digression into Jewish history? I want to describe one instance of state-supported anti-Semitism to illustrate how the theme of disguise has persisted. For 4,000 years, throughout a history of vilification and defamation, Jews have grappled with the social, economic, and political forces shaping assimilation. Often our survival has depended on assimilation and invisibility. "The British ambassador in Warsaw reported that anyone in Poland with a Jewish appearance was in danger," says Paul Johnson in his 1987 best-seller, *A History of the Jews*.

Each generation of American Jews comes to terms with absorption into the prevailing Christian culture. Between 1880 and 1914, during unrestricted immigration, my grandmother (in 1904) joined those Eastern European exiles who laid the foundation for American Jewry. Reading American culture in 1937, she believed that nose jobs would enable her daughters to make better (upwardly-mobile) marriages. To her, embedded in the Philadelphia immigrant community of Russian Jews, there was no danger of "losing" one's Judaism; becoming a more "pleasing" commodity was a fiscal asset, not a lifesaving one. Nevertheless, the proximity of the Holocaust suggests that my grandmother was not insensitive to the peculiarly protean forms of American anti-Semitism that she anticipated for her children and grandchildren. That a nose job involved shedding an inherited, familial characteristic, a mark of ethnic belonging, did not figure into my grandmother's discourse. Besides, she was used to "losing" things – a country, a set of expectations about women's roles – so what was a piece of skin to her? By contrast, my grandmother occasionally remarked on her eldest daughter's dark complexion, bragging to family and friends that strangers who met my Aunt Syde (a tourist) in the Caribbean sometimes took her for a "native." Looking back, I think that my grandmother enjoyed the slippage that identity manipulation permitted. She took pleasure in "exoticizing" her daughter, a harmless joke that might have become a useful tool in times of persecution. Perhaps she could indulge in this playful masquerade because my aunt remained so firmly fixed on the arm of her Jewish husband.

My sister's images of attractiveness did not include the face she saw when she looked in the mirror. When offered rhinoplasty, she wanted the chance to "feel beautiful," hoping, I think, that an outward change in appearance would shift the burden of self-loathing she carried inside. As I recall, most of the adolescent girls I knew had nose jobs during the summer, when the long separation from school friends made the transition from old face to new face easier. The distance between perceived economic necessity and perceived aesthetic choice (and accompanying emotional gratifications) follows a familiar route: one "greenhorn" secures an economic foothold so that successive generations may have financial stability and social mobility. Thirty years separated my mother and sister's nose jobs. However, like repressed emotions, noses "return." Today I wear the nose I imagine my mother would have had if they'd left hers alone.

Between 1992 and 1994, Jewish lesbian artist Deborah Kass created a series of paintings based on two images of Barbra Streisand: "Jewish Jackies" and the "Yentls." Self-consciously imitating Andy Warhol's multiple-image paintings, Kass creates her own version of the American cultural hero, echoing Warhol's well-known celebrity canon that includes Jackie Kennedy Onassis and Elvis Presley. Kass's decision to celebrate a powerful Jewish-identified woman (whose "Jewish" nose is part of her celebrity) offers a decisive alternative to assimilationist strategies. In Kass's large silkscreen, cross-dressed as a young male Yeshiva student in "Yentl" (a film she produced and directed), Streisand holds a book and gazes with a studied calm at the viewer. When I look at this image, I think of my grandmother – forbidden, as a girl child, to go to Yeshiva – and how she was valued for her cooking and sewing skills, her ability to minister to the men in the household. Later, in America, she was seen as a "progressive" woman: someone who did not look backward with regret to the "old country," but someone who embraced the new. All too frequently, however, the "new" isn't so new. *(Nu?)* Reviewing the museum show called "Too Jewish" that opened at New York's Jewish Museum in March 1996, Michael Kimmelman says of Kass's "Jewish Jackie" series: "Barbra Streisand, with her 'Jewish' nose, is the antithesis of the pert Jackie, a funny distinction until you realize that your laughter depends upon a stereotype of female beauty that doesn't accept Jewish looks like Ms. Streisand's."

4

Epilepsy is not, like sickle-cell anemia or Tay-Sachs disease, associated with a particular population. Faced with my sister Jill's neurological disorder that bewildered and frightened them in 1957, my parents coped the best they could. Like certain other neurological disorders, epilepsy takes a visible form, subjecting the epileptic (and her family) to the reactions of those around her. What motivated me to study the text accompanying my sister's medication was a talk I had with my mother. "You are to discuss your sister's problem with no one. We're taking care of it, and it is a family matter." Writing these sentences today, forty years after they were spoken, I feel the guilty shame of the "betrayer." I do not know if my mother actually thought I could "keep" such a secret, but in truth I could (or would?) not. Class clown, bossy schoolyard tomboy, I told friends at school and on the street that my sister had epilepsy. For a time, I feared that I would catch it and have the "staring" episodes that I later knew to call "petit mal," my sister's non-convulsive form of epilepsy.

During a seizure, my sister would abruptly depart – from a game, a conversation, a book – and drift away, staring into space, hearing and seeing nothing. Sometimes her seizures were brief, sometimes they lasted several minutes. As a young child, I was angry at her withdrawal. *Where are you going? Come back, come back,* the abandoned child inside me cried. I clapped my hands, I shouted, I danced around her, trying to bring her out of her trance. Other children watched, curious. I knew nothing, then, about the myths surrounding epilepsy, the association of epileptics with mysticism and possession by the devil. I knew that I went to overnight camp alone, that the camp directors were afraid to take responsibility for my sister, should she have a seizure at the lake.

One Thursday night, while my sister slept and my father passed "men's night" at the country club, I heard my mother weeping. I went in and stood by her bed.

"What is it, Mom?" I asked.

"It's nothing, honey."

"Come on, Mom. You can tell me."

"I said it was nothing," she repeated.

"Mom, you're not in here crying about nothing!"

"All right, then," she said. "It's your sister." And she sobbed into a kleenex.

"She'll be OK, mom," I said. "She'll be OK."

Much shame has come to my parents through their children: the shame of having a child with a neurological disorder; the shame of having a lesbian daughter. During my adolescence and young adulthood, I conflated these two "shames." I saw them both as psychological and social disorders, medicalized by science and tinged with pseudoscience. My sister's disease (and the side effects of her medication) caused terrible social problems for her throughout her life. I never heard my sister utter the word "epilepsy." To the best of my knowledge, she never spoke of her disease except, on rare occasions, to my mother. Her shame was complete, internalized, and ongoing.

When I left my family to go to college, I had already learned the ways of the deceiver: I had lived for several years in my parents' house revealing little about myself or my activities. I was in the habit of secrecy, and lying (about where I was going, with whom, what I was doing) came naturally to me. My desire for an intimate relationship with a woman required that I find another "family" in which to live. I took my secret into the world, in 1969, just as the Stonewall Riots forged the gay and lesbian liberation movements. For my sister, there was no liberation movement, no release from the prison of her disease, though the Disability Movement (one result of which would be the Americans with Disabilities Act) was also beginning. The women's movement didn't speak to my sister who stayed within the embrace of an ashamed and shaming family, breathing the stale air, dependent upon our parents for emotional and economic support. The claustrophobia I experienced at home sent me on a decades-long journey for a family of friends, for a way of reformulating myself as a Jewish lesbian-feminist. My sister was not so lucky. When she took her own life in 1987, she took our shared sibling-memory with her. I miss remembering together or reconstructing the household in which we grew up. Despite our differences, I still hoped for talk that could heal us both. I kept imagining that we could still be friends, as we lay on the floor, ages eight and ten, playing Chinese checkers for hours. I miss having an adult friendship with the woman she might have become.

*   *   *

I had not seen or spoken to my sister for three years, when I received a phone call from my mother telling me that she was dead. During those years, I badgered my parents to tell me where she was; I begged them to let me call her, write to her, speak with her doctor or therapist. They refused. They said she had insisted that they keep her whereabouts secret from me, and they would not betray that promise. My friends urged me to hire a private detective to track her down, but I never did. Was I afraid of angering my parents by circumventing their decision? Ashamed of my own role in the family's craziness? Was I protecting myself by *staying out* of the family drama, the strategy that saved my own life?

A month after my sister's suicide, my parents and I spent several days together on Martha's Vineyard. For the first (and last) time, I listened to my parents describe my sister's peregrinations during the last three years of her life. They told me about her hospital stays, her moves across the country. They told me that my sister did not want to see me or speak to me. She did not want me interfering with her life in any way. And they wanted to respect her wishes. They hoped that by doing so my sister would see their faith in her, their belief that she could chart her own path back to family, work, friends.

For a long time I believed that secrecy caused my sister's death. Secrecy about mental illness. And shame. My sister spiraled down, without adequate help, without a pharmacological workup, without a first-rate medical team evaluating her depression and her epilepsy. Had she received this help, my sister might have joined the hundreds of thousands of people who – coping with various forms of mental illness – get by, struggle along, survive. Or perhaps she might have taken her life anyway.

5

My father is an old man in a Florida supermarket, checking the price of milk. My mother, since her aortal valve replacement, tires easily, spends most evenings lying on the sofa watching TV. When my partner and I visit, they rally, they take us to dinner. My mother will wander around a museum with us and then treat us to lunch. Sometimes I try to talk to my family of friends about the unspoken, inarticulate sadness that fills me when I spend time with my parents. Certainly my sister's suicide casts a shadow over their days. I used to think, after her death, that I should have a child – to bring body and noise and movement into their hushed rooms. I thought a grandchild might stimulate a long-dormant longing they dared not have: for life. Instead, I came up against my own resistance to life's big, messy, unplanned ways.

In the household of my childhood, only my father was permitted to express opinions. I thwarted his design by speaking my mind, holding contradictory perspectives. From an early age, I was his combatant. Once, after an argument with my father, I ran into my room and locked the door behind me. I must have been thirteen or so. I remember the sound of his footsteps, as he came after me, and the sight of the splintering wood as he kicked a hole in my bedroom door. "To show you that you can't keep any secrets in this house!" he shouted. Familiar images of revenge swam through my mind: my father stricken by a heart attack; my father tied to a chair as I screamed my hatred into his ears; my father humiliated by a mock trial, in which the judge decrees he is a cowardly bully and must atone for his sins against me.

My parents never repaired the hole in the door. Year in and year out, it remained, a symbol, my father believed, of his ongoing efforts to suppress *secrecy*. As in any dictatorship, the despotic power he exercised engendered reactions he could not control. While he wished to subdue me, I eluded him. When he prohibited particular activities, I lied and did whatever I'd planned. Whatever *secrets* he desired to keep within the household, I carried outside. Beliefs he found unacceptable, I cultivated.

I don't see it that way, Daddy, I used to say, bravely, trying to defend my position (about Vietnam, or the work of the American Friends Service Committee). *Well, no one asked you how you saw it, so just keep your mouth shut and listen to people who know better than you. 'Ya hear me?* I risked his rage and the withdrawal of his affections, but deep inside I had accepted this risk. I would give up his love long before I'd give up my chance to have a voice of my own.

I have never spoken to my father about his beating me when I was a child. My turning away from men has pained him, I know, and we have long since given up the political arguments in which I annoyed him, and he bullied and intimidated me. We have agreed to live, unreconciled and unreconciling, in a drama of submerged feeling. For me, a deeper and more meaningful relationship with my father is part of my sacrifice: I offer up intimacy for autonomy. For *survival.*

I broke up with a woman I loved very much, because I did not want to raise a child with her. In my own therapy, I worked hard to transform the terror I experienced when I imagined *having a family.* I tried to picture the joy and pleasure of childrearing; I could not stop imagining a baby crying in the next room. I tried to feel the pleasure of strolling with a child in the park, but I felt the resentment of having to put my own writing and reading aside. I tried to picture my lover's happiness; instead, I saw my mother, drowning in others' needs, incapable of maintaining her own projects. No matter how hard I fought for a new image of myself *in a family,* the past haunted my present. I couldn't get away from images of anxiety, compromise, regret.

If one Jewish impulse is to keep secrets, another is to tell them. Perhaps this is why Yiddish is filled with words like "kibbitzer," and "yenta," words for people who tease and gossip and entertain with stories. I recall the great Jewish comedians – Eddie Cantor, Lenny Bruce, Buddy Hackett, Mike Nichols, Jackie Mason, Milton Berle, Jerry Lewis, Mort Sahl, the Marx Brothers – whose gags depended on rambling stories with unlikely juxtapositions, self-mockery, jokes at the comedian's expense. Often, the jokes cast one type of Jew against another: sophisticate vs. greenhorn, religious vs. secular. They spoof family relations, politics, the priest and the rabbi, a clever Catholic response against an even more clever Jewish one. The entertainment industry gave us Fanny Brice and Sophie Tucker and Joan Collins. Like Streisand, they are our public, female, Jewish "tellers," putting – with their words, and stories, and songs, and appearances – a Jewish face on public life.

Scholar and critic John Limon believes that stand-up comedy enacts *abjection.* The first era of stand-up replaced vaudeville – with Bob Hope and Milton Berle. By 1955, Limon says, 80 percent of all stand-up comics were Jewish men. Historical proximity to the Holocaust cast their *comic abjection* in a particular light. Now *Lettermania* (Limon's word) has displaced Carson, who, Limon argues, learned from Brooks, Bruce, and Hackett. In stand-up, Limon says, the comic plays with his own power by referring to his own *dweebness. Letterman,* he says, *is caffeinated when he should*

be sleepy; vertical when we are prostrate. The American joke, Limon
offers, *is that faced with alienation, we perform it.* *

Our Jewish-American writers have been "telling" since I. B. Singer
wrote *In My Father's Court,* the "inside" story of his Polish family
before WWII, headed by a patriarchal rabbi whose neighbors
come to him to settle disputes. They come with their secrets and
their shame, their hopes for remedy and their intractable person-
alities. And we have these stories because someone "told," because the rabbi's son listened to the comedy and the heartache
and recorded it, exposed it, put it "out" – beyond the reaches of
his father's court and the Jewish community that contained the
characters. Think of Grace Paley and the confessions of her Jewish pharmacist who, at the end of his life, loves and raises his
African-American grandson. I don't know if there is a perfect
relation for "keeper" of secrets to "teller" of secrets, but I do
know that they need each other.

My mother calls me to tell me that my uncle's insurance policies
and pension and investments have left my aunt a rich woman. As
long as I've known her, she's lived like someone poor – buying
secondhand clothes, never making a long-distance phone call,
clipping coupons. "Who would guess she would be rich at the
end of her life?" I ask. "It won't make any difference," my mother
replies. "Her self-denial is so strong she won't enjoy the money
anyway." Family secrets continue to bloom, like perennial flowers. Time proves my mother correct, and my aunt does not change
her ways. No one knew my uncle had so much money; what's
next? I brace myself for surprise.

* John Limon, "Journey to the End of the Night: David Letterman with Kristeva,
Céline, Scorsese," forthcoming in *Journal X,* University of Mississippi, fall 1996,
vol. 1, no. 1.

Helen Papell

Kaddish

It was the day forsythia suddenly
bulged eyes of yellow.
The sixth day after the spring equinox
my sister died

and my mother called upon her ancestor Eve
to complain that here in exile
death is the second bite
of the fruit mothers eat
from the tree of knowing good and evil.

Eve opened the wall
of the Garden of Eden.
There were the animals
as they had been created.
No one was reading a book
or building a boat.
No one was old or ill.

Eve said "In exile
giants nibble me.
In the garden the animals
never die
and I am loved."

Near the tree
Eve's murdered son Abel played
with a lion cub.
My mother said "Give me a garden also"

and another wall opened,
a dog and cat slept entwined as grass.
It was the seventh day of the week.
My sister in a scarlet dress
rocked upon the roots of the tree.

Judith Skillman

Asylum

A flutter of notes,
the *tic-tic* of beak on wood, and
a redheaded woodpecker tapping, knocking
at the door of a madrona,
looking for grubs.

Come in, I say.
Enter the tree, a feminine quantity.
Penetrate the mystery of daughterhood.

Always the soft fluff of forgiveness.
Always before or after a war.
Always in a deep wood flooded with memory,
the ticking, the twitching. Eyes everywhere,
etched in the bark of madrones,
on mothwing. In the decorative motion
of flower and bush, and the water
retreating from yards of beached wood,
I recognize the neurotic impulse.

But it's not *neurosis* anymore. In one
of Freud's dreams he lost a tooth,
and that tooth is the one we must discuss,
the way it fits in the palm
like a cigarette or a pill.

Sad Breed

My father meant to be kind when he cussed.
His cussing couldn't be helped.
The consonants had to come out,
at breakfast, lunch, and dinner, especially
when Mother served his favorite meals, pot roast
or veal stew simmered slowly
all afternoon over the gas burner.

I don't mean to be unkind to my father
by calling attention to his disease.
Kindness is a difficult thing to measure.
It could be that helpfulness
is out of order. The wind knocks
but doesn't enter, knowing
we are better off without its testy breath
in our houses.

The wild rose
scratches at our walls as if it wants to come in,
but it would bloody our sheets.
Shoes are full of odors,
and windows rattle,
but there was never a man as kind
as my father, who could only say *shit.*
That word *shit* he held onto like a lifeboat
in bad weather. A hatless fellow,
a short Jewish man, hissing.

Ruth Behar

Your House

for David, with sharp edges

Sometimes I don't think you've given
your life for me.
Sometimes I think I've given
my life for you.

Don't presume you know what I'm going to say.
I'm talking about more than giving up
the fellowship that time in California,
the one I'm always reminding you about.

Don't worry, I'm not blaming you. Did I say it was
your fault I no longer speak very much Spanish?
You say I should just talk, that the walls will listen.
Pity these nice suburban homes don't answer back.

Try to understand what a sacrifice it is to live
with someone who finds contentment in peanut butter
and bananas and does not know the meaning of guilt.
I come from a long line of exiles. I need drama.

You do so much for me, I feel cruel complaining.
Ironing the silk blouses my mother is addicted to giving me.
Putting them back in my closet without a word.
Sleeping soundly while I read late into the night.

You are just too good a guy, too nice a goy, leaving Jesus
for a martyred life with a woman carrying too much history
on her back. I know I've given my life for you.
I can't tell you how, but I have, I have.

Even when I am pushing you to the limit
to see if what my mother never stops saying is true:
Watch it, because men get tired, and they leave.
Especially then, I'm giving it all up for you.

My House

for me

This is what I wanted:
A house totally my own.
Me at the head of the table.
My salad on a separate plate.
And no suffering from dishpan hands.

I sit at the head of the table now.
In the house I bought
With my own money.
All mine: oak desk, feather mattress,
Mahogany piano, pictures on the wall.

It is my house, I remind him,
So you'll leave when I say so.
That's how I talk when my father
Gets into my mouth.
Then I'm only good for eviction notices.

I used to think it was feminism
That made those words
Pour out of me
Like wine grown rancid
From being too long in the glass.

When I speak like that
Demanding he pay
For what men have done to women
There is a sad little girl
Doing a bad imitation of her father's voice.

A girl who wants to give a home
to her Mami. Because
She never answered back
All those years he'd tell her
She had nothing, was nothing.
Nothing without him.

Shaken After Receiving a Letter from a Miami Poet with a Mean Tongue Who Doesn't Want a Bridge to Cuba

The letter arrived on heavy linen bond,
the kind where the tree is still breathing.
It was three pages long and typed on a laser
printer in ink so sharp it wanted to bite.
The poet said he had received my invitation
for the special volume about bridges to Cuba
and without even saying please or thank you
to cross him off my list immediately
to cross all his friends and enemies off too
and never again to write to him for anything.
Was I crazy or stupid or was my head stuck
in one of those academic Michigan clouds,
to think there's anything left in Cuba
except hunger and jails and mulatas
with half-peach tits like you'll never have?
And to hurt where it really hurts, he said,
Tell me, would you have stretched a hand
toward Hitler? Tell me, do you like Nazis?
I was never able to answer his letter. . . .
Europe, green from the bones of six million.
I tell you my femur is there, trying to walk.
A poet cruel to history is cruel to poetry.

Janet Sternburg

Trochaic

Earth, receive an honored guest
William Yeats is laid to rest
Let the Irish vessel lie
Emptied of its poetry.

It was the beat that got me. I first encountered Auden's "In Memory of William Butler Yeats" in my aunt's back room. I loved my aunt, but conversation couldn't compete with the lure of the room behind the kitchen. Feeling strange and shy, I made my way through pungent cooking smells, across a slippery lino-leum floor to her seldom-used room. My aunt had left behind a card table with a stack of paper, a folding chair, and a shelf of books. Each time I returned, I took down the anthology that held Auden's elegy.

The trochaic tread, stately, processional, seemed to usher in a meaning that I didn't hear in the lyric lilt of iambs. That I knew the difference between poetic measures was due to Girls' Latin School where I learned to scan poetry, diagram complex sen-tences, translate Cicero, and commit to memory the diameter and circumference of all the islands in Boston Harbor. I also memo-rized comparable figures for all the then-known planets in the solar system during a year-long course whose semesters neatly paired geology and astronomy. While I can't remember any of these measurements, by now probably much-revised, I do retain a sense that islands in my hometown waters are hinged to plan-ets in space.

When I was in the corridors and classrooms, I didn't feel strange. I was at ease with my love of trochees and my lesser love of iambs, and my fondness for their relatives, the dactyl (which made me think of vast wings attached to a lizard body) and anapest (which I imagined as a city in Eastern Europe). When my family moved away, I transferred to a large high school where I wanted to fit in. I hid my absorption in poetry but when I came home after school, I made up writing assignments for myself:

Janet, compose a poem in formal verse on a randomly chosen subject. With my eyes closed, I ran my fingers back and forth along our set of Collier's Encyclopedia and drew out a volume. Keeping my eyes shut, I opened the book somewhere in the middle, which turned out to be an entry on Vermont. I read until I came to the legend of native son Ethan Allen, who returned on moonlit nights in the shape of a white horse. In my poem, I set farmers on a porch, talking of humdrum things, until their vision was illuminated by the apparition of a horse made of light. Now that I had a subject, where was I to find the music? There, in the paragraph on Vermont's principal products, I found *Lumber, eggs, and hay.* Once again, I responded to that trochaic beat.

Years later I showed that poem to a psychoanalytically inclined friend who maintained that the poem wasn't random at all. She said I had written the myth of my own life. The farmers were my parents and I was the horse, charged with bringing radiance into their lives. She was right, to the extent that writing is built up around the armature of the writer's life. But she was wrong, too. That horse was outside of me. He was moving to the cadences of history, a rhythm I had first heard in Auden's poem.

Until then, history was either too close or too far away. It was much too close when I was four or five and my mother befriended a Polish refugee who had been an inmate at Auschwitz. After she was released, Mrs. Landsman had walked across Europe in search of her family. Eventually she found her husband and daughter, but her three other children had been killed. Through an arrangement that I still don't understand, Mrs. Landsman cleaned our house, although we were not in a position to afford a cleaning woman, and besides, my mother always worked alongside her. My mother was pretty and stylish. Mrs. Landsman wore a housedress that smelled of steam and sweat; over her hair she tied a scarf as red as her face; her Yiddish was guttural and shrill. She and my mother bent down into a soapy bucket. Later that evening my mother would say, "We washed the floor with our tears."

History, when it took shape in Mrs. Landsman, seemed full of sorrow unredeemed by beauty. I knew that I should pity Mrs. Landsman for what had happened to her, but instead I thought if this is history, get me away from its smell, its suds, its mournfulness. History was too distant when war appeared on our Zenith television screen. I didn't understand what was going on, but I did feel a pang for an old man who seemed sad. When I heard him say, "I shall return," I knew somehow that, unlike Jimmy

Durante who walked sorrowfully away from the audience as he said goodnight to his long lost Mrs. Calabash, this man would not reappear on our screen next week. One thing I understood: history was able to make people disappear.

Poetry, though, brought the past alive. When I read and reread Auden's elegy, I envisioned cold bridges over curved rivers, people huddled in dark coats as they waited for streetcars that would take them out beyond the city limits where they lived in "ranches of isolation." This Europe was overrun by murderous hordes that only a bardic voice could keep at bay.

> Follow, poet, follow right
> to the bottom of the night.

I heard the imperative in the trochee. Do it. Make it.

> With your unconstraining voice
> Still persuade us to rejoice.

Somewhere there were vineyards. Mrs. Landsman's tragedy might be met by song, trilling in the arbors of hope. No dying fall; instead, an emphatic beat at the end of a line, "rejoice." The palm of my hand came down onto that last stressed syllable, which I heard not as an iamb but as the conquering chord of the trochee. In that back room, I was conducting an orchestra of language.

At those moments I also sprung free of my own history. I was for a brief time not a solitary little girl, not sickly, not Jewish. I was part of a great line, in which I myself might become "an honored poet." But "Mad Ireland"; what did that mean? And what about "Paul Claudel"? An asterisk below a stanza directed the reader's eye to a footnote. Where the asterisk appeared, it turned out there had once been another stanza: "Time will pardon Paul Claudel/Pardon him for writing well." Paul Claudel had done something wrong, something connected to the war that spilled out in Mrs. Landsman's tears. At one point, Auden must have believed that this man's gift would absolve him, then Auden changed his mind. I was face to face with another aspect of history: revision. But the evidence of the poet's change of mind hadn't been erased; the stanza had survived, in a footnote that I went back to each time I shut myself in the back room. I felt surreptitious, as though the reference to Claudel were tinged with erotic scandal.

I knew that the madness of Ireland was very different from what I saw in the state mental hospital where my mother took me to visit her brother. In a ward for catatonics, he was eventually lobotomized and released to my grandmother's apartment where, for ten years, he sat silently in front of the television screen turning the pages of *Life* magazine. One day, standing on the back porch with my aunt, he casually remarked on the hair ribbon of a little girl playing below; it was, he noted, the same one she had worn the day before. Once he had broken back into speech, he had a decade's worth of jumble to tell. Eleanor Roosevelt whispered secrets in his ear; the downstairs neighbor had built the atom bomb; Harry Truman followed him to the barber shop. But Yeats's Ireland was a place where passions were not extinguished. They ruled, and their sovereign was a poet who could "survive it all." Was it words, then, that offered people relief from their history? If the seas of pity were "locked and frozen in each eye," was poetry the heat that liquefies pain, letting it roll down Mrs Landsman's cheeks?

History. Elegy. Poetry. The words ask for one more syllable. They need *time* in order to see beauty in other measures. As I now see Mrs. Landsman, scrubbing away at the stains, her hand circling again and again over that enveloping soapy floor.

His Regular Fare

One hand cupped to the side of his mouth, the other on the crook of a metal cane, his body ovoid in profile, swelling below his belt from an inoperable hernia and above from a brace that holds together his permanently fractured back, my father is calling at the top of his still strong lungs, "Marianne. Marianne."

I am aware, as always, on our way now to an Italian restaurant he used to frequent in his cabdriving days in Boston's North End, of worry: that he'll slide, right here on the street, from an engaging if loud attempt to locate his old friend Marianne, to a rage born of frustration, for it has been at least ten years since he has seen her, and she may well have moved.

He's not certain which building is hers, and sends me across the street (three or four steps is all it takes) to check names on the bell. "Look on the left," he calls out . . . "Read me the names." At the top of the brick stoop, I see that there is no register of names on the left, and the ones on the right – Giglio," I call out, "McCann/ Stewart" – are not the ones he is looking for.

"Marianne," he shouts, and my worry is compounded: will he be disappointed by this expedition to his old territory where, as a child, I used to imagine him strolling the streets like the mayor of a small town in Sicily, greeting the barber, stopping to say hello to Mrs. Caggiano, the florist. I know now that "mayor" was wrong; I gave him a position and an authority he never had. Even then I must have had my doubts, because the concern I feel now is old, like a continent re-emerging with my father's volcanic call, "Marianne, Marianne."

He was an outsider, an obliging Jewish cabdriver from another part of Boston, who helped maneuver a wheelchair down a steep stairway so that Marianne's bedridden mother could get some air, and later carried massive funeral wreaths out of the car. Five days a week for more than twenty years he drove Marianne in his yellow Checker cab to her job at the Registry of Motor Vehicles; she was his regular fare, a single daughter who lived at home with her ailing parents and was greeted every day by my father's interest in how her mother was doing that morning. I am worried now, as always, that he will be hurt, his affection not returned, or given in a perfunctory or condescending way, that on this one night of return from illness and retirement, this night when I am taking him out to dinner at a favorite old haunt, he will be forced to see that his earlier life is over, and that it hadn't possessed the qualities he'd attributed to it. He is getting red in the face as he shouts up at a window in a building that I think is not the right one.

Meanwhile, a little farther up the street, poised on the sidewalk like a bird on its perch, is my brittle-boned mother. On this visit to Boston, I've noticed that her shoulders are rounding as though to protect the little rib cage underneath. Walking is difficult for her; so too must standing be; so too is her acute embarrassment: maybe he'll draw attention to himself, be a target of disapproval and hurt her timorous dignity. She would like nothing more than for him to cease, recognize that the past is gone, anything to stop that bellowing into vacancy. "Sh-sh-sh . . . " And now I am in age-old alliance with him against her, liking his capacity for action, his embrace of the past and his ability to make noise, his appetites and desires, focused now on that window.

We have to leave, we have a reservation for dinner . . . the owner, now partially retired herself, has promised me that she'll come specially to the restaurant at that hour, to greet him.

A third-floor window opens, a curly gray head peers down and calls "Sid, Sid! I'll be right there," and Marianne, now in her sixties, comes running, pure pleasure on her face, broad gums showing in a vast smile of welcome. They stand on the curb exchanging long "and then" tales of chronic illness, of conditions that caused other conditions, of the one who died or the one who moved away, of her better supervisor, her new juicer.

Marianne has lost fifty pounds. My mother, ever vigilant in matters of appearance, compliments Marianne and reminds her of the time she couldn't get a black dress large enough for her to wear at her mother's funeral. Marianne beams at us all. Innocent of guile or seduction, she says to my mother, "You had him, but I had him too." She hadn't moved away. My father had been bellowing into love.

Rodger Kamenetz

Grandfather Clause

for David Kamenetz, z"l

If only you'd done what you'd been told to do.
If only you'd not been lifted by a chance wind
blown west across the wheat tips of the Ukraine
the thunder of knouts, the Czar's knappers.
If you had stayed instead to be murdered
by the Einzatsgruppen, then old men like you
fingers palsied on the trigger, bellies shaking at the recoil
would have shot you dead at the edge of a pit
slaughtered you on the outskirts of a town
Jews could not enter after sunset.

There is a clause that refers to you
in the inner lining of a foreign language
where Jew is the dirtiest word ever.
This clause prepared in advance of your name
is the secret history of your death
decreed in a grammar strange to your Yiddish
as the language I struggle to speak is inflected
by the death that might have been.

Yet you entered America like a pilgrim or a germ –
Which was it? Or both, as America decided
with your Jewish heart and lungs and your Jewish disease
and two strong fingers and a needle.

Why should I tell that old story again?
I'm still immigrating into this moment, this day
learning that the words applied to you apply to me.
Even after all this time, I will not allow anyone
to annihilate your name and mine.
I am grandfathered in.

Gabriel's Palace

(for Howard Schwartz)

Forests. Sleeping on a cold bed of leaves.
Ticking of grubs in the mulch. The inner ear
intimate with balance, whorls like a thumbprint
like a whirlwind. The dream, thick as syrup
oozes into the wound. Deep – always deep
in the forest – always forest – the cabin no one knew.
The wise man, the weird troll, the angelic woman
beckoned, threatened, dropped your name down a well
of whispering voices, vanished into a pile of glowworms
her nightgown shimmering electric silk.
Dazed, you stumbled into the center of the story
spoke your lines like a proverb
took your place in the order that penetrates order
that wheels through the circuits of moon, earth and sun
the great wheel of the Milky Way, locked and turning
with perfect force all the great weight of song.

The Broken Tablets

The broken tablets were also carried in an ark.
Insofar as they represented everything shattered
everything lost, they were the law of broken things,
the leaf torn from the stem in a storm, a cheek touched
in fondness once but now the name forgotten.
How they must have rumbled, clattered on the way
even carried so carefully through the waste land,
how they must have rattled around until the pieces
broke into pieces, the edges softened
crumbling, dust collected at the bottom of the ark
ghosts of old letters, old laws. Insofar
as a law broken is still remembered
these laws were obeyed. And insofar as memory
preserves the pattern of broken things
these bits of stone were preserved
through many journeys and ruined days
even, they say, into the promised land.

Alvin Greenberg

My great-grandfather, the poet David Greenberg (who published under the name ben Y'Shai), emigrated from Russia early in the 1880s, settled with his wife and young children in Cincinnati, and promptly suffered the fate of many a poet and pariah: banishment from family history. This was not because he was a bad man, at least not by my standards, but because he was, perhaps even worse by some standards, a poet. He took up one of the most common immigrant professions – that of an itinerant peddler – but what got him his bad reputation in the family was that, in order to write, he put his peddler's pack down almost as quickly as he took it up.

He peddled his small items – needles and thread, eyeglasses and scissors, the usual stuff – up and down the Ohio River Valley until he had enough money to support his young family for a while; then he came home, turned the cash over to his wife, and turned himself to writing and to his literary cronies. And there he stayed until the money ran out and his wife was forced to come nagging after him to hit the road again. In other words, while more typical Jewish peddlers were building the business, opening the little dry goods stores that would eventually expand into department store chains, great-grandfather Greenberg was . . . writing poetry. It was not a career choice designed to produce a poetry-loving family.

And so far as I knew until very recently, none of his poetry, published or unpublished, remained – nor did much of him, except for his bad rap as a poor provider, the erroneous report that he wrote in Hebrew (actually, it was Yiddish), and the strange rumor that he was supposed to have been a pastoral poet. So eventually I took it upon myself, the next poet to appear in the family, to attempt to recover this man, the poet whom the family had been only too happy to obliterate from its history. And what I did, lacking his own poems, was to try to write them for him, the poems of my predecessor addressed to me over the gap of the intervening generations that chose to pay no attention to him.

240

These things that I call *transverses* (a transverse line being, in geometry, one that intersects two or more other lines) are my attempt, then, to give voice to someone who has been silenced; to struggle with the irony that even if I had his poems, given my ignorance of Yiddish I couldn't read them; and perhaps not least of all to talk to myself in the understanding, sympathetic voice of an other with whom I'd like to believe I had much in common and who certainly has a lot to say to me.

the old country

sooner or later you had to know i'd grow morose,
mumbling old country this and old country that . . .
all things you couldn't be expected to understand

even if you could understand the words i mumbled them in.

we're locked in a immigrant trunk of language no new world
can free us from, not even this one, that thought it could
translate us all into the same idiom, the same desires.

my old language tells you where my desires still live.

so don't try to make sense of it. even i don't anymore.
together we'll just follow wherever it wants to go:
back, back: to a world we can't get back to: you

because you can't get back to where you've never been

and me because: because back there . . . just isn't
anymore. we know it, yes, we know it: we even
set down these words that say how much we know it, but

language is the container, not the cure, for our longing.

to the translator: 3

just spare me your flippancies, kiddo – them i know too.
you ache for the wisecrack like – wait, i can do it as well as you –
like the blintz aches for the sour cream! how about that?

didn't i have a great-grandfather once myself? o generations!

so what am i doing here? begging? of course: because i know
you'll make me come out sounding just like you (although maybe
with a little real work – something from your own imagination –

you could at least make me read like a translation.)

de rerum natura

some day they'll count how many times i've used the word 'cow'
(one more time right now) and add me up to be a nature poet.
is a cow nature? and whoever heard of a jewish nature poet?

what does a jew know of nature? (except for the nature of jews,
and even that's a whole taxonomy.) what's nature in the ghetto?
in the synagogue? the sweat shop? is poverty nature? poetry?

we're all immigrants from nature, but immigrants to what? i'd

gladly write you in forests, hills, and clouds, but all i have
are words, words in a language you can't read: that's *your* nature,
this is mine: to be what i am, to say the things i seem to say,

no matter how they add up: even 'cow,' 'cow,' 'cow,' . . .

immigrants

birds first. and certain animals. desert nomads.
sailors, peddlers, concert pianists, mailmen.
itinerant preachers, doctors, gamblers, lawyers,

even the sun, whose constant comings and goings
govern our lives, down to the finest detail,
telling us when to wake, what to wear and eat.

yes, just as your frightened congressman fears,
the nation's in the hands of the immigrants,
and not just the nation, the world: everything

moves: and aboard this cosmic steamer, earth,
most of us huddle in steerage, a bundle or two
of possessions at our feet, stomachs queasy,

children crying: only knowing where we've been.

trouble

the two most difficult things i know: peddling and poetry,
a pair of jewish curses, each one harder than the other,
routines of the troublesome self: but we do them, don't we?

for the world's hard, too: harsh and unpolished in its

coarse routines: a plotless, long-running, difficult show
even the toughest audiences rarely applaud . . . or endure.
surely trouble shall follow thee all of thy days, saith

the world's first critic: those prophets studied their text

well, but even without a script they knew what came next:
more of the same: just like peddling, just like poetry.
the hardest part's going on to another town, another line,

inserting yourself into the unexplained air of the future,

trying to do something with it, sometimes just to be there.
that's trouble. we're trouble. trouble's everywhere.
the trouble with you's your lack of practice with obscure.

the trouble with me's i'm always searching for the cure.

the trouble with all the others both is and isn't clear:
something that clearly troubles us, something very queer.
the trouble with the dead's they're dead and do not mind

that the trouble with the living is: they're left behind.

the trouble with now's it's now, a babble of strange voices,
the unfamiliar everywhere, bad weather, way too much to see.
the past's of course less trouble than it used to be,

but the trouble with the future is the future isn't me.

Eileen Pollack

The Pool

from *Paradise, New York*

I always suspected I'd been chosen by God for some special fate, but I didn't receive proof until I was nine. It was summer, mid June. Where could death hide on such a bright morning? Nowhere, I thought, and poked one bare foot out the bungalow door. How soft the grass looked! I longed to turn cartwheels, climb the old oak, perform a few miracles to take up the hour until the pool opened and I could show off my new lime-green two-piece.

"No," my mother told me. Her fingers closed around my suit straps.

"Why not?" I demanded.

"Put on your shoes first."

I wrinkled my nose.

"You heard me, Miss Piss."

In my mother's opinion, deadly microbes were breeding in every warm puddle. The germs of paralysis were tiny sharks teeming in each muddy drop.

"If you go around barefoot, you might pick up TB."

For years I'd assumed she was saying Tee *Vee*. The current ran through the earth like a snake of hot sparks. If you stepped on the snake with bare feet, the pictures shot to your brain. One afternoon, when my mother wasn't looking, I took off my sneakers and searched for the spot. I planted my right foot, paused, saw no pictures, planted my left foot a few inches over, stepping and pausing until I'd signed every patch of the Eden with my own special footprints. But I couldn't find the current. I even tried pressing my ear to the ground and listening for voices – Fred, Ethel, Ricky, and the red-headed Lucy for whom I'd been named, or so my brother Arthur told me.

I kept doing this until Arthur discovered me down on all fours, ear to the ground. He jumped on my back and wouldn't let me up until I admitted what I was doing. Then he laughed so convulsively I could feel my body shake beneath his. He sputtered his last laugh and took pity on me, explaining the truth: that our family's hotel once had been a refuge for patients who coughed furiously and spat blood until they choked to death, eyes bulging, tongues black. Their mucus, Arthur told me, still wriggled with germs, which waited to crawl in the blisters on my feet. He thought this would scare me, but it excited me to think that the Eden was haunted with the germs of dead people, and that these lived on, unseen, awaiting a chance to make contact with me, inhabit my blood.

"Put your shoes on this minute," my mother ordered, "or no swimming for a month."

I didn't bother to tell her that I wasn't afraid of catching TB. What would that matter? TB was only one of a hundred virulent devils waiting to prey on a girl in bare feet.

"If you step on a rusted nail you'll get lockjaw."

I savored this tragedy. Arthur would be chasing me across the front lawn. I would step on a nail and stumble. He would catch me and threaten to pull down my bathing suit, as he'd often done before, and when I tried to beg for mercy my jaw would lock shut. Slowly, Arthur would realize what dreadful affliction had silenced his sister. He would beg my forgiveness, which of course I wouldn't grant.

Not that I believed I would die. How could such puny villains – a microbe, a nail – strike down a girl of rare visions and dreams? If anything, I sensed on that brilliant June morning not death but a challenge, an occasion to prove my powers at last.

I put on my flip-flops and dodged past my mother.

"Come back here!" she shouted. "Those things are so flimsy, a piece of glass could go through!"

But she didn't have time to run after me and tie real shoes on my feet. Flip-flops smacking my heels, I ran to the camp house, an unpainted shack with a dozen old mattresses piled high inside. The raw wooden walls were inscribed with the signatures of campers now in their fifties: YUDEL LOVES EDITH; SHEL CLOBBERED MILTIE 8/10/32. Standing on my toes, I was just able to reach the top cubbyholes. Wasps dove from the eaves, but I wasn't afraid; I'd given them instructions to strafe all intruders and leave me unstung. From the only cubby with a door I withdrew a shabby book with warped covers. My grandfather had given me the book the year before, on my eighth birthday. He'd bought it, he said, when he arrived in America; he'd wanted to own a copy of the Bible in English, and the Bibles for adults were too hard to read. OLD TESTAMENT FOR CHILDREN, EDITED, ABRIDGED the title said in block letters. A smiling man and woman posed behind a tree; I recognized them as the couple tossing the beach ball on the Eden's main arch. In his soft stumbling voice, my grandfather started to read aloud the story of Moses on Sinai. I interrupted to ask why he pronounced the w's as v's.

"Vell," he said. A troubled look passed his face. He leaned forward. The book slipped from his lap. He opened his mouth, and I sat waiting for an answer until my parents appeared in the doorway with a cake, which we didn't get to eat. Though my grandfather lived another ten years, he couldn't move or talk, so it seemed to me as if God bestowed the Torah not on Moses, but on me, then lay down to sleep while I studied His gift, preparing for a test I knew would come soon.

The more I read the Bible, the more I believed that Moses and I were two of a kind. Hadn't a bush with flame-red leaves ordered me to kneel by the shuffleboard court because the ground there was holy? And that same afternoon, hadn't a radio emitted a wail, after which the announcer, in his resonant voice, commanded me to await instructions regarding the mission God had reserved especially for me? I heard God speak often, praising my deeds. I asked Him favors: *Please, God, let the sun stand still so I can swim one more hour.* My prayers sometimes worked, but never when any witnesses were near.

And so this was the puzzle that occupied my mind in the camp house that morning: how could I prove how special I was? I lay on my back, studying the baffling words on the wall above the toilet, preparing for the day I would be called on to translate the warning God had written on some other wall, as Daniel was asked to explain MENE MENE TEKEL UPHARSIN to wicked King Belshazzar.

"Attention, attention!" My mother's voice rang from loudspeakers on poles all over the grounds. "Ladies and gentlemen, the pool is now open for your aquatic enjoyment."

I replaced my book in its cubbyhole and jumped down all four steps to the sidewalk. Slowed by my flip-flops, I left these behind, two bright red footprints. For a moment, I stood on the hot concrete deck surrounding the pool – good training in case I was ever flung into a furnace, like Daniel. Then, with a cry, I raced to the edge and threw myself over.

Cold as perfection. I frog-kicked underwater. When I emerged on the other side I felt cleansed, though of what I wasn't sure. Maybe the chlorine would sterilize my skin so no ugly hair would sprout between my legs, as it did from the crotches of the women on the lounge chairs, black tendrils creeping down puckery thighs. I levered my body to the deck, exalting in the strength of my lean, freckled arms. I pinched my nose, rubbed it – if Arthur saw snot, he would blow his whistle and call out his findings. The pool walls were painted turquoise and the water reflected the sun like an enormous gem sunk in the pillowed green acres of the Garden of Eden. Arthur, the Eden's lifeguard as well as its headwaiter, was as obsessed with keeping the pool clean as he was with scrubbing blackheads from his face. He dumped in chlorine until deadly vapors rose from the surface. Any moth or beetle that fluttered too close dropped like a pebble.

I breathed deeply, then dove. Emptying my lungs, I sank to the bottom, where I lay with my belly scraping the rough steel. My blood throbbed so loudly in my ears, the watery world pulsated with it: *How long can you stay here, how long, how long . . .*

Forever, I answered. I could live without breathing, explore the world's oceans with no need for tanks. I flipped onto my back and floated there, between bottom and surface, the sunlight a spatter of gold drops above, the fir trees curved wings. I told myself no one had seen the world *this* way.

And when I grew bored with floating, I climbed from the pool and tossed a penny over my shoulder.

"Arthur! Hey, Arthur! I bet I can find it in less than a minute!"

Not that my brother ever would time me. Not that he paid any attention. Like most children, I equated attention with love. But my brother thought the highest form of attention a brother could bestow was relentless correction. And because he did love me, he feared I would become what he most hated: a woman who thought she was special. He classified people according to whether they demanded special treatment – "Waiter, make sure the fish has no bones!" "I want colder water!" "Artie, dear, get me a fork whose tines aren't bent!" – or whether they sat quietly and ate what they were given. I knew I couldn't please him. From my orange hair to my feet, whose nails I painted scarlet, I was too loud, too brash. But praise is most precious when given by those who dispense it most rarely. If my brother had commended me for finding the penny I'd thrown into the pool, I might have become a pearl diver. And when I rose from the depths and saw his turned head, I felt cheaper than the coin in my fist. With no special talents, I must be the same as every other girl, as one drop of water is exactly like the other drops. This scared me so profoundly I had no other choice but to turn to the staff, who paid me attention because my last name was Appelbaum, a fact I tried hard to forget.

I climbed from the pool and shouted insults at the busboys until two of them grabbed my ankles and wrists, and – one, two, *three* – tossed me into the depths so the water rose from the pool and flattened the hairdos of the women playing cards.

"Lucy! Don't splash!"

To protect their bouffants these women wore kerchiefs with hundreds of petals or tall hats whose filaments waved in the wind like the tentacles of spiny creatures on rocks by the sea. Some women played canasta, tapping their heels as they waited for cards. (Their legs were shot blue, like the celery stalks my teacher propped in an inkwell the year before, in third grade.) Other women played Mah-Jongg – fast fingers, fast tongues, the ivory tiles clicking: "Two bam," "One dragon." But if I drew too near their table, one of these women would grab me by the shoulders, exclaiming *zise mammele tayere* – sweet, dear little mother! – while the other women chimed:

"What bottle did that red hair come from!"

"Someone is going to wake up and find herself with a lovely little shape any day now!"

I was desperate to grow up, but the crepe-paper skin hanging from their necks made me queasy, and I had to admit that growing up didn't stop at fifteen, or even at my parents' age, but kept on and on until you began to grow *down*, the old women's spines curving until they were shorter than I was.

My only hope that old age needn't be frightening came from the Feidels. Each afternoon they appeared at the pool, Shirley in a trim maroon one-piece, Nathan in trunks neither baggy nor too tight. Shirley had the figure of a much younger woman, with smooth skin and long white hair, which she wore in a bun. Nathan had a thick, square-cut, silver mustache, a cleft chin, and a nose that came straight from his brow. He and his wife would step down the ladders on opposite sides of the pool and, without hesitation, even on the chilliest day, slip into the water and swim toward each other, pass and keep swimming, twenty laps in counterpoint, strong rhythmic strokes, as the numbers on their wrists, written in an ink that never washed off, rose from the water again and again.

When they finished their swim Nathan and Shirley climbed from the pool, and Nathan draped his wife's shoulders with a thick purple towel they must have brought from home. Then they kissed. No parts of their bodies touched but their lips, but I felt so unsettled I was attracted more strongly than ever to the waiters who lay sunning on the deck.

An outsider might have thought the boys were sleeping, but I knew they were actually using the sun's rays to recharge their batteries. How else could they find the energy to work seven days a week: out of bed at six to get ready for breakfast, clear the tables, serve lunch, set up for the next meal, a few hours' break before serving dinner, which took until eleven-thirty to clear? The steel trays they brandished might have been shields for an army of knights. Loaded with dishes, such a tray couldn't be lifted by two ordinary men. But a waiter could swing a tray to his shoulder and dart between the tables so the steaming soup flew above the heads of the indifferent diners. I didn't think it fair that the guests, who did no work, should lounge on cushioned chairs while the staff had to lie on the concrete deck. When I ran the Eden – and I never doubted I would – things would be fair.

I stood above Herbie, the knight I loved best, Sir Herbie the Scrub-brush, bristling with black hairs. Beside him lay Larry, with a pink hairless chest and nipples like pink candy dots, and Steve, Michael, Bruce, all of them sleeping so soundly I almost regretted what I had to do next.

Almost. Not quite. The night before, the busboys finished work early and decided to hitchhike to town for ice cream. When I begged to go with them, Herbie said, "Loose, you won't miss much. The waitress at HoJo's will bring us our sundaes. We'll try to imagine what she looks like without that hair net, we'll pass out in our butterscotch syrup, and when the place closes, we'll get up and crawl home."

So why didn't they stay at the Eden, with me, and go to sleep early?

"We have to, that's all. It's the law of our nature."

I'd heard of many strange laws – like not eating spare ribs, or that other law, the one about slicing the penis from an eight-day-old boy – but nothing about having to gawk at girls in hair nets.

"It's this way," Herbie said, rubbing the bristles on his chin, "when guys get together, they do certain things. Maybe those things aren't so great. But it's worse for a person to be by himself."

This I understood. When no one was watching me, I felt my life was a movie projected on air.

I scooped icy water from the pool, then uncupped my hands above Herbie's belly. Though he tightened his muscles, his eyes remained shut. I hated myself but I had to keep going.

The third scoop of water made Herbie reach out and pass me to Larry, who, in his sleep, passed me to Steven, who passed me to Michael, then on to Bruce, whose arms closed around me, a carnivorous plant with a fly in its leaves. I squealed and squirmed, flesh to hot flesh, until I heard a whistle.

"Stop that!" Arthur commanded from his lounge near the diving board. "Don't pester them. Go play with your dolls."

His voice stung as smartly as if he'd squirted chlorine in my face. I told myself again that Arthur didn't really hate me, he hated the hotel. He was always complaining that the Eden was ruining his health and souring "his chances." He couldn't take time off to visit his roommate from his first year at Princeton, though this roommate's family owned a house at a place called Martha's Vineyard. No, Arthur was just too tired to let his love show. Seeing him now, twisting this way and that as he tried to massage his own shoulders, it came to me that he truly did need me.

I freed myself from Bruce, who rolled over immediately and dropped back to sleep. I took a few steps toward Arthur. I would rub his sore back and tell him the jokes that Maxxie Fox, the comic, had taught me that morning. *I was wrong*, Arthur would say. *The minute you touched me, the pain disappeared.*

I'd just reached the diving board when Linda Brush scooted past and sat on the lounge chair right next to Arthur, without even asking. How could he stand to have her that near? Linda Brush was one of the middle-aged mothers who brought their children to the Eden for two or three months, leaving their husbands to work and sweat in New York. Her hair was a shiny black ball; a person could poke two fingers in those black-circled eyes, a thumb in that round mouth, and send that head rolling. She wore a two-piece bathing suit like my own, but orange; a scar crawled down her belly into the panties. I grew ill, thinking where that scar led and how the two Brush twins had lived in that stomach until the doctor slit it open and lifted them out.

The twins were identical. As a young child, I'd thought this meant they were alike not only on the surface, but the same through and through. I couldn't see them lying next to one another without feeling compelled to draw a blanket over one baby's face. Having a twin cheapened your worth; for all anyone could tell, your twin was the real you and you were the fake.

As the Brush twins grew older, I saw, to my relief, that they weren't the same. Samuel, the younger twin, followed Mitchell wherever he went, so dreamy and slow he seemed to be mocking Mitchell the way Arthur mocked me, repeating everything I said with a retarded child's slur. ("Stop doing that!" I'd scream, and Arthur, thick-tongued, would mimic "thtop doing that.") For as long as I knew him, Sam Brush retained an infant's blank face, whereas even by six Mitchell had hardened his features, sharpened his gaze, as though to help everyone tell them apart. Today he was pressing a scalloped bottle cap into Sam's bare arm, as though cutting dough for cookies. Sam sat there and smiled.

Their mother didn't notice. She was squeezing lotion across my brother's chest, teasing him about his dark skin and kinky black hair. "Why, if Ah didn't know bet-tah, Ah'd think one of the Appelbahms had slept with they-ah dah-kies."

Why didn't my brother slap her? He just grunted, and Linda slid her hand toward his navel. I saw her pink nails slip beneath the elastic waistband of his trunks.

I jumped in the water, swimming and swimming. I wouldn't even touch the bottom or the sides.

At four o'clock my mother came to the pool for her one-hour break between running the front desk and running the dining room. She stood beside the water in her gray housedress.

"You're chattering like a skeleton," she said.

"Oh, Mom, how can a skeleton chatter? A skeleton is *dead*."

"And you will be, too, if you catch pneumonia."

I swam to the shallow end and climbed the steps as slowly as it is possible to climb steps.

"Quick! Go and change! If you stay in a damp suit you'll end up a cripple."

I rolled my eyes. "How could a damp suit – "

"Don't argue. Sylvia Siskind's daughter got polio from just a quick dip. Of course, that was a public pool, her mother had to be crazy to let her near it. But we don't have to tempt the Evil Eye by walking around in damp suits."

I had no intention of changing to dry clothes so early in the day. I would get a snack; by the time I returned, my mother would have left or forgotten her order. I hitched up my bottoms, marched across the front lawn and right through the lobby, defying a sign that said NO WET SUITS, and then I marched out the side door and up to a window in a ramshackle booth called The Concession.

"The usual," I said.

Mrs. Grieben, the cook and concessionaire, reached one flabby arm into the freezer and brought out three chocolate-covered marshmallow sticks, so frigid they hurt my teeth when I bit one. Then she opened the red cooler.

"Orange hair, orange soda," she said sagely, as if God had decreed that dark-haired children must drink Coke and blond ones cream soda.

The Orange Crush tasted like summer itself. I gulped half without stopping.

"Who gave you that *chazeray*!"

The voice made the bottle shake in my hand.

"Who gave you that pig food!" My grandmother raised a fist at Mrs. Grieben. "You want her to get fat as a pig, as a *chazer* like you?"

"You don't call me pig!"

"Pig! *Chazer*! Pig!" Nana whirled. "And you! Don't run around barefoot!" She said this in Yiddish – *gey nit arum borves* – and I wanted to laugh because this last word sounded like "boobas," but I knew what was coming.

"You go without shoes, your feet get stepped on!"

I jumped back in time to prevent Nana's heel from grinding my toes. As far as I could tell, this was the only real risk of going barefoot.

Nearly everyone I knew was terrified of Nana. As a toddler, Arthur had picked up a block and hurled it at her. He missed; she retrieved it and hurled it right back. Though the block split his scalp, Arthur was too stunned to cry, even when the doctor was stitching up the wound.

My grandmother couldn't hear a word an enemy shouted in her ear, but if someone whispered a bad word about her, even in the next room, Nana would scream: "You should burn in Gehennah for such a lie!" She didn't speak, she ranted, punctuating her sentences with goaty snorts – *naah, naah* – which made me believe this was how she'd come to be called Nana in the first place.

"Don't run with that bottle in your mouth, naah, you might trip, naah, naah, you'll knock your teeth out."

"I don't *have* any teeth."

But even when confronted with the gaping truth, my grandmother wouldn't relent. "Stay here until you're finished, naah. You don't walk, you can't fall."

I guzzled my soda and set the bottle on the counter. "I don't think you look like a pig," I assured Mrs. Grieben, then ran back to the pool.

What luck! My mother was playing canasta. I slipped quietly down the steps, but the waves spread like radar.

"Lucy, you'll get cramps!" She turned in her chair. "You need to wait an hour after eating, at least."

"But I only ate soda!"

"Then why is your face covered with chocolate?" She unrolled a tissue from her sleeve. "Here, spit."

I refused; she spit for me, scrubbing my cheeks and the skin beneath my nose until I could smell my mother's sour saliva. I squirmed free. Had Herbie and the other boys witnessed my shame? No, they'd left to set up for dinner.

"Come on, Mom," I pleaded. "Just a little while? Can I?" I was whining, I knew, but the sun already was touching the hill behind the Eden. "Now? Can I? Please?"

My mother's eyes strayed to the new hand of cards on the table. The other women's heels were tapping the deck. "Oh, all right. Just don't go into the deep end."

I promised. But even before she'd played her first card I'd ducked beneath the floats and was heading toward the marker that proclaimed 7 FEET.

The sunbathers were the first to pack up. The pinochle players stubbed out their stogies and hectored their wives into bidding their last hands. The canasta games ended. My mother stood and stretched. She saw me in the water. "Lucy, come out of there this instant!"

"Just one more lap."

"I can't stand here arguing, you know that."

Though Nana ruled the kitchen and my father served as her steward, my mother's job was hardest since she mixed with the guests, scurrying from table to table and enduring their complaints about cold soup and spoiled liver. They'd paid a flat sum, which earned them the right to gobble all they could, three meals a day. Most of them tried to wolf down enough food to recoup their investment, and, if they could, accumulate interest.

"You're old enough to understand," my mother said. "Even with all our work . . . The prices these days! And how can we pay off our debts if we're only a quarter full? What will your father do, at his age . . . All I ask is, please, don't do so much to aggravate me."

The sadness in her voice, and the setting sun, which was throwing sad shadows, made me want to run to my mother and comfort her. But before I could climb out she said, "What's the use?" and hurried away.

Other than the Brush twins, their mother and Arthur, only my grandfather remained at the pool. He lay on a special wheeled lounge chair beneath an afghan his wife had crocheted, the yarn fuchsia, red, and orange, a neon advertisement of his helplessness. I liked to sit beside him and tell him the events of my day. My grandfather never teased me, he was never called away to attend crises. I would stretch out beside him and lie without moving to see what it felt like. Arthur, I knew, should have rolled Grandpa Abe to the kitchen so someone could feed him. Instead, my brother turned his recliner so he and Linda Brush could follow the last rays of the sun.

"I've got to go," he said blandly.

"Your busboy can do what needs doing. You work too hard, Artie. You don't want to die young."

I dove underwater. The surface squirmed with pink and red lines. I'm a magic fish, I thought, and swam up to eat the worms, closing my fish lips over each squiggle. When the worms disappeared, I decided to swim the length of the pool one more time and get out. I swam to the deep end, and on my way back was startled to find someone had joined me. With the sunlight so weak and my eyesight so blurry from all that chlorine, all I could make out was the person's shape. He was smaller than I was, unless this was a trick of the way the pool bottom slanted.

Whoever it was, he could hold his breath longer than I could. I came up for air. My head and lungs ached, but I dove down again to see who could beat me at this skill I'd been practicing for so many years.

When I saw the boy's face, I was drained of jealousy. *Your lips are blue*, my mother always said when I'd stayed in too long, and I thought she was lying, how could someone's lips turn blue? But this boy's whole body was so blue he blended with the water. I couldn't pull him up so I dragged him by his shorts. These began to come off, but my feet touched the bottom.

I burst to the surface. "Arthur!" I shouted.

I knew he would come running. I would get all the attention I'd ever wanted, though even in that instant I knew it wouldn't last.

He was there, beside me. He grabbed Sam; my brother seemed to leap from the water without touching the wall, and when he lay Sam's body on the deck I could see that it was covered with angry red circles, as if a fish with sharp teeth had sucked him all over. I remembered the bottle cap. "Mitchell," I said.

Their mother was shrieking and shrieking. Arthur bent over Sam, one dark palm to the boy's thin blue chest, the hand rising each time Arthur blew in the boy's lips, though whenever Arthur paused the hand would just lie there. "Get help!" he yelled. "An ambulance!"

If I thought anything at that moment, I thought I could help Sam more by staying than by going. Hadn't I found him and dragged him to safety? If no one else had been there, wouldn't I be the one blowing in his mouth? I tried to remember a prayer from my Bible, but all I could think of was, "Please, let Sam live."

"Goddamn it, Lucy!"

Arthur's voice set me moving, but it didn't stop my praying, and ten minutes later, when the ambulance pulled up, Linda Brush was still shrieking and I was still pleading, "God, let him live."

The volunteers carried Sam on a stretcher as Arthur walked beside them, lips pressed to Sam's. Linda Brush ran after them. She tripped on my flip-flops, cursed and got up. I saw blood on her knees. She and Arthur, half-naked, climbed into our Pontiac and followed the ambulance. Only when the siren had died in the distance was I able to stop praying. I saw my mother and Nana standing at the edge of the road, gesturing crazily at each other.

I walked to my grandfather's lounge. I'd been told he couldn't move, but one of his feet had poked free of the afghan. The ankle was bare, the foot itself covered by a brown backless slipper. I knew he had a "problem with sugar" and somehow had lost two toes to this problem. I'd always wanted to sneak a look at the stumps, but I was too scared to do this now and tucked his leg beneath the afghan.

It came to me that my grandfather must have seen Sam fall into the pool. What did that feel like, straining so hard and not being able to do more than wiggle one foot? My grandfather seemed so helpless I climbed on his lounge and pulled the blanket over us both.

I heard my name. "Lucy!" Then, even more loudly: "Lucy, where did you go!" A sharp whistle followed – TU-TU-TU-TU.

My mother said, "No, Ma, leave the boy. No, stop that."

I peeked from beneath the blanket. My grandmother was holding Mitchell Brush high above the walk, trying to shake the whistle from his clenched mouth.

"TU-TU-TU-TU."

Nana shook him sharply and the whistle went flying across the lawn. Mitchell's face was contorted in defiance and pain, but he wouldn't cry.

"Stop, Ma, you'll snap something, you'll kill him."

I lay my head against my grandfather's chest. He murmured *there, there*, unless this was only the rumbling of his stomach, and his fingers traced a message of love on my back.

Jay Rogoff

Grandma's Cooking

Plaster, plaster, slap the soup!
Fall from the ceiling, make it good.
Give it flavor, give it spice.

Times Mom's mother cooked she'd raise
her eyes to heaven as she plopped
platters down. My sister whispered,
"This chicken's got *hair*," and dumped
salt straight from the big kosher box.
My cousin choked down by the quart
her homemade odorless applesauce
full of skin, seeds, and water. When
she turned her back we'd spoon our helpings
into Arthur's bowl. He'd gag
and ask for more. Once she surprised us –
chopped liver – and we chewed and chewed:
she'd forgot to cook the meat.

She moved about her house as if
some weight would crush her, like the safe
in silent movies. She smelled of mothballs,
sometimes worse. The doctor tried
to diagnose: "Why are you always
sad?"
        "I have two lovely daughters.
I have six grandchildren. Sad?
Who is sad?"
        Nobody asked
about Grandpa, rotund
and silent in his undershirt,
settled like a seal before
the TV set, set to devour
her sclerotic meals, to eclipse

them with indifferent, stubbled lips.
He was built of *Don'ts*: "Don't cross
the street, Don't go near –, Don't spend – "
When I finished junior high
he dropped a gold watch in my palm
without a word. I felt it gleam,
its cool Art Deco grace, and thought,
Where did he get this from?
Outliving her eleven years,
he still bitched about
a twenty she once lost.

In the ward's bright lights one young woman
flapped her wings and soliloquized,
while a teenage boy with a scarred
face tongued the air like a lizard.
An older man stared like an owl
and never said a word. All
creatures, predators and prey,
dwelled peaceably atop Mount Sinai.
Grandma struggled around the ward,
every step achieved as hard
as Everest, all uphill.
We watched her slippers slap the floor.

They upped the knob to 6; she buzzed
with fear that blotted out – like static's
sweep across the radio –
all regularly scheduled programs.
It swept and dusted Grandma's soul
and rearranged the furniture.
A man with a beard and monocle
angrily stubbed out his cigar
and turning on his humpbacked aide,
shouted, "Enough! Turn off the power!
You want to have her dropping dead?
I wash my hands – it's on *your* head."

"Yes, master. Don't beat me any more."
The room glowed blue. Straps undone,
Grandma sat up on the table,
bolt upright. Just audible,
as angels once appeared in telescopes:
"Can I go home? Can I go home?"

My grandmother began life simple,
then had simplicity simplified.
If the body is a temple,
how can it not become defiled?
If instead it's a machine
how could she have understood
how loose springs, a broken bed
can grind our dreams to bone?

My grandmother ate Vita herring
and borscht and sour cream from a jar.
I don't believe the soul endures.
It bears enough. It drives the car,
takes out the garbage, laughs, despairs.
It shivers my heart
how Grandma's kindness was tolerated
by all of us, the way you listen
to your host's child mangle Mozart.
You clap. We'd kiss, and eat her cooking.
It was her way of looking
after us, forever longing
for paradise, with grandchildren,
for some shell to crack open
and sing, enfolding her in singing.

Jinx

Even now, I can't think of Slippery Rock without a little revulsion. For years I hated the entire state of Pennsylvania simply because it contained Slippery Rock. Later, I decided I liked the eastern half of the state because Philadelphia was a mitigating factor.

We had moved to Slippery Rock after my father's death and my mother's return to school to earn a Master's degree. This was her first teaching job: Slippery Rock State Teacher's College. One sometimes heard the unlikely name of Slippery Rock on the tail end of sports reports across the country – partly because Slippery Rock had a good football team and partly because newscasters liked to say Slippery Rock.

Slippery Rock is located about seventy miles north of Pittsburgh, and supposedly its name derived from an unlikely incident in which a settler, chased by Indians, led them across the creek, where they all slipped on the stones in the river, save the wily settler, who knew his way around. "Watch out for the slippery rocks," he yelled back at them. If Slippery Rock had a tourist industry, one might produce large quantities of coffee mugs depicting such a hilarious scene. Or not.

In 1969 Slippery Rock had about three thousand residents and perhaps as many students. The nearest big town was Grove City – it had an ice cream parlor – that's what made it big to me. Slippery Rock had one main street, one restaurant, a newsstand, a town drunk who doubled as the town artist, and freshmen at the college wore beanies around campus, to make them feel silly, I suppose. We lived in an apartment complex, and my friends consisted of neighborhood kids who doubled as classmates. The neighborhood kids wanted to know right off where I was from, where I was born, and I told them New York City. They had heard of New York City, but Slippery Rock was their world, and in a strange reversal of THE NATURAL LAWS OF THE UNIVERSE, they started calling me a hick.

"No, you're the hicks," I insisted.

My main friends were a red-haired kid named Joe, a tall kid named Dick, and a blond kid named Steve. Their families: The Smiths, The Stones, and The Minks, did not believe in wasting syllables on either first names or surnames. Steve Mink spat all the time – all the time, even indoors – Steve never had much spit in him as a consequence; he never allowed moisture to accumulate, but I remember him spitting once on our carpet. "Don't do that in here," my mom told Steve. "That's disgusting."

"I do it at home," Steve said.

"You're not at home," she told him.

We used to go to Steve's house down the road to play football. Steve had a go-cart and a grandmother who beheaded chickens while we played football, like she was part of some kind of surreal and evil cheerleading squad. I was generally the quarterback because I was too skinny to actually tackle anyone, but pretty much fun for the other guys to tackle. I played without shoes and was rarely tackled because I was so terrified that I did all kinds of amazing maneuvers to avoid any body contact whatsoever – leaping over my opponents as they lunged for me, zigzagging and whirling with the grace of a pro. But I soon tired of this play, figuring the odds would eventually get me, and I retreated after school each day to my room, where I tried to memorize Hamlet's soliloquy – I'm not sure why I chose this – while below my window my contemptuous friends yelled up at me, demanding that I play football or they'd beat me up.

"Whether tis nobler in the mind to suffer the slings and arrows of outrageous fortune," I replied.

At that time, I wanted to be an actor – who doesn't? – and I thought that memorizing Shakespeare would lift me out of Slippery Rock. It didn't, and I suffered my share of slings and arrows at the hands of my friends. One night, on my way home from Boy Scouts, Dick, Steve, and Joey ambushed me near our apartment complex: for refusing to play football anymore, for being a hick, a Jew, a Boy Scout (they hated Boy Scouts, too). Joey and Steve grabbed me and held me against a wall while gangly Dick started beating me, but with an improbable object, a gigantic inflated inner tube. It *kind of* hurt, but not much. It surprised me more than anything, and it was awkward for him. I think it wore him out before he could hurt me. "Goddamn hick," he kept yelling, until finally I broke free. Joey called me a kike as I fled. He had previously served notice that he could no longer play with me – his parents had told him I had killed Christ.

"No, you killed Christ," I told him. These kids had everything backwards, so I figured they had that wrong, too.

My revenge came later that fall when I scored the only copy within the county of The Archies hit single, "Sugar, Sugar." I bought it in Grove City for less than a dollar and taunted Dick with it, who was desperate for the single. He offered to buy it from me, but I wouldn't sell. Finally, he offered me $25 for it. I didn't ask where he got the money and I didn't care. But who knows. Maybe it's worth $25 again by now, if Dick still owns the record. I suppose he still lives in Slippery Rock and does things backwards. Maybe he owns the booming tourist concession, selling those mugs that read, "Watch out for the Slippery Rocks," to all those hicks from New York blowing through town.

I hated Slippery Rock because in 1969, to an eleven-year-old boy from an oddball intellectual family, it was a hateful place.

I know I'm being mean to the past and present citizens (denizens?) of Slippery Rock, that I'm being unfair, that I'm being petty in condemning them with such a broad brush. I tell you, I would not mind if God broke off Slippery Rock like an icicle from a roof and tossed it over his shoulder. I know it's irrational, but when you're eleven years old and in despair, you carry a part of that despair for the rest of your life. There's a sharpness to life at eleven that later you're inured to. And you cast around for blame even when you know that the source of your hatred, fear, and sadness is not, in all likelihood, solely where you live.

Maybe it has to do with the death of my father four years before, but not even that completely.

Maybe it has to do with the death of my friend Tommy Alfazy, earlier that year. Tommy was my best friend from Long Beach, New York, where I spent all my summers at my grandmother's beach house. Tommy and another friend, Vince, had been building a fort in the sand on the beach. They dug a hole, piled boards on it, and covered it with more sand. They had asked me if I wanted to do it with them, and I said no, that I thought it was stupid, but they went ahead and did it anyway, and the boards and sand collapsed on Tommy and smothered him. I was in Slippery Rock when I heard the news, and maybe this is in part why I still hate Slippery Rock. The town is death to me, broiling skies and coal veins underneath. I started forming a theory after

Tommy's death that I was some kind of jinx, and that people I loved died, especially when I was away from them and couldn't be there to help. Three years earlier I had been sent to a friend's house when my father suffered his heart attack. I had been away from home when I learned the news. The same was true of Tommy's death – I was stunned when I heard that Tommy, only ten years old, had died. It didn't seem possible. My father's death was possible, but a ten-year-old's death was something I had never been prepared for.

At eleven, death was so real to me that I tried to kill myself. Maybe I shouldn't have been reading *Hamlet.* One afternoon I went to the bathroom cupboard and swallowed as many aspirin as I could before my throat swelled up and I could swallow no more. If I'd been older, I suppose I would have used something more powerful than aspirin, but even aspirin in large quantities can seriously fool with your metabolism. The intent to kill myself was there. Attention wasn't what I sought. After that, I went to sleep and didn't wake up until the next morning when it was time for school. I must have slept for fourteen or fifteen hours, and I'm not sure why my mother didn't try to waken me, or if she did, why she didn't realize that I was more unconscious than asleep.

When I awoke, I felt slightly ashamed of myself, and really wasn't sure why I'd done this – I just felt lonely. The only person I ever told was a boy named Donald who stood in front of me in the lunch line the next day at school.

"You know what I did last night," I said as we slid our trays along. "I swallowed about seventeen aspirin."

He turned and gave me a skeptical look. "Why'd you do that?"

"I don't know," I said.

"You could have died," he said. "That's pretty stupid."

I agreed and felt chastised, but at least he said something that wasn't backwards, that I could understand. I didn't feel like telling my mother. My mother wouldn't have understood. She would have overreacted. But this kid Donald reacted just right, with just the right amount of disapproval. My mother set no limits for my older brother and sister and me when we were kids, and we were often told by relatives that we were spoiled and unruly – all true – but my mother had her hands full after my father died, simply trying to make a living for us. I hardly remember seeing my mother during those days in Slippery Rock. Or my brother and sister.

My sister Nola had graduated from Ohio University on the same day in 1968 as my mother received her Master's. Nola, who was Phi Beta Kappa, went off to Brandeis for a Ph.D. in Philosophy. This was my brother Jonathan's freshman year at O.U. He was sixteen, following in the family tradition of attending college without graduating from high school. My father had attended Amherst at fourteen. My mother started college at sixteen, and Nola had started at seventeen. In fact, I'm the only high school graduate in my immediate family – a strange intellectual joke, a reversal of the normal meaning of such a statement – there's something slightly embarrassing that the only thing my family had to overcome in its education was boredom.

Most of my memories of that time are of me alone, watching TV in the basement or sitting up in my room, memorizing *Hamlet*. I guess, in such a vacuum, I needed to create my own limits – and that, perhaps, is what the aspirin was about. I had successfully negotiated a limit.

I invited Donald home that day and we listened to my recording of the musical soundtrack from *Hair*. We sat on my mother's couch and sang along. "This is the dawning of the Age of Aquarius." Donald liked to sing and he liked to talk about books, both activities I was used to. Donald and I became best friends, *only* friend for me, and we went sledding together or stayed indoors and sang songs from *Hair*. He lived on Elm Street, and I asked my mother what an elm looked like. She said it was a kind of tree, and I asked what kind of tree, and she said she couldn't really explain – most of them were dead anyway. That seemed appropriate for Slippery Rock. I don't remember any of the other street names in Slippery Rock, not even the street on which we lived, only a street named after a diseased tree. I still take nightmare journeys up the hill to our apartment complex sometimes. In my dreams, Slippery Rock is built on frosty terraces with slippery roads and rickety stores that look like the faded wooden structures on the surface of coal mines. Of course, Slippery Rock looks nothing like this, but my dreams build the town into a rockpile of metaphor.

I developed all kinds of compulsions in Slippery Rock. When I ran up the stairs, I had to take them two at a time. On the way down, I skipped the third stair because three was evil, I decided, and if I stepped on the third stair something bad would happen. When returning a snack to the cupboard I had to return it to the exact spot where I had found it. The rules kept changing, appearing in my head like flash cards a moment before the necessary action had to be taken.

Place your spoon on the right side of your bowl. Leave one green Lucky Charms marshmallow floating alone in the milk.

When I think back to that boy I was, I'm almost worried for him, amazed that he ever made it out of Slippery Rock alive, that he survived into adulthood. Now I see what I was trying to do at the time, how I was trying to give my life some order, but back then I could only await the next commands in this mental boot camp in which I existed.

My grandmother was living at the time in Hollywood, Florida, with my Uncle Joe and my Aunt Rose, and after I started getting D's in school, someone suggested (whether my grandmother or my mother, I'm not sure) that I might go down to Florida and finish the school year there. I was ready. The week before we left, there were two hijackings of planes bound for Florida to Cuba. I didn't mind the danger. Even Cuba seemed preferable. I understood the hijackers. I understood why someone might want to risk jail to leave a place they hated living, why death might be preferable. I didn't understand the politics of it. To me, this was a simple case of needing to get away from where you lived, desperation.

My mother and I went down to Florida together over the winter break and stayed the first few days with a woman in Miami named Marjorie, whom my mother had known in college. Marjorie was the editor-in-chief and restaurant critic for *The Miami Star* – the paper's stationery proclaimed it as "One of America's Most Interesting Newspapers." Certainly, Marjorie was one of America's most interesting people, at least to me. In a letter to my mother not long after my father died, Marjorie complained nonstop: about her asthma, a growth that might be cancerous, and a "daughter who will not even take me to the hospital when my ankle is broken." She claimed to write every one of her restaurant columns in five minutes: "In spite of the 'flighty' way of composing, I've gotten compliments on some of my columns . . ." Marjorie fascinated me. She told me that none of the restaurateurs knew her identity, and that they were always trying to find out. She ate out every night. She had a pool, and a mini sauna in her bedroom – the sauna looked like something out of "Get Smart," a chamber that you sat in with your head poking out.

We went to a restaurant one night where Marjorie ordered frogs' legs for me. As we ate she told my mother and me a story.

"In this very restaurant, I saw a man die. He was eating some fish and he swallowed a bone."

"My God," my mother said.

"And you know what, no one helped him. There were doctors in the restaurant, four of them, and not one of them helped the poor man. They were all afraid of being sued. I mentioned that in my review, but it's still a fine place to eat."

I think I've remembered that scene for so long because I was so horrified. We sat at a corner table and I could see the entire restaurant. The restaurant was large and airy and low-lit. We sat by the porch, and I could see waiters carrying their trays, and men and women, a few children sitting at tables, laughing and talking – I focused on one man, a little large, a little red in the face, and imagined him falling out of his chair, coughing, grasping his hands around his throat.

Maybe I hadn't escaped Slippery Rock, merely taken a detour.

The next day Marjorie drove us around on the freeway. I was sitting in the back seat and Marjorie and my mother were chatting up front. Marjorie drove a Mustang, about sixty-five miles an hour, and as she roared up the road I noticed what seemed like a hundred cars heading toward us. I screamed, "Marjorie, look," and for a moment we all looked at the cars in a line four lanes wide heading straight for us – none of us quite sure what was wrong with this picture.

"Those fools!" Marjorie yelled and swerved her car onto the median, between two palms, and made her own entrance ramp onto the right side of the freeway.

I was the first one of us to develop the Hong Kong flu. Until my mother took my temperature, I wasn't quite sure what was wrong with me, why I felt so lightheaded. I had attributed this feeling to spending the night with Marjorie's grandson – he was an avid Elvis fan, the first I ever met, and, like all REAL ELVIS fans I've met since, he left me vaguely unsettled. All night long I had to hear Elvis songs, and not even early Elvis, but late Elvis. Not *too* late. Not puffy, sweaty jumpsuit Elvis, but Comeback Elvis. Suspicious-Minded Elvis. Kentucky Rained-on Elvis. Spanish Harlem Elvis. My theory is that people don't really care about his music anymore – they just can't stop saying Elvis. Elvis, like Slippery Rock, is fun to say.

Slippery Rock Demolishes Elvis, 140 to zip.

What *I* liked was worse, far worse, of course. "Sugar, Sugar" by the Archies, who didn't even exist – At least Elvis once walked the earth, or so it has been told. "Spinning Wheel" by Blood, Sweat, and Tears. I had watched Barbara Feldman from "Get Smart," on whom I had a terrific crush, do a knock-off of "Spinning Wheel" on the Ed Sullivan Show.

"Watch all your troubles by the riverside/catch a painted pony let the spinning wheel ride," she sang while caressing a painted pony on a carousel.

To a literal-minded eleven-year-old, it seemed like the perfect staging for the song.

Now it's funny, but it wasn't funny at the time. And The Archies weren't all that funny either. Not even Elvis was funny. Now all that stuff is dead, no matter how much people want to resurrect it, even Elvis. It's so dead it's laughable.

We didn't stay long with Marjorie after that. Marjorie and my mother came down with the flu, too, and though Marjorie begged us to stay to take care of her, we couldn't. We couldn't even take care of ourselves. We had to move to my grandmother's place so that she could help nurse us back to health. I hope someone took pity on poor Marjorie and helped her, if not her daughter who wouldn't take her to the hospital for a broken ankle, then some other more merciful relative or friend. I've probably never met a person more terrified of death than Marjorie, though comically unmindful of it at the same time. We never saw her again, and as far as I know, she and my mother never communicated after that disastrous stay.

The next two weeks I spent in bed at my grandmother's place with the Hong Kong flu, a fever that broke at 104. My mother had it too, and she was in the bed next to mine. While my grandmother waited on us, we read to each other and played games. My mother introduced me to a play by the French writer, Jean Giradoux, "The Madwoman of Chaillot," about an elderly woman in Paris who, together with her destitute and powerless friends of the street, trap a group of ruthless oil magnates and developers in the sewers of the city because they want to drill for oil under Paris.

Strangely, being sick with the Hong Kong flu, on the brink of death and dementia, is one of my fondest memories of childhood. Sure, what leaps to mind are the obvious Freudian reasons – my mother all to myself – in the next bed ha ha! – and while I won't deny these possibilities, I also simply have to say that the reason those two weeks were enjoyable was because they were so enjoyable. I liked things of the mind, still do, and this was the first time I could relax and do what I enjoyed doing in a long while. Not that I disliked playing football – though I did, intensely. Not that other kids weren't more normal than me – spitting on the carpet, beating people with inner tubes, going ga-ga over Elvis.

I was allowed for two weeks to be sick, abnormal. And so, I did things that I wasn't supposed to do as a kid. I read and memorized a part in a play. I read poetry aloud. I played a poetry game called "Exquisite Corpse." Appropriate for a boy transfixed by and obsessed with death.

I'm always suspicious of people who say they had a normal childhood. What happens to those people? I think maybe they're in a restaurant one day and they see someone choking on a fishbone, and they don't know what to do. They have no frame of reference. They write an unfavorable review. They're afraid of a lawsuit. They're tempted by the frogs' legs.

I know I'm being unfair to those people who live idyllic lives. I admit it. No, they're the ones who save the person's life. I'm the one who watches, glad it wasn't me this time. I'm the one who has no frame of reference, no experience with safety. That blue pallor looks almost normal to me. I'm the one who orders the frogs' legs.

After my mother and I recovered from the Hong Kong flu, she returned to Slippery Rock and I was left to spend the rest of the school year with my grandmother Ida, my great Uncle Joe, and my Aunt Rose. Actually, I wasn't related to either Joe or Rose, though I considered them my aunt and uncle. Joe had been married to Ida's sister, my great Aunt Frances, and after Frances died, Joe married Rose, a Hungarian Jew who had survived the death camps. It was impossible not to like Rose, who had the cheeriest personality of anyone I've ever met, bar none, despite the fact that she lost her entire family in the Holocaust, with the exception of her son, whom she didn't know had survived until thirteen years after the war when she ran into him by accident on the streets of Tel Aviv. Rose had owned a newsstand in Manhattan in front of a restaurant frequented by the Gabor sisters, and Rose was always telling us about her Gabor encounters – she liked them both immensely. She looked like a slightly older, zaftig version of the Gabor sisters, with dyed blonde hair, what they might have looked like if they had owned a newsstand in midtown Manhattan and sat on a stool all day, and been through death camps and had blue tattoos on their wrists.

Rose was one of those people, chiefly women of an older generation who, once they've identified a favorite food of a favored grandchild, niece, or nephew, will forever make it for that child whenever she or he visits. With Rose and me, it was apple strudel. My grandmother Ida was a lovely person, and had the same idea, but with her the signals somehow got crossed, and she thought my favorite food was meatloaf – which I have nothing against, but it's not what I'd order for a last meal.

Joe was completely the opposite of Rose, a dour man who always looked concerned or worried. Joe was built like Barney Rubble, with white scrub-brush hair and a white mustache. He had been a signalman in the Navy in World War I and had a ship sunk from under him. He and my Aunt Frances had met and married in the thirties, and had run a little soda fountain in Jamaica, Queens. Frances was always considered the great beauty of my grandmother's family, but when I knew her, she was old and pretty dotty, having suffered a stroke. At seven, I liked talking to her because she was so funny, inadvertently so, but I didn't know any better, and couldn't understand why the adults looked so unhappy when she said something funny. One night Joe fell asleep at the wheel of his car and hit a utility pole – and Frances was killed. To most of the family, her death was a relief. Sad, but a relief. No one, of course, ever talked about Frances or her death after she died. I learned about her death on a train ride – my grandmother told me, and said I shouldn't say anything to Joe because it would make him sad. This is one thing I learned about death at a young age, that after someone died, you were never supposed to mention them again. If it had been the other way around, Frances would have talked. She would have babbled happily about Joe, maybe thinking he was still alive, because of her *condition*, because she didn't know any better.

For four months I lived with Joe, Rose, and Ida in their retirement community in Hollywood, and I loved it. By any yardstick other than a conventional one, I was essentially an elderly person. I ate Meals on Wheels, nightly played a Hungarian version of canasta called Kalooki with my relatives, and played shuffleboard with Joe every day – we had a shuffleboard court right outside the door! I really liked being old. Age, I decided, is wasted on the elderly. None of my relatives seemed aware how much better it was to be old than young. They even complained about it.

And I enjoyed the school I attended. Classes were held in open-air metal huts. The walls would drop away when the weather was good, which was almost every day. I went from D's in Slippery Rock to A's in all my subjects. This was a little idyll for me – shuffleboard at home instead of football, and the entire school went bowling on Fridays right after the Spelling Bee, which I always won. The only sore spot in this happy time was one boy named Frank Parker, who I disliked for one reason or another. So I put a curse on him. I took a piece of notebook paper and drew two swords crossed like the Wilkinson swords, and I made up a name for an honorary society, The Silver Sword Society. In between the swords, I wrote the initials of this secret society. Underneath this picture, I made up my curse:

> A curse upon Frank Parker. Something bad will happen to him.
> So sayeth Robin Hemley, President of the Silver Sword Society™

After I wrote the curse, I put it in my desk, but it must have fallen out when I removed one of my books because Frank Parker found it on the floor.

"Did you write this?" he asked me, rubbing the top of his head. I expected him to get into a fight with me, but he didn't look angry. He told me that he was reading the curse as he stepped out the door, and a tile fell off the roof and knocked him in the head.

"Really?" I was quite pleased with myself.

"Take the curse off, okay?" he asked.

"Sure, okay," I said. I made Frank stand completely still and I advised him that an invisible sword was sticking through his gut. Carefully and elaborately, showing much strain, I tugged the sword from Frank's belly.

In the way of the kid world, Frank and I became good friends after that. I could afford to be generous. I had some control. I could direct some of the bad things that seemed to follow me, could make them stick in someone else's gut if I wanted.

That day, contented, I went back to the retirement village, ate some Meals on Wheels chow and watched my favorite TV show, *Dark Shadows*, about a good but still deadly vampire named Barnabas Collins, who was always traveling back and forth in time trying to save the world. I identified with Barnabas, still do. But he scared me and he scared himself, like I scare myself sometimes. Barnabas was always fighting one monster or another, when he wasn't fighting himself and his own tendencies toward self-destruction. This week, it was something called The Leviathan. The worst thing about the Leviathan was that no one had yet seen it, but you could sure hear the damn thing. Its breathing was labored and intense and hollow, and it made splashy footprint sounds as it walked. It lived in water and always left puddles of it, like so much pee, wherever it went.

That's how you could tell The Leviathan had been around – that and the fact that whenever you saw that puddle of water, you knew that The Leviathan had snatched another victim. But you never saw it, and you never saw its victims, and that's what killed me. It was, by far, the scariest monster around.

I had to turn the TV off. I couldn't watch anymore, and I never watched *Dark Shadows* again after that week.

One day a letter arrived in the mail from an Assistant Counsel to the Attorney General of the United States. I had written to President Nixon because of an incident I had seen on the TV news one evening when Joe and Ida and Rose were watching in the living room.

> Dear President Nixon,
>
> You don't know me, but I am a concerned boy. Tonight on the news I saw some people throwing rocks at little kids on a bus going to school in Arkansas. How can you let this happen? Children should be safe when they go to school. Please do something about it right now! I am eleven.
>
> Sincerely,
>
> Robin Hemley
>
> P.S. – I am a boy, not a girl even though my name is Robin. Boys in England are called Robin, even though I am not from England that is my name.

The scene on TV had shown several orange school buses being pelted with rocks by angry parents – some of them were trying to tip the buses over. The picture was shot from a little distance from the bus, but you could clearly make out children on the buses, and you could hear them screaming as the windows shattered and the metal was dented. The scene transfixed me. I couldn't understand how adults could throw rocks at little children. Wasn't childhood dangerous enough? Kids terrorized one another just fine – they didn't need any help from adults. I didn't know a thing about busing or integration, and only a little about the civil rights movement, but I knew a lot about children feeling unsafe, feeling that death was right around the corner.

The letter I received back from the government was addressed to Master Robin Hemley, which I didn't understand until my grandmother explained that this was a term of respect used when addressing boys.

March 2, 1970

Dear Master Hemley,

President Nixon has asked me to respond to your letter of concern in regards to the incident in Fayetteville on January 21 of this year. The President shares your concern. However, appropriate action was taken by the state of Arkansas, and so it does not seem fitting at this time for the federal government to intervene.

Sincerely,

Harold W. Varina
Assistant Counsel to the Attorney General

Ida read this letter aloud to Rose and Joe that afternoon, and I was treated like a hero. Rose didn't understand English perfectly and was convinced that the President had signed the letter himself, and that Harold W. Varina was indeed the President. Ida wanted to frame the letter, and even Joe seemed happy – the beginning, he said, of a distinguished life in politics for me. I was happy for all the attention, but not really satisfied by the letter. The man who answered my letter had not, after all, answered my question. How could this happen? I wasn't only asking for a solution or an excuse. I wanted a reason.

My grandmother and I went to Miami Beach a couple of weeks before I was to return to Slippery Rock. She said that we had to go to a hotel where Cousin Ruth was dying of Lou Gehrig's Disease. I didn't even know who Cousin Ruth was, and visiting someone who was dying did not seem to me a suitable activity for young or old alike. The less said about death, the better, and watching someone die seemed like an embarrassing activity, akin to watching them on the toilet.

"What am I supposed to say to her?" I asked my grandmother. I wasn't going to tell her I was sorry she was dying. When my father had died, someone had told my brother Jonathan that they were sorry, and he'd said, "What are you sorry for? You didn't kill him." And that's the attitude I adopted afterwards. That seemed properly embattled and hostile. I imagined Ruth would say the same thing if I told her I was sorry. "What are you sorry for, kid? I don't even know you." And then I'd be humiliated and would plunge a silver sword in her for revenge.

"You don't have to say anything," my grandmother told me.

"There will be a lot of people there, and Ruth can't speak anymore. Just say hello and smile. Everyone loves your smile."

"Should I tell her I'm sorry she's dying?"

"That's not polite," my grandmother said. "Don't mention it. Pretend to be happy to see her."

To seal my approval, my grandmother offered me a death bribe. I was familiar with death bribes – to make death more palatable, you were given something that you wanted. When my father died, a friend of our family took me downtown and said I could have any toy I wanted. She seemed dismayed when I couldn't think of anything, so I pointed to a model car in a drugstore window. The car was wrapped up for me and my mother's friend seemed relieved. I tried to put the car together, but gave up halfway through the project. Wheels on a chassis, that's all it ended up as, nothing at all like the perfect picture of a Camaro on the box.

My grandmother's death bribe was a banana split, the largest, she claimed, that could be found anywhere, big enough for two people. And, as an added bonus, the soda shop where the banana splits could be had was located on the bottom floor of Cousin Ruth's hotel. Ida and I sat at the counter with a giant boat of whipped cream, bananas, ice cream, and syrup, fortifying ourselves with dollops of sugar before we met dying Ruth. Ida kept asking me if it tasted good, and I kept having to reassure her that this was indeed the best banana split I'd ever eaten. We gorged ourselves and then went up to Ruth's room.

Though other people milled around the room, it was the dying person who immediately captured my attention. She sat in a recliner, her legs propped up, covered up to her neck with a loose, colorful blanket. And then I looked away, forcing myself not to stare. The windows of the room were open and people were quiet. My Aunt Carrie was there, and my Uncle Morty, and a few other people I didn't recognize. A friend of the family named Anne Deutsch sat on the bed near Ruth. Anne was not simply a friend of our family, but a kind of camp follower, a fanatical devotee. She was the same age as my great aunts and uncles, in her sixties at the time, and wherever they or my grandmother went, she went too. She was always around. I can hardly remember an occasion when she wasn't there. I didn't mind her. She was a very sweet woman, sweeter than many of my relatives by a long shot, but I was not happy to see her because of a falling out of sorts we'd had the previous summer. We were walking to the store near my grandmother's beach house when she asked me if I'd start calling her Aunt Anne.

"You're not my aunt," I said.

"I know," she said, "But I'd like it if that's what you'd call me from now on."

"I don't want to," I said. No one in my family liked to be called Aunt or Uncle. I once tried it out on my Uncle Allan and Aunt Rene and they told me to stop immediately.

"How about this, Robin," she said. "If you call me Aunt Anne, I'll treat you like one of my own, and you know what that means?"

"What?"

"Presents."

This whole conversation made me uncomfortable, and the more she pressed me the less I was inclined to call her Aunt, or even Anne.

"Just say it," she said. "Just say Aunt Anne."

"No."

"I mean it, Robin. I'm only going to make this offer once."

But I hadn't relented. Now I saw her on the bed looking forlorn and I felt sorry for her. I approached and she gave me a little hug and peck on the cheek and I said, "Hello, Aunt Anne." She smiled faintly at me.

Weeks later, my grandmother reported to me that this gesture of mine hadn't gone unnoticed or unappreciated – I was surprised that Anne's request was known by the entire family. I never called her Aunt Anne again. Soon she had a grandchild anyway, and I was left in the dust.

Next, I approached Ruth. I had to face her sooner or later. I remembered Ruth vaguely now. She had a nice face and a gentle smile. I had already been told that she couldn't talk, but that didn't seem necessary. She looked at me and I didn't feel so frightened of her, though I could see she was weak and dying. We didn't touch, but I smiled back and made a gesture that I hoped no one else noticed. I grabbed the scabbard of a sword and pulled it from her body, gently, almost imperceptibly. To the uninitiated, it might have looked like a half-hug, pulled away from at the last moment.

I didn't want to return to Slippery Rock, and made every attempt to avoid going home, but my mother missed me too much, and in April she came down to Hollywood. I missed her, too, but not enough to want to return. I was having a great time as an old timer. And my shuffleboard game was getting really good – I even started winning at Kalooki.

There used to be a picture of me walking around a fountain in Miami wearing sunglasses, a Naugahyde vest, a Nehru shirt, and a sun medallion as big as my face. A destructive dog of mine chewed it up several years ago, but that's just as well. It's an embarrassing picture, not simply because the styles are so laughable now. Of course, we laugh at whatever isn't current, whether music or fashion. And why not? We all want to be young, or most of us anyway.

The photo was embarrassing because it was so fake. This was my impression of a young person, not the real thing. I was an actor, and I was sure that I was going to be discovered as I walked around that fountain. I knew that someone important must be watching, someone who'd recognize I had the exact look they wanted.

I was so sure, just as I was sure that this time the plane would be hijacked and my mother and I would begin a brand new life in Havana.

The first night back in Slippery Rock my mother told me she had something important to tell me. We were halfway through dinner.

"Your friend, Donald," she said. Then she said something I couldn't hear, but I pretended to hear it, pretended it made perfect sense.

"Oh," I said and kept on eating.

But my mother wasn't finished. "I'm sorry I have to tell you this, Robin. Did you hear me?"

"Yes."

"I know you were close."

I kept eating.

"No one is really sure what happened. It happened during the winter. Apparently, Donald and his younger brother . . ."

"You mean Fred?"

"I don't know which one."

"He only has one."

My mother was looking at me and then she looked at her plate. "They were down near Slippery Rock Creek. A man started chasing them or something, no one's really sure, and Donald fell through the ice. His brother . . ."

"Fred?"

"Yes, Fred. His brother saw the whole thing happen and he hasn't spoken a word since."

Then my mother told me an alternate version of Donald's death, that they had been climbing trees, a branch had broken, and Donald had fallen through the ice. I didn't need to hear an alternate version. However he died, however he came to be there, the results were the same. He'd fallen through the ice, and unable to find his way out again, had drowned. I understood that. I nodded. I understood that. They shouldn't have been out there on the ice alone. I understood that. But it didn't sound like Donald. It didn't sound like something he'd do. He was so cautious. He never got in trouble. He thought death was stupid.

I understood his brother's inability to speak, to shed light on the true story. I understood that, in the face of death, no words were necessary, no words were appropriate, no words could suffice or describe. The less said the better.

We finished dinner in silence and then my mother went to the living room couch and started sorting through her mail. I stood up slowly from the table, turned around, and ran to her. I collapsed in her lap and cried. "I wasn't home again," I said, sobbing. She stroked my head, not sure what I meant, what being home had to do with anything. If I had been there, I thought, this might not have happened. Somehow my being there could have saved him. There was no comforting me and never could be.

Donald was the only one I cried for. I didn't cry for my father. I tried. I knew I was supposed to, but I couldn't. I didn't cry for my friend Tommy, smothered earlier that year in the sand fort he'd built – though I remember his face much more clearly than Donald and knew him longer. But Donald, who I barely knew, who had shown me the kindness of disapproval, who told me it was stupid to die, he was the one I couldn't stop crying for. Even now, nearly thirty years later, the grief smothers me like so much sand, like ice I can't find my way out of. Donald's death convinced me once and for all that I was, indeed, a jinx, that whoever I loved would die – and I haven't seen anything to convince me otherwise – except that now I know we're all jinxes.

When I think of Slippery Rock now, the picture I invariably see is a storm rolling in from the vantage point of the kitchen of our apartment – I see hills with skeletal trees. I don't know why it's this image, unremarkable and bland, not even fixed in a specific moment of memory that stays with me so deeply, that seems to embody all my terror and angst over the place – except that what terrifies me most about life are exactly those moments that are unremarkable and bland, that are erasable. Loss of memory terrifies me. Loss of identity terrifies me.

The world is supposed to make sense, that's what childhood is about, what at least we pretend it's about. That's when we give our children all the explanations for why things work and how they work, or if we can't, we stay silent and, by our silence, ask them to try to figure it out. We try to keep them away from things they won't understand, things we can't understand, pictures on the news, atrocities, the deaths of parents, of young friends, of siblings. We give them explanations, but still they crawl into our bed at night and tell us they're afraid, they've had a nightmare, even the young ones who have survived relatively unharmed so far, our children who we wish we could protect forever, whose childhoods we want to be an idyll.

We don't even need to know what their nightmares are about. Nightmares are all the same. You're being chased – that's all you need to know. Or you're in an unfamiliar place. Or a familiar place with stores that look like coal mines, streets that are slippery, frosted terraced hills, a drum kettle sky and winter in the air.

I know what it's like to wake up in terror, alone, unable to catch a breath. I still wake up hating myself many nights. For unspecified reasons, for many reasons that don't even always make sense. This is Slippery Rock's legacy. This is where I still live.

Sanford Pinsker

Dares, Double-Dares, and the Jewish-American Writer

In the diversity-conscious 1990s, one would think that little daring would be required for a young Jewish-American poet to submit his or her work to national literary magazines, but such was not always the case. For Karl Shapiro, who served for many years as the editor of these pages, literature – pronounced *liter-a-toor* by them in the know – had the look of a closed Anglo-Saxon shop. Outsiders were not only *not* welcome, but in a culture dominated by T. S. Eliot's poetry and his cultural pronouncements, Jews in particular were at best declassé and at worst a considerable threat. In Shapiro's case, well-meaning elders suggested that he change his name to something more acceptable, more "British," more like A. J. Archibold – anything, in short, that didn't scream out his "Jewishness" as Shapiro obviously did – before he submitted his poems to places like *Poetry* or the *Atlantic*.

Those were the bad old days at their snootiest; but if things have changed, it is also true that they have largely remained the same. Jewish-American writers had an uphill struggle during the 1940s; now they discover that they aren't the fashionable minority fashion-conscious editors are looking for. Write about the barrios of east Los Angeles or inner-city ghettos in Chicago, about an Indian reservation or growing up on one of the Aleutian islands, and the diversity industry will extend you a welcoming hand; but fiction about Jewish-American life has a way of generating yawns: been there, done that, as Gen-X'ers like to put it. As with so much about American culture, only Yiddish quips seem earthy enough, ironic enough, for the occasion: *Shver tsu zein a yid, aber zayer schver tsu zein a yiddische schreiber* – It's hard to be a Jew, but it's doubly hard to be a Jewish writer.

Which brings me to the dares and double-dares of my title. At its most obvious, most literal level, dares are anchored in the world of the playground where early contests about manhood are given expression in vivid rhetoric and escalating hyperbole. One could be "dared" into an eight-year-old's version of fisticuffs, but most of the time dares meant doing the unthinkable, and the dangerous – say, climbing a seemingly unclimbable tree. Double-dares raised the ante exponentially. "OK, OK, you climbed," your nemesis would grudgingly admit, "but I *double-dare* you to filch a few apples from the top." Double-dares were scary because the people who issued them meant business and also because what they said and what you did (or did not do) always pulled in a crowd.

Perhaps I remember the dares-and-trees business (which may or may not have biblical resonances) because my parents had a special term for climbing trees: *pasht nit* (not proper). It was rather like playing football or doing anything else that involved the body. When my eight-year-old frustrations reached the breaking point, I appealed to my grandfather as a court of last resort. "Why," I asked *zeyde*, "did God give us a body in the first place, if not so that we could run and jump, play sports, and most of all, climb trees?" He seemed momentarily stunned by my poser, but was hardly rendered speechless: "God gave you a body," he confidently replied, "so that your head shouldn't roll off."

About dares, much less *double* dares, my *zeyde* would have had little to say because such foolhardy behavior was subsumed under the large umbrella called *goyische nashas*, those things that gave pleasure to non-Jews but that had no place whatsoever in the world of prohibitions I occupied. Not until much later, when I first read *Portnoy's Complaint*, did I realize how deeply rooted fears of the body were in the immigrant Jewish ethos. And later still, when I published one of the early critical books on Roth's fiction, my dedication tried to capture the mingled strands of love and disappointment that I felt toward my mother and that she no doubt felt toward me. "To my mother," the dedication reads, "who hoped I would write about somebody else."

I suppose that some might have called my decision to major in English "daring," but as I remember it, the words my uncle used were *Vemen baristu* – Who do you think you're fooling? At the same time, however, my family boasted to everyone with ears about my A papers and regular appearances on the Dean's List. In short, they *kvelled* in public even as they continued to worry in private.

Some have pointed out that my doctoral dissertation on the schlemiel constituted an act of scholarly daring, and perhaps during the mid-sixties it was; but I prefer to think that good timing and dumb luck had more with the how-and-why my thesis glided almost effortlessly into a book. After all, I was merely doing some clean-up work in a field that earlier critics – most of them *without* Ph.D.s – had pioneered. Here I am thinking about people like Alfred Kazin and Irving Howe. Their writing not only created the climate in which writers such as Saul Bellow and Bernard Malamud could prosper (and Henry Roth's extraordinary novel, *Call It Sleep*, could be rediscovered), but the work, taken as a whole, also carved out an academic space in which people like myself could stand bedecked in mortar board and doctoral hood.

True enough, some grad school chums wondered if I weren't kissing my career goodbye with this "Jew-lit" thing. Don't throw your academic eggs into one tiny basket, they cautioned, and then went on to mispronounce the basket as SHLIM-el. They were hardly alone. Many of my graduate professors (rather like my mother) would have preferred that I write about something else: the surface and symbol of American transcendentalism or perhaps a good brisk study of some fourth-rate local colorist. But I persisted, or, if you will, *dared*. In truth, though, the time was ripe for a sustained look at Yiddish and Jewish-American writers because, as a prominent ad once proudly declared, "You don't have to be Jewish to eat Levy's Jewish rye."

For a generation of Jewish immigrant sons and would-be writers, the dare was to write directly about the experience at the end of their collective noses. And that's precisely what Henry Roth and Alfred Kazin, Delmore Schwartz, Saul Bellow, and Bernard Malamud did. Granted, they also yearned to be fully American writers, and as critics began talking a bit too glibly about the ethnic triumphs of the Jewish-American "renaissance," they responded by issuing what looked for all the world like a collective No! in thunder. True enough, we are Jewish, and, yes, we often write about Jewish neighborhoods populated by Jewish protagonists, but there is something reductive, limiting, just plain parochial about calling us "Jewish-American writers."

Saul Bellow could get especially exercised on this point. "I am a hockey fan," he once told me, "but the critics never mention *that*." Fair enough, I suppose, although I am not convinced that the fact Moses Herzog follows the Blackhawks is a significant detail in a novel that captures the pathos and comedy of a Jewish intellectual under great stress. Isn't the immigrant world of Napoleon Street, one that Bellow recreates with enormous fondness, much more telling in terms of understanding what makes the Herzog heart tick? Besides, when I suggested to Bellow that there was an easy remedy to his problem – namely, to write his next novels about hockey players and then look forward to reviews in *Sports Illustrated* – he was, rather like Queen Victoria, not amused. But the point is worth repeating: critics respond to the books before their eyes, and when writers choose to write about Jewish neighborhoods, Jewish characters, Jewish foods, and particularly Jewish foibles, it is hardly surprising that critics feel an obligation to point this out.

Better yet, ethnic Jewish culture became so pervasive, so popular that Leslie Fiedler, a critic known for combining bravado with daring, gave one of his essays the following title: "Zion as Main Street." Slice the bagel as you will, Jewishness was In – often for dubious reasons and sometimes with cheesy results. The best Jewish-American writers were, of course, better than the hoopla that often surrounded them, but when the bandwagon of the Jewish renaissance got rolling, most critics found it hard to locate the brakes. The daring ones did, by pointing out that Jewish-American literature must be more, much more, than a laundry list of ethnic detail: corned beef sandwiches washed down with celery tonic, a smattering of Yiddish curses, or the hauling out of stereotypes running the gamut from Jewish-American princesses to ever more extravagant bar-mitzvahs. Let *Marjorie Morningstar* stand for dozens of these ersatz Jewish novels, all pumped out during a time when virtually anything "Jewish" could get published, and more important, would get read.

Small wonder, then, that ethnically driven Jewish-American fiction collapsed from its own weight, or that during the last few decades talented young Jewish writers had good reasons to be depressed. They were *persona non grata*, which, translated into lingo of the Manhattan streets, meant that they couldn't get arrested. True enough, stories such as Grace Paley's "The Loudest Voice" gave the tensions of assimilation a touch so artfully delicious that it could not be ignored, and to our collective benefit, feminist critics brought extraordinary Jewish-American writers such as Tillie Olsen or resurrected ones like Anzia Yezierska to wide, well-deserved attention. Nonetheless, the 1970s was hardly a boom time for Jewish-American fiction on what people like to call the cutting edge.

Cynthia Ozick may strike some as the notable exception, and they would surely be right – that is, if critical attention rather than general readers is the benchmark. My early book on Ozick was followed by a handful of thicker, more fashionably academic studies, but, taken together, what generated papers for scholarly conferences or articles for literary journals couldn't keep her works in print. Why so? Because Ozick almost singlehandedly moved Jewish-American fiction beyond the dare of ethnic Jewishness to the more complicated, more demanding *double-dare* of a fiction firmly couched in Jewish ideas and rendered in liturgical rhythms.

Ozick once claimed that her goal was to dream "Jewish dreams," and to that end she has consciously steeped herself in Jewish learning. It is an honorable effort, but one that a writer like I. B. Singer never had to undertake. Every dream he had was, by definition, a *Jewish* dream – including, I would argue, many that struck traditional Yiddishists as scandalously pornographic. By contrast, one feels an effortfulness in Ozick's fiction that is entirely absent from her brilliant essays.

What may ultimately matter, however, is the new generation of Jewish-American writers that her double-daring made possible. Irving Howe once speculated that as the emotional and aesthetic distance from the immigrant Jewish experience widened, we could only look forward to ever-thinner slices of Jewish-American social realism; and, as such, that it was probably time to close the book on what he regarded as a rich chapter in the larger history of regional American writing. The work of Steve Stern (*Lazar Malkin Enters Heaven*), Gerald Shapiro (*From Hunger*), the remarkable – and remarkably young – Allegra Goodman (*Sudden Immersion*), Joseph Epstein (*The Goldin Boys*), or recent MacArthur winner Rebecca Goldstein (*Mazel*) suggests otherwise, but in large measure Howe is probably right, as he was right about so much that would come with the very American story of cultural assimilation.

What Howe hadn't counted on, however, was the staking out of fictional claims on essentially new territories, ones that an older generation of Jewish writers largely ignored or only addressed from oblique angles. I am referring to Israel and the Holocaust, subjects fraught with peril and a rich potential for controversy, but that also engage the contemporary Jewish imagination in ways that yet another rendering of suburban meretriciousness does not. Consider, for example, Philip Roth's *The*

Counterlife and *Operation Shylock,* novels largely set within Israeli society and out to raise provocative questions about the Diaspora. For far too long, what can only be called "Jewish correctness" has insisted that American Jews write generous checks, perhaps make obligatory visits, but most of all, keep their silence with regard to Israeli politics. After all, they argue, American Jews do not have to live, or die, with the consequences of their opinions. By contrast, Israelis do.

Against this background so long familiar that its outlines hardly require elaboration, Roth performs a "Jewish mischief" (his term) that, in the case of *The Counterlife,* so inverts the usual distinctions separating life in Israel from its equivalent in galut that the New York Jew turns out to be the confident, self-assured type Zionism had promised while an average Israeli becomes the skittish, frightened ghetto Jew of Mitteleuropa. *Operation Shylock* gives this essential beat an even more bizarre twist by introducing an impostor "Roth" who preaches that only Diasporism – that is, the voluntary return of most Israeli citizens to the Poland of their cultural roots – can save the Zionist state from an impending Second Holocaust.

Talk about chutzpah! About double-daring! Roth had never been more self-consciously subversive, not even in the days when he enraged people with his satiric portraits of gold-bricking Jewish soldiers, sex-starved Jewish adulterers, or smothering Jewish mothers. Granted, the official Jewish community has never quite forgiven Roth for his smart-alecky early work, but I would argue that they are child's play when compared with his more recent novels. In a lesser way, so too are Tova Reich's wickedly comic profiles of American Jews who turn up in Israel as religious-political fanatics. True enough, *Master of the Return* and *The Jewish War* make heavy demands on their readers. One needs to know a good deal about Hasidism (and especially about Nahum of Bratzlav) in the first case and about right wing ultra-Orthodoxy in the second, but that is what double-daring consists of: the assumption that Jewish fiction is, well, *Jewish.*

Writing about the Holocaust is even more problematic. Theodor Adorno's stern injunction that there should be "no poetry after Auschwitz" is certainly understandable. To create objects of aesthetic beauty in the last years of our nightmarish century seems, on the face of it, obscene. By this reckoning, Holocaust fiction is not only an oxymoron but a travesty – especially if attempted by Jewish-American writers who were not there and who could not possibly know.

In recent years, however, this territorial stronghold has relaxed as it becomes increasingly clear that the imagination can also be a witness – not, to be sure, the same as the testimonies and memoirs of survivors, but important nonetheless. Once again, it was Ozick – in her riveting, absolutely unforgettable story, "The Shawl" – who opened up the territory now occupied by younger Jewish-American writers such as Melvin Bukiet and Thane Rosenbaum. What separates the children of survivors from the survivors themselves is that the former are significantly darker than their literary forefathers. True enough, the older writers' world was shattered, but they could recollect the world before the cataclysm. For the second generation, however, there is only *After*, a word that shivers even as it perplexes – and that figures significantly as the title of Bukiet's recently published novel. As he puts it, in an expression of double-daring in perhaps its purest form, "In the beginning was Auschwitz."

Interestingly enough, both Bukiet and Rosenbaum choose *not* to write about the Holocaust directly. There are no scenes of selection, no gas chambers, no mass graves. Instead, what their fiction explores is the long shadow that the Holocaust continues to cast. And it is here that they run into yet another instance of Jewish correctness – namely, the instance that the Holocaust is a subject so wrapped in the veils of piety that only sanitized portrayals are acceptable. In the case of Thane Rosenbaum's *Elijah Visible*, a young man named Adam Posner is given a number of different identities, here a lawyer, there a painter, yet all of these Adams in some way live under the burden of the murder of their families and the pain of their ambivalent Jewishness. They are in one sense thoroughly modern, completely assimilated characters, yet in another, they are consumed by the Holocaust as a defining, psychologically altering event. This is writing explicitly of and by the second generation.

By contrast, Bukiet's *After* is much more disturbing because it begins at the moment the camps are liberated, and follows a group of survivors as they scheme their way through a destroyed, thoroughly chaotic landscape. Bukiet allows his characters the full range of humanity, from the noble to the base, and in the process his vision will surely offend those who feel they need only pony up a ticket stub to *Schindler's List* and a "Never Again!" button from the Holocaust Museum to be certified as Holocaust-sensitive. *After* is not only double-daring because it might be fairly characterized as a work in which Primo Levi meets Thomas

Pynchon, but also because it is relentless in its fury toward God and history, yet written with a tone of deliberately disconcerting humor. The combination will undoubtedly upset self-appointed spokespersons for American Jewry because Bukiet upends the apple cart of piety that has until now attached itself to hushed discussions of the Holocaust. But Bukiet, I hasten to add, is not out to outrage merely for outrage's sake (in this sense he strikes me as quite different from the controversy-seeking Philip Roth), but rather to re-humanize Holocaust survivors by allowing them to make jokes, make love, and, yes, connive for money just like other human beings.

My hunch is that versions of Jewish-American double-daring are likely to be with us for some time, and that if the net result does not entirely recreate the literary atmosphere we associate with the salad days of Saul Bellow, Bernard Malamud, and the early Philip Roth, it is likely to come close. One thing at least is clear: the demise of Jewish-American writing has been much exaggerated. What was once a "dare" is now out for redder, more Jewish meat. *Double-dare* may be as good a term as any to describe what the new crop of Jewish-American writers is doing, and gives every promise of continuing to do.

There are days like this, when the dry air
of the desert, with its billowing clouds
of sand and heat, less real than mirage,
the merest shimmer, suddenly
ignites the mind
where a tall column of salt
stands like a sentinel
at the edge of the Dead Sea.

And sheep come to it,
goats and their kids,
and lick and lick,
so that slowly,
from all those
tongues, it begins
to suggest a figure –
forgotten, forbidden
from the beginning,
a graven image
a linga
standing between
sand and sky
at the edge
of a salten sea,
nibbled and licked,
tongues
shaping it
to the endless
animal need
to feed the red sea
of the interior.
It is mute and faceless,
pure shape
without speech –
and it shines, the crystals
of salt turning light
into brilliance, so that
for miles and miles
it burns like a beacon,
and legions come
and fall down before it,
bring it small gifts
and offerings, until soon
around the glittering pillar, piles
of stones and the litter of prayers grow higher
and higher, until at last nothing can be seen
except a mound of pebbles, and nearby,
a sheep bleating, salt-starved,
abandoned by the edge
of a dead sea, stunned in the hard light,
its dirty fur a blur of gray in the eye.

Eleanor Wilner

The Pillar

Now we must – one by one – remove these pebbles,
not because it was wrong to have brought them,
    nor because the offering was unworthy,
        nor their placement here entirely without cause –

    but because it must always happen again:
one generation to bring gifts, another
    to carry it all away again; one
        to bury what they came to honor, another
            to bring it to light again; and always,
        standing alongside, sending its small round
cries into the night, the desolate sheep
        bleating for salt, its need driving us
            as we bend our backs to the task.

Contributors

ART

Double Red Yentl (My Elvis) ©1993. Silkscreen ink on acrylic, 72x72".
Deborah Kass is an artist who lives and works in New York City. Her
work has been exhibited nationally and internationally and is in the col-
lections of the Museum of Modern Art, the Whitney Museum, the
Guggenheim Museum, the Jewish Museum, the Museum of Fine Arts,
Boston, and the Cincinnati Museum, among others. She has lectured and
taught throughout the United States, at the Whitney Museum, the Jewish
Museum, Museum of fine Arts, Boston, Cincinnati Museum, Kansas City
Art Institute, Rhode Island School of Design, California Institute of the
Arts, Art Institute of Chicago, and Skowhegan School of Sculpture and
Painting and elsewhere. She has received grants from the National En-
dowment of the Arts, The New York State Council on the Arts, and Art
Matters, Inc.

PROSE

Robin Becker is an associate professor of English at Pennsylvania State
University. She is the author of *All-American Girl* (U of Pittsburgh P),
Giacometti's Dog, and *Backtalk*, was a 1995–96 Fellow at the Bunting Insti-
tute of Radcliffe College, and has received fellowships in poetry from the
Massachussetts Artists Foundation and the NEA; she also serves as po-
etry editor for *The Women's Review of Books*.
Michael Blumenthal is currently associate professor of English at the
University of Haifa in Israel and was formerly senior editor of Central
European Press in Hungary. He has five books of poems including *The
Wages of Goodness* (U of Missouri P). His novel, *Weinstock Among the Dying*
(Zoland Books), won the 1994 Harold U. Ribelow Fiction Prize from
Hadassah magazine. His poems have appeared in *Poetry, Antaeus, New
Republic, Prairie Schooner*, and *The Nation*, among others.
Rebecca Goldstein, a 1996 MacArthur Foundation Fellow, has published
Mazel, The Dark Sister, The Mind-Body Problem, and *Strange Attractors*, all
by Viking Penguin.
Robin Hemley is professor of English and creative writing at Western
Washington University and editor of the *Bellingham Review*. He has pub-
lished a novel, *The Last Studebaker* (Graywolf), and two collections of
short stories, *The Big Ear* (John F. Blair), and *All You Can Eat* (Atlantic
Monthly Press). He is a winner of the Nelson Algren Award.
Irena Klepfisz is a teacher/activist poet, essayist, and translator of Yid-
dish women's writing. She is the author of *A Few Words in the Mother
Tongue*, a book of poems, and *Dreams of an Insomniac*, Jewish feminist
essays. She currently serves as the editorial consultant on Yiddish and
Yiddish culture for the North American feminist magazine *Bridges*.

Faye Moskowitz, director of creative writing at George Washington University, is the author of *A Leak in the Heart* (Godine), *Whoever Finds This: I Love You* (Godine), and *And the Bridge Is Love* (Beacon). She is also editor of *Her Face in the Mirror: Jewish Women on Mothers and Daughters* (Beacon).

Sanford Pinsker is Shadek Professor of Humanities at Franklin and Marshall College. He is best known for his study *The Schlemiel as Metaphor* and for co-editing a prize-winning encyclopedia of Jewish-American history and culture. He publishes essays, reviews, and poetry in a wide variety of literary journals, including *Partisan Review, Sewanee Review, Georgia Review, Virginia Quarterly*, and *Salmagundi*. He is the senior judge of the Edward Lewis Wallant Book Award.

Eileen Pollack is the director of the undergraduate creative writing program at the University of Michigan in Ann Arbor. Winner of an NEA Fellowship and two Pushcart prizes for fiction, she is the author of *The Rabbi in the Attic and Other Stories* (Delphinium Books).

Daniel Stern's most recent book is *Twice Upon a Time: Stories* (Norton); his other collections of fiction are *Twice-Told Tales* (Paris Review Editions) and *An Urban Affair* (Simon & Schuster).

Steve Stern's most recent books include *A Plague of Dreamers* (novellas), *Harry Kaplan's Adventures Underground* (novel), and *Lazar Malkin Enters Heaven* (stories, Syracuse UP). He is an associate professor of English at Skidmore College.

Janet Sternburg's books include *The Writer on Her Work, Volume 1* (1981) and *Volume 2* (1991) published by Norton and recently selected for *500 Great Books By Women*; her poems and essays have appeared in numerous journals and anthologies. The pieces in this issue were excerpted from the book she is now completing, *Phantom Limb: A Memoir of the Body and the Human Heart*. She teaches in both the Writing Program and the Film School of the California Institute of the Arts.

POETRY

Ruth Behar is a poet, ethnographer, essayist, professor of anthropology, and a MacArthur Fellow. Her poems have appeared in *Tikkun, Witness, Michigan Quarterly Review*, and in the anthologies *Little Havana Blues* and *Sephardic-American Voices: 200 Years of a Literary Legacy*. She is the author of *Translated Woman: Crossing the Border with Esperanza's Story* and *The Vulnerable Observer: Anthropology that Breaks Your Heart*. In addition, she is the co-editor of *Women Writing Culture*.

Marvin Bell's *A Marvin Bell Reader* (selected prose and poetry) was published in 1994 (UP of New England). His most recent book is Volume 1 of *The Book of the Dead Man* (Copper Canyon). Volume 2, subtitled *Ardor*, is in progress.

S. Ben-Tov's poems have appeared in *Partisan Review, The Antioch Review*, and *The Jerusalem Report*. Her book, *During Ceasefire*, was published by Harper and Row. Ben-Tov is currently completing a new book of poetry, *The Recoilless Cannon and Other Inventions.* "How Your Father and I Built Israel's First Rocket," published in this issue, is based on a true story. Preparation and publication of research work on the Israel Science Corps was supported by the Memorial Foundation for Jewish Culture.

Naomi Feigelson Chase was a reporter for *Village Voice.* She has written a book on child abuse called *A Child is Being Beaten,* a book about the sixties, and a book of poetry, *Waiting for the Messiah in Somerville, Mass.*

Richard Chess is associate professor of Literature and Language and director of the Center for Jewish Studies at the University of North Carolina at Asheville. He is the author of a collection of poetry, *Tekiah* (U of Georgia P); his poems have also appeared in *TriQuarterly, New England Review, Bellingham Review,* and other journals.

Scott Coffel's poetry has been published in *The Antioch Review* and he has work forthcoming in *The American Scholar, Paris Review,* and *The Wallace Stevens Journal.* He is an ex-employee of the Boeing Company, "downsized but not out." He lives with his wife and young son in Iowa City.

Norman Finkelstein is a professor and the chair of the English Department at Xavier University. An essay on being a Jewish poet/critic appears in the anthology *People Of the Book: Thirty Scholars Reflect On Their Jewish Identity* (Wisconsin, 1996). Other publications include *The Utopian Moment in Contemporary American Poetry* (Bucknell UP) and a collection of poetry, *Restless Messengers* (U of Georgia P).

Alvin Greenberg writes and teaches at Macalester College. His most recent books of poetry are *Why We Live with Animals* (Coffee House Press) and *Heavy Wings* (Ohio Review Press).

Marilyn Hacker is a writer, editor, and teacher. In 1995 she received the Lenore Marshall Award of the Academy of American Poets and The Nation for *Winter Numbers.* Her *Selected Poems* won the 1996 Poets' Prize. (Both books were published by Norton.) In 1996, Wake Forest University Press published *Edge,* her translations of poems by Claire Malroux.

Mark Halperin's collections of poetry include *The Measure of Islands* (Wesleyan UP), *A Place Made East* (Copper Canyon), and *Backroads* (U of Pittsburgh P). Work has appeared in *Iowa Review, Northwest Review,* and *Prairie Schooner,* among other magazines.

Norman Harris, now retired, was the Editor-in-Chief of the *Daily Nebraskan.* Along with his wife, Bernice, he is a major funding source for the Norman and Bernice Harris Center for Judaic Studies at the University of Nebraska-Lincoln.

Barbara Helfgott Hyett is a teacher, public lecturer, and the director of the Workshop for Publishing Poets. She has published four books: *The Tracks We Leave, The Double Reckoning of Christopher Columbus, Natural Law,* and *In Evidence: Poems of the Liberation of Nazi Concentration Camps.* Other poems have appeared in *The New Republic, Hudson Review, The Nation, Partisan Review,* and elsewhere.

David Ignatow has two new books, *I Have a Name* (Wesleyan UP), his sixteenth book of poetry, and *End Game and Other Stories.* He won the Bollingen Prize in 1977.

Rodger Kamenetz will appear in a documentary feature based on his book, *The Jew in the Lotus* (Harper Collins). He is a professor of English and director of Jewish Studies at LSU. He has also published *The Missing Jew: New and Selected Poems* (Harper Collins).

Ann Z. Leventhal's poems have appeared in the *Georgia Review* and *Kalliope*. She has published a novel, *Life-Lines*, with Music Circle Press, and *Three Genres: The Writing of Poetry, Fiction and Drama* with Prentice-Hall. Her short stories have appeared in *Vignette* and *Christopher Street*. Among her accomplishments: her forty-one-year marriage, four children, and six grandchildren.

Cynthia Macdonald is a writer, professor, opera singer, and psychoanalyst. Her special focus as a psychoanalyst/psychotherapist is writing blocks. In 1997 Knopf will publish *I Can't Remember*, her new book of poems. She has previously published *Amputations, Transplants, (W)holes, Alternate Means of Transport: New and Selected Poems* (Knopf).

Jerry Mirskin is professor of writing at Ithaca College. He has published a chapbook of poems: *Picture A Gate Hanging Open and Let That Gate Be the Sun* (Camellia) and is finishing a collection of poems by the same title. He has been twice nominated for the Pushcart Prize and has published widely.

Alicia Ostriker is the author of *The Nakedness of the Fathers: Biblical Visions and Revisions* (Rutgers) and *Feminist Revision and the Bible* (Blackwell). Her most recent book of poems is *The Crack in Everything* (Pittsburgh), which was nominated for the National Book Award in poetry. She is a professor of English at Rutgers University.

Helen Papell is a librarian, storyteller, and puppeteer. She has published in *Jewish Women's Literary Annual, Mildred, Negative Capability, Outerbridge, Verve,* and *Visions.* She also appears in the anthology *Sarah's Daughters Sing.* A new book is forthcoming, *Talking with Eve, Leah, Hagar and Miriam* from the Jewish Women's Resource Center.

Linda Pastan's ninth book of poems, *An Early Afterlife,* was published by Norton in 1995. *Carnival Evening: New and Selected Poems* is due in 1998. She recently served as Poet Laureate of Maryland.

Marcia Pelletiere's work has appeared in *Southern Poetry Review, Kalliope, Quarterly West,* and *Painted Bride Quarterly.* She is a writer, singer, and teacher of creative writing.

Mark Perlberg is the author of *The Burning Field* (William Morrow) and *The Feel of the Sun* (Swallow/Ohio UP). He has a third manuscript of poems waiting for publication, *The Color of the Spirit.*

Doris Radin is the recipient of two Fellowship Grants from New Jersey State Council on the Arts. She has had poems in *The Nation, Massachussetts Review, Prairie Schooner, New Letters, Confrontation,* and *Midstream.* Her book, *There Are Talismans,* was published by Saturday Press.

Jay Rogoff's poems have appeared in *DoubleTake, Kenyon Review, Paris Review, Prairie Schooner, Sewanee Review,* and elsewhere. He won the 1994 Washington Prize for his book-length poetic sequence, *The Cutoff* (Word Works). He is a lecturer in Liberal Studies at Skidmore College.

Liz Rosenberg teaches at SUNY Binghamton. She has published two books of poetry, most recently, *Children of Paradise,* and a novel, *Heart and Soul* (Harcourt Brace).

Mark Rudman's recent books include *The Nowhere Steps* (Sheep Meadow), *Diverse Voices: Essays on Poets and Poetry* (Story Line Press), a long poem, *Rider* (Wesleyan UP), which received the National Book Critics Circle Award in Poetry for 1994, *Realm of Unknowing: Meditations on Art, Suicide, and Other Transformations* and *The Millennium Hotel,* the latter three from Wesleyan. He is a Guggenheim Fellow for 1996/97. He teaches at Columbia's School of the Arts and is a poet, essayist, translator, and teacher.

Ira Sadoff teaches at Colby College and in the MFA program at Warren Wilson College. His recent publications are *Emotional Traffic* (Godine) and *An Ira Sadoff Reader. Delirious: New and Selected Poems* is forthcoming.

Steven Schneider is an assistant professor at the University of Nebraska at Kearney. His poems have appeared in *Jewish Currents, Jewish Spectator,* and *Beloit Poetry Journal.* He is the author of *A.R. Ammons and the Poetics of Widening Scope* (Fairleigh Dickinson), and is an avid tennis player with a 4.0 USTA rating.

Harvey Shapiro is a journalist and author of nine books of poetry, the most recent of which is *A Day's Portion.* A volume of *Selected Poems* will be published by Carcanet in England in June 1997. He will be reading his poems in the International Poets' Festival in Jerusalem.

Judith Skillman is the author of two books, *The Worship of the Visible Spectrum* (Breitenbush) and *Beethoven and the Birds* (Blue Begonia Press). She is a writer and teacher, and was a recipient of a Washington State Arts Commission Writer's Fellowship in 1991.

Ruth Stone is the author of *Second Hand Coat* (new and selected poems), *Mother Stone's Nursery Rhymes,* and *Who is the Widow's Muse.* Her work has appeared in *Boulevard, American Voice,* and *American Poetry Review.* She teaches in the English Department at SUNY Binghamton.

yermiyahu ahron taub is a project archivist at the YIVO Institute for Jewish Research whose poems have appeared in *Backspace, Evergreen Chronicles,* and the *James White Review.*

Emily Warn's poems have appeared in *Kenyon Review, Poetry East, Southern Poetry Review, The Cream City Review,* and *The Seattle Review.* Her books include *The Novice Insomniac* (Copper Canyon Press), *The Leaf Path* (Copper Canyon Press), and a chapbook, *Highway Suite* (Limberlost Press).

Roger Weingarten teaches in and directs the MFA program in writing at Vermont College. He has eight collections of poetry, most recently *Ghost Wrestling* (Godine). Winner of Ingram Merrill Foundation and NEA fellowships, he is also a contributing editor for the *Prague Review.*

Henny Wenkart is a writer and editor who, though Vienna-born, now makes her home in New York City. She is the editor of the *Jewish Women's Literary Annual* and several anthologies; the author of children's books, philosophical articles, a book of poems, and a novel in progress. She holds the Ph.D. in Philosophy from Harvard for her dissertation on *The*

Philosophy of Matter and of Mind of George Santayana. She teaches philosophy in Dorot's University Without Walls.

Eleanor Wilner, a MacArthur Foundation Fellow, is author of five books of poetry. The latest, *Reversing the Spell: New and Selected Poems*, will be out in 1997 (Copper Canyon Press).

Lisa Yanover spent two years in Israel studying Hebrew and Yiddish after her B.A. Since completing her M.A. at Davis she has been in the Ph.D. program in Creative Writing and Literature at the University of Houston. She has published her poetry in *Prairie Schooner, Amelia,* and *International Quarterly*.